One of the things that I think is so overwhelming for most people about estate planning is decision fatigue. There are so many decisions that have to be made. If you don't have a clear overall intent, every one of those decisions is painful. Once you have that clear overall intent, those decisions just flow, and you can just carry out the action steps rather than having to decide at every single point. Now because of *Seven Generations Legacy Coaching*, we have clearly articulated family values and clear intent around how we want to engage our children in discussions about money, finance, being responsible, and being a good steward of all resources. This clear intent makes it so much easier to make the micro decisions. One of the big surprises that has come out of coaching is that we have much more opportunity in the present moment to set our family up for success in future generations than we realized.

—Dr. Sabrina Starling, Founder of Tap the Potential,
Author of *The 4 Week Vacation* and the *How to Hire the Best* Series,
Keynote Speaker

I was so overwhelmed with "estate planning" until Rachel broke it down into bite-sized pieces, helping me create a plan BETTER than I've ever imagined. Checking the "done" box on a legacy plan felt AMAZING! Riveting from the start, Rachel reveals the secrets that made her wealth plan stronger and how you can too. Don't wait; let *Seven Generations* FINALLY give you the same peace of mind it gave me.

—Eileen Wilder, Founder of Confident Closer,
Elite Speakers, Two Comma Kit

For years, I've struggled with the challenge of how to best transfer my wealth to my children. I know what it took for me to build it from scratch; it was hard, painful at times, disappointing, long hours, and lots of study and learning. What I've become and learned in that process is the true value. Of course, I want to bless my heirs with what I've built—to give them a great life. I also don't want to create entitlement, laziness, or spendthrifts. I want them to go through the growth process and not give them any shortcuts; at the same time, I want them to live their best lives and use the money to create opportunities and multiply it. Rachel's book came like a gift from God at the right time, with the perfect plan. Anyone that reads this book will be able to move confidently in the direction of creating enduring family wealth, not only a legacy but a blessing to ongoing generations.

—Jack Gibson, Founder of Indestructible Wealth

Whether you are a parent or a relative, you will rarely, if ever, come across a more gripping story or one that can be as useful to you in your own life. If you care about those who come after you, this is a must-read.

—**Mitzi Perdue (Mrs. Frank Perdue), Author of**
How to Make Your Family Business Last **and** *How to Communicate Values to Your Children So They'll Love It*

Through her own personal story, Rachel Marshall, author of *Seven Generations,* shares the raw reality of the fragility of life and how it can be gone in an instant. The deep love she and her husband have for their own children led them to research and design the legacy they will leave them. This book is the practical guide needed for any family looking to leave a legacy that lasts far beyond the next generation. Don't be fooled by its simplicity, for that is the beauty of this how-to guide. I urge you to get this book, read it, and use it as the tool to jumpstart your own plan.

—**Barbara Stackhouse, RDH, M.Ed.;**
Consultant and Author of *Profit First for Dentists*

Talk about a life story! I am so impressed! Having known Rachel for over ten years, I can attest that she is ahead of her time in dealing with important, but too often neglected issues of legacy. She goes beyond giving you a definition of legacy by giving you a true understanding of what it means to be part of a legacy. I can tell you that most people do not learn what she has until it's late in the game–not over, but late. Don't wait any longer to get started building your legacy.

—**Jeffrey W. Ganthner, DSL, AIA, Burns and McDonnell,**
Mid-Atlantic Region Vice President & General Manager

"Start at the end" is where Rachel begins, and as an advisor who nearly lost her life in childbirth, Rachel personally knows the power of this perspective. *Seven Generations* is itself a labor of love that offers inspiration and practical advice to readers of all levels of wealth. If you want to create a legacy that promotes your descendants' true freedom and reflects your faith that life is about more than money, *Seven Generations* is the book for you.

—**Keith Whitaker, Ph.D.; President of Wise Counsel Research and Co-Author of** *The Cycle of the Gift, The Voice of the Rising Generation, Family Trusts, Complete Family Wealth,* **and** *Wealth of Wisdom: The Top 50 Questions Wealthy Families Ask*

Rachel's book opened my eyes to the huge GAPS that were missing from my estate planning. My wife and I are rushing to take care of the important matters and going through Rachel's exercise to leave the legacy we've always wanted to build. Thank you for this incredible resource, Rachel!

—Craig Ballantyne, Author of *The Perfect Week Formula*

High achievers, thought leaders, entrepreneurs, and investors who have a huge motivation to make the world a better place for your kids and prepare them for the best opportunities, this is for you! You are creating your legacy right now by the way you invest for meaningful impact in the most important relationships right in front of you. Instead of just hoping your efforts make a difference, plan out exactly how to use your successes to equip your children for success! *Seven Generations* will show you the way!

—Anna Kelley, Impact Investor, Author, and Real Estate Coach, Greater Purpose Capital

If you're looking for a practical discussion about how to make a lasting difference for generations to come, look no further. *Seven Generations* gives you the inside scoop and all the tools you need to design your own family legacy. People who know me know that I am all about leading the way. Rather than just telling you it's possible, Rachel shows you exactly how she did this for her own family. Well done, Rachel.

—Michael Cobb, Chairman and CEO of ECI Development

Finance . . . Wealth Building . . . Legacy Wealth are all such important and relevant topics for our times! They have a bit of mystery and confusion about them for many. Rachel writes her powerful message and testimony in such a beautiful way that I felt like I was right there as a witness. Her teaching approach of first tell the story, second teach the lesson of the story in an informative, practical way, and then "you try it" really speaks to my learning style! Praying for this wonderful mission/journey that you are on!

—Julia Jordan, Senior Director of Success at Real Estate Investor

Rachel went through a scary healthcare crisis and turned it into the launching pad for a rich family legacy. Why wait to create your own legacy? Here's everything you need to leave the means and the meaning to make generations after you better, starting right now.

—Dave Chase, Co-Founder of Health Rosetta

There are many so-called "experts" discussing the topic of "legacy planning." However, there are very few who can actually discuss how to put those ideals into motion. Rachel is able to take a refreshingly straightforward way to overcome the challenges of passing on wealth to future generations without creating beneficiaries who are destroyed with feelings of entitlement. This is a book for anyone interested in passing on more than just the money. Highly recommended!

—Andrew L. Howell, Esq., Managing Partner of York Howell and Guymon, and Co-Author of *Entrusted: Building a Legacy That Lasts* and *Riveted: 44 Values That Change the World*

Seven Generations outlines a formula for not only living at your best but also "pre-scripting your legacy" ahead of time. By stepping back to really understand the meaning of money, you will see how you can use it to empower your children instead of disempowering them (which, unfortunately, is so often the case). Empowering your children to create wealth will give them the foundation for lifelong success and flourishing— and Rachel can help you with this targeted, intentional work. You'll not only be able to clarify your own "family guidance system" but also gain valuable insights for setting up your estate planning and organizing your financial life to support your value system. At the core, your eyes will be opened to the power you hold right now to make a difference, not only for yourself but for generations to come.

—Jon and Missy Butcher, Founders of LifeBook

What's cool about *Seven Generations* is that the principles work for everyone! Whether you have young kids, adult children, or even no children, you'll see exactly how you can strengthen your family, navigate estate planning, and leave the greatest gift behind to continue making an impact long after you're gone. Everyone needs to read this book!

—Mark Podolsky, The Land Geek and Author of *Dirt Rich*

It's really simple—the freedom to live where you want and provide the experiences you crave for your family all for one purpose: to create the life you want with the ones you love. In *Seven Generations*, Rachel helps you get really clear on WHY you do everything you do so that you can make it last. With a gripping personal story and clear steps to create a legacy, you'll be able to not only live your best life but also guarantee that your legacy will last.

—Mikkel Thorup, Host of *The Expat Money Show*

I help business owners reach breakthrough success and live soul out. Because of the deep work that I've done to reinvent myself and help my clients to stop making things so hard and complex and receive how simple and easy it really is . . . I have to tell you, Rachel gets it! *Seven Generations* is comprehensive and soulful. But most importantly, it's the guide to legacy planning that moves you to do all the planning you've never found time for because it's really that simple, easy, and maybe the most important thing you'll do with your life. She shows you how to live up to your best and create a family culture that creates and thrives on financial freedom. Get this book today and dive in! You'll be a thousand times better for it!

—**Mike Kitko, Executive Coach, Speaker, and
Author of** *The Prosperity Principles*

As entrepreneurs, we are in constant reinvention . . . and as much as we like change and evolution, there are always proven systems and recipes to scale and grow the right way. With *Seven Generations*, Rachel has laid out a simple yet comprehensive recipe to take care of your family, empower your kids, and write your legacy ahead of time. This book is the cure for leaving money that destroys people and the antidote to lifeless estate planning. You're creating your legacy already, so make it as strong, enduring, and effective as it can be.

—**Cesar Quintero, Founder and Visionary for The Profit Recipe**

Rachel walks you through the three critical pieces needed to invest profoundly in your family for generations to come. *Seven Generations* will lift the lid of your possibilities and empower you with everything you need to leave a brave legacy using the raw materials of your life right now!

—**Kary Oberbrunner,** *Wall Street Journal* **and** *USA Today*
Bestselling Author, and CEO of Igniting Souls Publishing Agency

A big part of asset protection is a proper legal structure of LLCs and Limited Partnerships, holding companies, and asset protection trusts. But no amount of legal planning will guarantee that what you want to happen will happen. *Seven Generations* is a brilliant look at how to infuse meaning into your legal planning. That's how you bring your legal planning to life and ensure your businesses, investments, and assets will make the biggest difference in your family and do the most good for the longest time.

—**Douglass S. Lodmell, J.D., LL.M., Managing Partner,
Lodmell & Lodmell, PC**

Rachel speaks the language of entrepreneurs! More than just reaching financial freedom, *Seven Generations* helps you accomplish the purpose you do all of this for—to create a life of significance, make a difference, lift others higher, and fulfill a mission that lasts past your own lifetime. There's no better time than now to get started!

—Ross Stryker, CEO of Smart Asset Opportunities,
Real Estate Investor, Developer, and Syndicator

Rachel is straight and to the point about what it takes to build Generational Wealth. Rachel builds on the concept that generational wealth is not making more money, buying more stuff, or leaving a larger inheritance. Instead, *Seven Generations* shows you how it's possible to create a lasting legacy and strengthen your family by doing the most with your money, investing in your children, and equipping them to produce and manage money well.

—Rodney G Mogen DBA, MBA, CRPC, AAMS, CAM,
Insurance Brokerage Director

To most, we are business leaders. But underneath that, family is such a huge part of your mission on this earth—being an example, investing well in our kids, and helping them become all that God's created them to be. That's why I'm so excited that Rachel has packed truth and practical wisdom into one book. *Seven Generations* is leading the way to help you create a legacy that truly makes the difference you are called to make.

—Brian Dixon, Marketing Mentor, Founder of Brian Dixon Agency,
and Co-Founder of Hope*Writers

I absolutely loved reading your book. It was written and well thought out, with examples and details of step-by-step instructions on the how-to. I especially loved hearing your testimony, and I was most motivated when you explained how to create lasting wealth and the strategic ways to do it. We are very much on the track of leaving healthy wealth to our children and generations to come, but there were parts I didn't realize or thoughts you mentioned that, in turn, gave me a different perspective as well. In a wonderful way!! So much great encouragement and wise advice. I loved it. We will definitely be adding and implementing this in our lives. Very impressed, and I'm so excited for others to read it!! This is so important for families!

—Gina Dizon, Owner of Remodel Life

SEVEN GENERATIONS LEGACY

Design a Multigenerational Legacy
of More Than Money

SEVEN GENERATIONS LEGACY

Design a Multigenerational Legacy of More Than Money

RACHEL M. MARSHALL

WITH LUCAS N. MARSHALL

Seven Generations Legacy, Design a Multigenerational Legacy of More Than Money
© 2023 by Rachel M. Marshall, with Lucas N. Marshall.
All rights reserved.

Published by Author Academy Elite
PO Box 43, Powell, OH 43065
www.AuthorAcademyElite.com

Identifiers:

Library of Congress Control Number: 2023911260
ISBN: 979-8-88583-225-0 (paperback)
ISBN: 979-8-88583-226-7 (hardback)
ISBN: 979-8-88583-227-4 (e-book)

Available in paperback, hardback, e-book, and audiobook

Scripture quotations taken from the (NASB®) New American Standard Bible®, Copyright © 1960, 1971, 1977, 1995, 2020 by The Lockman Foundation. Used by permission. All rights reserved. www.lockman.org

Any Internet addresses (websites, blogs, etc.) printed in this book are offered as a resource. They are not intended in any way to be or imply an endorsement by Author Academy Elite, nor does Author Academy Elite vouch for the content of these sites for the life of this book.

Cover design: Debbie O'Byrne

Images credit: Andres Arturo Chavez Montoya, Mikey Marchan, Mikael Kevin Marchan, Ronald Cruz, Ma. Jenica Alexis Llanes, Louie Gio Ocsena, and Evan Joshua Tiu Ng with DesignPickle, and Zahra Tariq.

This book is my true story. I am an entrepreneur in the wealth industry. This book is educational; however, reading this book does not constitute legal, tax, or financial advice and should not be used as a substitute for advice. Some names and identifying details have been changed to protect the privacy of individuals.

I dedicate this book, first and foremost, to my family:

To Lucas, my wonderful husband, leader of our family, brilliantly deep thinker, and champion of truth—I am so proud to build our family team together.

To Avalynn, Olivia, and Eli, who made my heart come alive and gave me a purpose—I love everything about you, and I'm so thankful for the gifts that you are.

To my father and mother, Brad and Teri, who gave me life and a love for Jesus and taught me to have principles and a good attitude.

To Lucas's parents, Kenneth and Ruth, for raising a good son. And to the memory of Kenneth Marshall, whose life taught us all how to make a difference.

To the ancestors before us, especially Grandma Sally Montagne, who, at age 92, still stitches love into every handmade quilt, scarf, and stocking, and is the world's greatest story preserver and host; and my Grandpa Ed Lemler, who was loyal and serving, cherished his deep roots, and was loved by his community.

To the descendants to come after us, we have lived with you ever on our minds.

And to you, dear Legacy Creator. What you are building matters.

TABLE OF CONTENTS

PILLAR 3: THE MONEY: FUNDING YOUR LEGACY 183

CONCLUSION: PUTTING YOUR PERPETUAL LEGACY IN MOTION. 239

FOREWORD

Rachel and her family have not only crystalized their own legacy planning to catapult their wealth generations ahead and prepare children and grandchildren to do the most with it, but they've also outlined a roadmap for others to complete this daunting task.

That's why when Rachel asked me to collaborate in her goal of helping a million families create a multigenerational legacy of more than money, it was a mission already in my heart. I knew that if anyone could spearhead this initiative, Rachel would.

This book you hold in your hands will introduce you to your power to create a profound legacy. It will take you to the deepest place within yourself, so you can step into integrity. It will transform you, strengthen your family, and increase your generational impact. And it will flatten your hurdles by giving you a clear strategy to make sure nothing slips through the gap.

Here's why I know.

As the CEO and Founder of the #1 largest association in the ultra-wealthy investor space called the family office industry, I have helped set up and create over 100 family offices with clients that range from a $5M net worth plastic surgeon to $1B+ net worth families. Out of 525 current investors under contract with us, our average client has a net worth of $28M, and most of our larger clients are $70M-$400M net worth.

My clients are operating at an elite level already in many areas.

I help them create or formalize their family office wealth solutions further and become more effective. We are under contract with billionaires, a shark from *Shark Tank*, on the board of a publicly traded company, and help our investors allocate capital into strategic opportunities.

One of our primary areas of value creation is helping families position themselves to consistently source and attract more high-quality deal flow that fits their investment strike zone.

To do that, I look for the slight adjustments they need that will have the greatest impact.

And, across the board, I often find one glaring problem.

To create the wealth and impact you are capable of, the most important thing is *integrity*—the *integration* of who you are, where you spend your time, what you focus on, your values, friends, etc.

Whether you are worth $3M or $300M+, the first place you should start when creating a family office solution is having high intent and maximum *alignment* through your daily life and after your life.

I find it so backward that many will have their Bentley or Ferrari serviced at a high-end dealership that charges $1,700 for an oil change. Yet, they won't take care of their health to the level of doing a blood biomarker test to see what nutrients they are deficient in.

The same goes for legacy planning.

Most plan out their summer travel, the ski trip for the year, or due diligence on investment #85 that they have completed to date, yet don't spend even 1 hour a year focusing on the legacy they will leave.

Most of us don't focus enough on legacy. Admittedly, dealing with trust and estate attorneys—or any type of attorney—is not most people's favorite activity.

On top of that, many don't know what the end goal should be, what process to follow, what models to emulate, or who to trust to get it done.

Those who do estate planning rarely keep it updated every few years.

But this huge oversight of what's beneath the hood and what happens beyond your lifetime severely restricts your capacity.

Because if you haven't fine-tuned and optimized these intangibles, you are *misaligned*, and you limit your ability to produce and create wealth that lasts.

That's where Rachel stands out.

Few people voluntarily step into legacy planning. It's even more rare to codify a guidance system that *aligns* you and your family to prosper for generations.

This book is your ticket to writing your legacy that's richer, bolder, and more fulfilling than you can imagine.

Use it.

Rachel will teach you a skill and a way of living that will elevate your trajectory for the rest of your life.

First, the mindset required to create a legacy that lasts. Secondly, the steps to put it in place, practically.

So don't just read. Take action and implement your legacy plan now. Go all in because this is the most important work you'll do in your lifetime.

Tune your alignment today by taking care of what matters most—making sure you and your family are healthy physically, mentally, and relationally—and you'll amplify your efforts to charge your biggest goals.

Richard C. Wilson
CEO and Founder of the Family Office Club,
Bestselling Author of *The Single-Family Office Book*

PREFACE

WHY LEGACY PLANNING FAILS

There's something that makes you press on.

You've experienced success. You've carved out time and financial freedom or are well on your way to reaching it. Everything you could ever want is in your grasp. You're no longer striving to earn more so you can access the ranks of the world's best producers, thinkers, and achievers—you are one of them.

Your desire for more is not about the money anymore. But still, you reach higher, evolve, innovate, scale, and advance. Why?

You feel the basic human longing to matter. To make a difference.

To *last*.

From your vantage point, you've learned something that evades people their whole lifetimes. It's that the point of the money wasn't the money at all.

It was significance and impact.

How can you lift others to reach their potential? How can you use not only your wealth but also the time-earned wisdom with which you created it to champion the success of your children, grandchildren, and great-grandchildren? These are questions not of success but of significance.

You know this feeling if . . .

- You've ever looked *down* and craved a deeper connection or a stronger bond with your kids.
- You've ever looked *up* and felt called to lead well.

- You've ever looked *within* and discovered the call to be a better man or woman.
- You've ever looked *back* to thank those who've come before you.
- You've ever looked *forward* to your great-great-great-grandchildren not yet born and prayed that they would prosper.
- You've ever looked *beyond* this life and ached to make a difference that lasts forever.

That longing to live life beyond the bounds of ourselves is at the core of human existence. It runs as deep as your DNA.

To love, to fully express ourselves, to contribute, and to truly *live*—that is the quest of a lifetime.

Those who honor that longing create a legacy.

The word *legacy* can rub us wrong, though. Tainted with guilt or sadness, it makes us consider inevitable loss. Or it can make us bristle with an uncomfortable defensiveness or groan under the weight of unmet expectations.

Maybe you're worried that gifting an inheritance will corrupt your kids. Or you don't think they deserve it.

If you didn't come from money and earned your own way, you may want your kids to develop the grit to earn their own way too. Or if you're resentful that you weren't given anything, perhaps you're set against giving anything to your kids. Maybe you've spent so much on your kids already, trying to win a relationship, that you feel you've met your obligations and given enough.

You might feel that the values and spiritual heritage you want to leave are the most important to you, and a legacy seems material and superficial.

You could find that you can't have children or never plan to, but you still want to make a difference for your spouse, sister, brother, niece, nephew, or a cause you believe in.

Or perhaps you're still on the way. Maybe you feel that you don't have enough to think about leaving wealth behind. Or you're smack in the middle of life, and each financial goal—retirement, kids' college, caring for aging parents—seems like another thing to juggle without enough of you to go around. It could be that trying to consider leaving a legacy is the one target you've told yourself you'll just have to be okay doing without.

But your legacy is needed—right here and right now. Creating it is the most important work you'll ever do. And I urge you to get started immediately.

Full transparency: I'm the least likely person you'd expect to be talking about legacy.

I am in my thirties. My husband, Lucas, and I have young kids, and we're squarely in the middle of our story with no standing ovations marking the completion. My lofty aspirations feel so big compared to where I stand right now, and I don't feel I've lived nearly all that I'm capable of.

I'm not at the age most people start thinking about death and hand-offs to the next generation. Those obvious contemplations seem better reserved for those at the sunset of their lives, like a glance in the rearview mirror to look back and remember what was.

But I experienced a wake-up call that changed everything.

I'll tell you all about it, but the important thing here is that it confronted me with a question: *What if I didn't get a lifetime ahead to finally arrive at the finished product of my life's work?*

What if I didn't need to wait to be able to share my lessons and my wisdom with my children and generations to come? What legacy could I forge right now out of the raw materials of my life to create a foundation for my children to thrive?

At the time, rather than providing answers, the questions created a tension and a sense of solemn responsibility that I'm just now finding words for. By leaning into that pivotal question, Lucas and I began to construct a family legacy of more than money that will last for generations.

Tragically, most legacy planning fails.

Most people never plan for what will happen after they die. They don't say the important words. They wait too long to consider their legacy because it just wasn't urgent enough, or they hadn't yet "arrived." Or they're waiting for a windfall moment before they do the financial planning. They don't buy life insurance, or what they did have already ran out because it was only temporary coverage. They don't have an estate plan. If they do, it was put in place twenty-five years ago, and since then, life has changed, making their old plan irrelevant.

But even most who do have the money and the planning intact miss the most important piece of legacy planning: forging a plan to mentor, develop, train, and equip the next generations with the skills and tools to grow family wealth in the coming generations.

And then the unthinkable happens. Someone dies way too soon.

If the blow isn't bad enough, there's a wake of heartache that follows.

Your minor children's living arrangements and livelihood could be determined by the state. Extended family may have to turn to GoFundMe to raise donations for college funds and pay for outstanding medical bills. Your spouse may have to liquidate your assets and unravel everything you'd put your heart and soul into building because they need the cash to pay taxes, buy out your business partner, pay bills, or distribute an inheritance evenly. Customers could suffer if your business falls apart, damaging relationships and dissolving the value of your most valuable financial asset. Kids might get your business and investments, but only after 40 percent or more goes up in smoke from estate taxes. Children may be left with money but no direction on how to use it well. The inheritance you leave could be wasted and squandered, leaving your children worse off instead of better.

Those who suffer the most are the ones left behind. And for most, the suffering could have been prevented.

The root of this problem is that if you are looking at your own legacy with the wrong lens, you'll never see why it matters, and you'll let all the hurdles get in the way.

The reason I know is that I, too, was guilty of all the same excuses that make most legacy planning ineffective.

1. It can feel **just too hard to think about the difficult things**: facing our own smallness and bigness at the same time, the meaning of our life, our values and how congruently we live them, whether we've done the best for our kids, whether our efforts will help or hinder them, and exactly what happens to everything we've created in this life if we suddenly vanished from the scene.

2. It's **overwhelming** to confront our own mortality. Staring it squarely in the mirror feels like a slippery slope that if we contemplate too long, we're inviting it in.

3. You're too busy handling the alligators that are closer to your boat—the **daily grind** with the endless array of life's challenges to overcome and problems to tackle—that the idea of using your time and mental resources to plan for something you don't even want to think about is just unrealistic and draining.

4. It can feel like trying to arm-wrestle all the worst-case scenarios. And instead of protecting us, **worst-case thinking just fuels our fears** and cripples our action.

5. There's **so much unknown** that it can seem impossible to draft a plan that works. Fate seems to laugh in our faces and mock our illusion of control. And it feels so ambiguous and amorphous that treading in this territory feels like drowning.

6. The **tyranny of the urgent** clamors for our attention and drowns out our ambitions. After all, we reason that if it's not urgent, nothing will probably happen anyway. So, we defer and postpone to a more convenient time, just to wriggle out from under the duress.

7. Cultivating this ground and pioneering a legacy **can make you feel small**, incompetent, and out of your league while you're in the process. And you'll probably doubt whether you had any business beginning in the first place.

8. You have **so many questions**—and **fears**, if you're honest. Maybe you have no idea where to start. Maybe you can't bear the thought of what would happen to your beautiful children if you weren't here. And even the word *legacy* can seem intimidating, like some grand, ethereal, philosophical utopia that doesn't have teeth, reality, or even definition, making it completely unreachable.

So we slip into living life on autopilot, expecting that we'll do all the important things someday.

But then, that convenient time never shows up. The thing we know we should do becomes the sore spot that keeps nagging, sapping our energy.

Friend, I understand. I was there too. But my insight was bigger than my excuses and caused us to forge a legacy that will stand like the rigging of an oil well—strong and indomitable, even when buffeted by hurricane-force winds.

Ultimately, we created the following:

- A **love letter** for our girls to read if anything happened to us
- A new **estate plan**
- A *Memorandum of Trust* to guide our estate plan that spells out the purpose of our trust, our family values, vision, mission, goals, and how to use our money to fulfill those aims
- **Relationships and transparent communication** with a carefully selected trustee, guardian, power of attorney, and contingent relationships
- The **upgraded life insurance** that would provide the most payout to fund everything we hoped for our family

- An **organization system** for all our documents, accounts, and everything our trustees and heirs would need to move forward after we pass away

This legacy is no ordinary legacy.

- It is the **compass** that points plainly to truth and reminds my children and their children who they are.
- It is the **funding** to launch and scale any opportunity.
- It is the **octane boost** to fuel my children's wise choices and the **restraint** against poor ones.
- And it is the boat that **carries them through our dreams**, whether I'm seated next to them or not.
- It is guaranteed to **expand** our family wealth in each generation.
- It will be the way that generations after us will feel our love, affirmation, embrace, and cheerleading as they **carve out their own life**.
- And whether the date we graduate from this life is tomorrow or 80 years from now, it will account for the immediate **fine details of our children's lives** and the long-range **purpose** of our family.

What we learned by doing this work for our own family became the Seven Generations Wealth and Legacy Formula—a simple system to help families like you move past their estate planning overwhelm and build a lasting legacy.

This three-step framework for creating a legacy of more than money that lasts for generations is what I'll teach you in this book by showing you exactly what we did:

- Pillar 1: The Meaning
- Pillar 2: The Mechanism
- Pillar 3: The Money

The Seven Generations Wealth & Legacy Formula™

9 clear steps to help you remove the fear of money ruining your kids, in 90 days, so you can create generational wealth and a legacy, without stress, overwhelm, or feeling that the only option is to give everything away.

First, I'll show you how to articulate your family guidance system, spelling out how your family lives and what you invest in.

Then, I'll help you ensure your estate plan is the most effective boat to carry your legacy between generations.

And finally, I'll show you how to guarantee the funding for your legacy so that there will be an inheritance to grant your children every opportunity you would have created with your life.

Let me introduce you to a few of the people we've helped to create a family legacy using the Seven Generations Wealth and Legacy Formula:

Dr. Sabrina and her husband Ned were overwhelmed with the many decisions that had to be made in the estate planning process. Through Seven Generations Legacy coaching, they realized that they had much more opportunity in the present moment to set their family up for success in future generations than they realized. Now they have clearly articulated family values and clear intent around how they want to engage their children in discussions about money, finance, being responsible, and being a good steward of all resources. This clear intent makes it so much easier to make the micro decisions.

Another client couple, Anna and Kent, thought it would be amazing to leave a letter to their kids about what they would have to do before they could have money, and who they needed to become in order to handle it. Seven Generations Legacy coaching was the perfect opportunity to jump into action, put pen to paper, and get it done, instead of just thinking about it. Now, they're not just going to hand them a trust and a will, but instead, they'll give their children a document that's a record of their own life and God's faithfulness, what they've learned, and what they want their children to learn the easy way instead of the hard way.

Through this journey, I've learned this simple truth: your legacy isn't just a postscript—it's the proactive, forward-thinking, future-focused designing of your ideal life. It's not the caboose; it's the *engine*!

YOUR LEGACY IS NOT THE CABOOSE OF YOUR LIFE—IT'S YOUR ENGINE!

And that means your opportunity to begin your legacy is *right now*.

You are in the driver's seat of your legacy. You can take the reins and guide the course of your memory and future generations in the direction you want to go.

So, don't drift and leave things buoyed by happenstance. Instead of *accepting* your legacy, you have the chance to *make* it—as wonderful, meaningful, fulfilling, and rich as you want it to be.

Do you hear that calling to be more, give more, and serve others more? Will you say yes to push through the uncomfortable and do the hard thing to elevate yourself so you can elevate the quality of your gift and its power to do good?

Whoever you are, and wherever you stand on the timeline of your life—whether you have a lot or a little, you're a newlywed looking forward to a family, a young parent, a parent of adult children, already a grandparent, or even if you have no children of your own—*now* is always the exact right time to create a legacy of more than money that lasts for generations.

Not only is this possible, but it's also the noblest aspiration and most fulfilling task you'll ever endeavor.

And rather than stumbling around in the dark, The Seven Generations Wealth and Legacy Formula will help you overcome your hurdles to estate and legacy planning. Because we've battled with every single one of those limiting beliefs, we're able to help you navigate around these giant obstacles. So, with a systematic and clear process to follow, you can accomplish all your dreams for your posterity.

1. Instead of feeling "too hard," legacy planning will become doable because this formula leads you, step-by-step, through the introspection and self-discovery you need to clarify exactly what matters most to you.
2. You'll have a hand to hold through the process of confronting your mortality, and you'll discover the right perspective, so you can lean in, and convert the fear into power to design the legacy of your dreams.
3. And rather than having to ignore what's right in front of you to plan for the far out future, this method gives you a proven pathway to remove the guesswork and get your legacy planning done exactly the way you want it, so you can focus your time and attention on what you do best.
4. Instead of wasting time guessing, the Seven Generations Wealth and Legacy Formula allows you to streamline the estate planning process, so you get your planning done faster, without the headache.
5. Rather than doubting whether you can actually do this, the process reveals to you exactly how strong, capable, and powerful you are to make a lasting impact that will bless and empower future generations.
6. Instead of your estate planning being something that's never really complete, with this method, you'll not only know how to get started, you'll always know the next thing to do, so that you can finally finish your estate and legacy planning.

7. And rather than being plagued by the endless loop of what-if scenarios that have no answer or solution, the Seven Generations Wealth and Legacy Formula helps you answer those questions once and for all.

8. And then you can quiet your fears, overwhelm, and frustrations about legacy planning, because when you've used this formula, you can finally sleep better at night with the peace of knowing that even the worst-case scenario will have the best possible outcome.

Are you willing to take full responsibility—the kind of responsibility that ignites the best within you?

I know you're here because your answer is *YES!*

HOW TO READ THIS BOOK

This book you hold in your hands is a special book because it came from a very personal experience. I'm going to tell you a lot of my story, because it's a part of the process that changed our lives and our perspective, and allowed us to create an indestructible, perpetual family legacy.

In the next three chapters, I'm going to tell you about that *kairos* moment where the space between ordinary life and eternity became paper thin for us—the moment that instantly revealed why it was crucial to begin here, in the prime of our lives, way before most people ever consider passing the baton to the next generation.

It was the darkest, worst day we'd ever faced. But it was also the pivot point that woke us up to what truly matters.

The good news is that you can adjust your reading experience to meet you exactly where you're at.

If you want to get to the bottom line and get to the actionable content to see how we help people like you, or if you simply want to save time by cutting to the chase, or if you're a bit queasy at medical trauma, or expecting a baby and reading a hard birth story might be too much, start at chapter 4.

If you're exploring new possibilities, would you commit to reading the first four chapters? This baby step will start you on a profound journey to recognizing the power you hold to write your legacy. And then you can decide what you want to do after that.

And if you are ready to play full out, let's dive in, and we'll journey together to chisel your legacy.

Life is about to become better than you'd ever dreamed. Let's go!!!!

Now, I'm aware that this work treads close to the most sacred, delicate, raw, and vulnerable part of our human existence. These facets of our lives can carry so much emotion and fear. As much as I believe we can do hard things, I think that wrongly entering this room of our hearts is catastrophic. While avoiding it altogether is a giant mistake, so is the opposite—barging in because of fear and guilt. Either way, we damage our efforts and ourselves in the process.

Friend, this is not a guidebook on how to live scared or imagine worst-case scenarios. Instead, my goal is to help you to see and step into your power to create the best future. I want to give you the courage to navigate life's realities and live the most in the face of them.

- You'll find out how to guarantee that your grieving family won't have to set up a Go-Fund-Me page to pay for everyday expenses when you're gone.
- You'll see what to do to prepare your assets and accounts to be used for your intended purpose by the people who will steward them after you.
- You'll see exactly how to establish an inheritance even if you don't think you have enough.
- You'll learn how to instill the values and character your children will need to receive their inheritance well.
- You'll discover the three fool-proof things you need to leave an impactful legacy.

This book is not a technical manual written in a professional voice of explanation.

Instead, you'll hear the heart of an everyday mom who loves her kids and wants to make a difference for generations to come. I'll show you what Lucas and I have done practically, step by step, so you'll see why we made the decisions we did and exactly how they benefit our life. You'll benefit from hearing my motivation: love, knowledge of what I have the power to create, and living fully. You'll get to watch how we wrestled through answering hard questions. And as I share my story, I hope you'll see yourself in my questions and searching and that my answers will help you discover, understand, and create your own.

I hope my story is the springboard to give you the words and courage to truly, extraordinarily craft your own legacy that lives on for generations. It will be your voice and your fingerprints, your family's story. It will be all about your mission, and it will express your love with a love uniquely your own. Because of this work, you'll live more consciously, awake to your value, aligned with your ideals, and stronger as a family. And your children will thrive and move their mountains and improve the world in generations to come.

If you read this book and decide you'd like help implementing its strategies as quickly as possible, or if you have questions, please book a call with our team here:

https://sevengenerationslegacy.com/strategycall

Helping people like you optimize your financial life, build multigenerational wealth, and design a multigenerational legacy of more than money is exactly what we do every day.

We're here to help.

To your success,
Rachel Marshall

KEY CHAPTER TAKEAWAYS

- Your legacy is not defined by other people after your life. Instead, it is your power right now to proactively design your ideal life, your memory, and your impact that will live on far after you're gone.
- Don't let all the hurdles like busyness, overwhelm, and the fear that it will take too long or be too painful keep you from taking care of your family and benefitting generations to come.
- The Seven Generations Wealth and Legacy Formula walks you through nine clear steps to design a legacy of *meaning*, with the right legal *mechanism* to pass on wealth most effectively, and as much *money* as possible to fuel the good you can do for future generations.

LEGACY PLANNING CHECK-IN EXERCISE

Before we continue with the rest of the book, let's pull over here for a minute and get an honest look at where your legacy planning is at today.

For each question below, rate yourself on a scale of 1–5, based on how true the statement is for you. If something is "not at all true," rank it a 1. If something is "most definitely true," rank it a 5.

When you've rated yourself for each statement, total up your scores, and use the Answer Key to find your next steps.

Legacy Planning Check-In Statement	Self-Rating
1. I have a spouse, children, future children, or family I care deeply about, and they would be impacted financially if something happened to me tomorrow.	

2.	I have a plan to financially protect and provide for my loved ones.
3.	If I passed away, the financial provision I've arranged for my family will provide the same level of lifestyle as if I were still here.
4.	I've completed an estate and asset protection plan with an attorney that includes at least a will, a trust, power of attorney and healthcare power of attorney.
5.	I've reviewed and updated my estate plan in the last 2-5 years, and it accurately reflects my assets, relationships, and knowledge of my children today.
6.	My family knows about the inheritance I've planned to leave them and I've prepared them to be good stewards of the resources they'll receive by teaching them sound financial management.
7.	I've written letters to my children that they have already received or will receive at an appropriate age to ensure they know how I feel about them, and about the inheritance I'm leaving them, communicating the meaning of the gift along with my philosophy and wishes to ensure it's not just a transfer of assets that enables dependence and entitlement.
8.	FOR THOSE WITH MINOR CHILDREN—I have thought through everything I would pay for during my children's lifetime and written down these instructions for my trustee and heirs.
9.	My values, financial philosophy, and the purpose of my estate planning are clearly written and communicated with my family and trustees in a Memorandum of Trust.
10.	I have a trust in place and it doesn't give outright distributions, so the inheritance I leave isn't subject to creditors, and won't negatively affect the future estate of my heirs.
11.	I'm confident my trustees and family will make financial decisions congruent with my goals, and my named trustees know my children personally and are capable and willing to mentor my children in financial stewardship if I am not here.
12.	All of my assets are titled properly so that they are not subject to probate.

13. My financial plan includes continuity of family wealth with assets that are guaranteed to be available for the next generation.	
14. My kids want to spend time with me and they ask me for my input.	
15. Our family values are written down, displayed prominently where everyone can see them, are in alignment with how we live our lives, and our family discusses our values at least once a week with children living at home, and at least annually with adult children.	
16. We have a family logo with shared family secrets embedded in it.	
17. My family has weekly meetings where we discuss important family matters if children are still living at home, or at least annually if you have adult children.	
18. My family has a regular family day each week and spends goal-oriented time together at least weekly if you have children living at home, or at least annually with adult children.	
19. Our family has a planning session every year to plan out our family calendar and goals, prepare for the personal development of each of the members, and ensure we progress towards our family mission.	
20. All of my bank and investment account access, passwords, safe access, and final wishes for burial requests are written down, organized, and the people designated to handle these matters have been given the correct procedure to access the information.	
21. My estate planning and asset protection attorney(s), tax strategist, CPA, and financial planner work together to coordinate strategies that maximize my cash flow and assets during my lifetime and after I leave an inheritance to my children, and one of these professionals quarterbacks my financial team so I don't have to do it personally.	
22. TOTAL YOUR SCORE:	

What Your Score Really Means

Score 21–39
The Fundamentals of Your Legacy Planning Are Missing

The bad news is that your family is missing core, fundamental elements required to sustain a lasting legacy. You may have the legal structure without meaning, financial assets without guidance, or a strong family without any contingency plans. You've let the hurdles to legacy planning stand in your way, and you probably already know and feel the pressure of this every day. No surprise there.

However, the good news is that all of that can be fixed, and even better, it means you get to redesign your family legacy so it empowers your family for generations and represents everything you'd want to be remembered for.

Read this book with an open mind. Consider how implementing the Seven Generations Wealth and Legacy Formula from the ground up will radically improve your family and your estate planning. It won't take much for you to experience a night-and-day improvement.

Score 40–69
A Simple Estate Planning Addition Could Make Your Life A Lot Easier

If your score landed you here, it means your communication about what matters most is the thing holding you back from leaving behind a legacy that will last.

You likely rely on status quo financial planning or estate planning to build and transfer assets, but lack the communication needed for your plans to fulfill your wishes and enhance the lives of your loved ones for generations.

You've done the work, but unfortunately, it isn't working for you and your family the way you hope.

Communicating your heart and desires is less of an aptitude or personality; it's a formula that you can use to communicate the right things to the right people at the right time. The Seven

Generations Wealth and Leagacy Formula will allow you to communicate everything correctly. All you'll have to do is just be honest and follow the process. You'll be able to eliminate your estate planning stress and overwhelm, and feel empowered throughout the process. Even more, because you're communicating completely, your plans will succeed in empowering your children and grandchildren.

Get ready to experience the joy of estate planning you know will work, so you can sleep better at night knowing that you've done everything to protect your family and prepare a legacy for your posterity.

Score 70+
You're Ready to Add the Finishing Touches to Your Legacy Planning
You've probably got your financial and legal planning done correctly, and your Memorandum of Trust dialed in and custom-tailored to your family's values. All you need is a systematic way to prepare your children to receive an inheritance by mentoring them in character development and financial stewardship.

For you, the biggest hurdle to overcome is to infuse your meaning and values into your everyday family culture.

That's where the Seven Generations Wealth and Legacy Formula comes in. We'll help you design your rhythms, stories, and traditions so that your everyday life is an environment to live out what matters most to you. You'll have financial tools with a built-in mentorship capacity to act as the training wheels for developing financial stewardship in your children.

Then, the more fuel you add to your legacy in terms of financial assets, the more impact you can leave for multiple generations, knowing that each generation will add to your family's wealth.

1

FIGHTING TO BUILD OUR FAMILY

Crisis in the Delivery Room

U p until that day in mid-May of 2019, I hadn't considered I was weaving a legacy with my life. I hadn't articulated what my children needed to know. I wasn't ready to pass the baton. The legacy I would have left was unclear. I would have left money but not the guidance to create wealth and steward family resources.

But that was all about to change.

As they rolled my bed past my husband and my newborn daughter into the hall, my labor exhaustion muddled with the anesthesia and I surrendered to the idea of surgery. Following the difficult delivery of my second child, doctors feared for my life.

I was a mom with space in my heart for more.

I'd always envisioned a full table, family photos with a multitude of similar but distinct faces, and holidays bustling with the laughter of a tight-knit extended family. Coming from my own large family, I had experienced its love as well as its dysfunction and fragmenting. I think that's why I always gazed starry-eyed at the big families that had stayed close, marveling at their magic.

Our daughter Avie was seven years of free-spirited and giant-hearted balm to the ache in my heart. Still, I longed to add children to our family that was perfect but not yet complete.

My husband Lucas's unwavering stance through the years had been, "One at a time." He quite possibly meant, "One is good," without wanting to crush me.

As resolute as his words, I'd seen the way he came to life when he had become a dad for the first time, and I wanted that again for him—and us.

Building a family, like everything we'd done in nearly thirteen years of marriage, had been intentional. Get married, finish school, reach income and financial targets, wait five years to start a family . . . . We had it all planned out. But I hadn't really seen what came *after* that. I hadn't predicted entrepreneurship or the effort it would take.

Then, in the chaos of having our first infant and an infant business at the same time, I had agreed that it had seemed like the best thing to wait to grow our family.

My words had come tumbling right out of my mouth to a dear friend before I'd even thought it through, "We'll probably wait seven years and then have a bunch more kids."

It was as if God himself had spoken the words to give me hope of more children to come while warning me that I'd have to be stiflingly patient. I'd resigned that more children were a promise for later, and that gave me consolation in the long waiting. Then those seven years careened by, and all the while, the idea of having more children felt like more than we had mental resources for.

Until, just as predicted, the timing felt right. Well, almost right.

Though mysteriously, we have faces that never quite seem to age, Lucas and I were both graying, and we felt anything longer than a seven-year gap between kids would make it hard for them to feel like they were growing up in the same world.

On the one hand, it would be completely resetting the clock and starting over with sleepless nights, babyproofing, and all the other things new parents fifteen years younger than us had the energy for. Who did we think we were anyway? We were finally hitting our stride in business and getting into a groove with our schedule, our sleep, and our life.

On the other hand, I felt the pull that maybe we would need to have another child before we felt ready.

The day of Avie's seventh birthday party—a magical day at an equestrian farm with sweet friends riding and painting ponies and devouring a unicorn cake I'd been perfecting until the wee hours of that morning—I just knew I was pregnant.

My heart skipped a beat when that second pink line appeared on the test the next morning.

It had been exactly seven years! I knew it was God tenderly chuckling as He confirmed His word, and I was overcome with extravagant gratitude. We would have the privilege of raising, parenting, and stewarding another child.

During the next nine months, radiant bliss swept me up in expectancy. I truly had never felt better in my life. That is every moment except my visits to the doctor, which riled up an irrational fear of all things medical, known as "white-coat syndrome," that had every midwife raising her eyebrows.

With Avie, I'd developed pre-eclampsia (a pregnancy disorder marked by high blood pressure, protein in urine, swollen ankles, and increased risk of seizure or stroke). Even though it occurred right at the end of that pregnancy, we'd had to induce early. The memory was the one black mark staining my first delivery experience. I hoped for redemption this time, but I couldn't shake the worry I'd end up right where we had last time.

I did everything I could to reduce stress, from daily meditation and deep breathing to applying and diffusing essential oils. I even checked my blood pressure at home multiple times a day to confirm that my baseline was perfect. Still, every time I went to the clinic, my numbers spiraled out of whack. It seemed almost hilarious every minute except when I was seated in the chair and they pulled out the exasperating blood pressure cuff.

Still, we planned, prayed for, believed in, and prepared for a gentle, intervention-free water birth at our midwifery center.

Avie was deeply invested in becoming a big sister. Sometimes I think the hundreds of prayers she whispered for a baby sister played a part in materializing this child. I let her skip school to tag along to almost all my prenatal appointments, and we planned to have her present at the birth. All was going well, and the baby and I were vibrantly healthy.

As my daughter grew inside, I fell even more in love with her. I came to know this little life as peace, as I felt her substance, deep grounding, and steadfast strength.

During the last month, I could no longer coax my blood pressure down in the office.

Then something happened that changed my life forever. Baby's growth started slowing, then shrinking. I was put on pelvic rest. Then bed rest. Then baby needed extra ultrasounds and non-stress tests twice a week. When I was nearly admitted at a prenatal visit during week 37, the door for a water birth in the home-like calm of the midwifery center slammed shut.

The midwife told me I was high risk. Again.

I cried stinging tears as I grieved, choking on the disappointment. I felt like I hadn't been mentally strong enough to conquer my blood pressure and my anxieties about having a birth that looked different than I'd hoped. My fears roared into an inferno of discouragement and defeat. It all seemed as fatalistic as a death sentence, wresting control out of my hands.

Ten days before my due date, the warning signs reached a climax. That morning's non-stress test showed the baby's heart rate too high—a cry of distress. A rushed ultrasound placed her in the third percentile for size, estimated to be about five pounds, and diagnosed her as Intrauterine Growth Restricted (IUGR).

At the time, I had no idea the impact this would have. The problem was that my placenta was calcifying and no longer allowing the baby to get enough blood flow and nourishment to grow in utero.

Exacerbating matters—and still unclear whether a cause or an effect—my dangerously elevated blood pressure now classified me as having pregnancy-induced hypertension, just one step down from the dreaded preeclampsia.

They said we needed to induce right away to allow the baby to tolerate labor.

I couldn't help wondering, what would it mean to *not* tolerate labor? Would it mean a C-section? That was a monstrosity of panic for me. Or did it mean something even worse, that baby might not live?

This baby who was the antidote to my anxiety, this one I had grown to know as graceful faith, full of victorious purpose, favor, radiant wisdom, and success. She was fighting to survive.

As the nurse pushed my wheelchair through the long, low corridor from the clinic over to labor and delivery, I wavered between serenity and debilitating anxiety. I knew we hadn't come this far for everything I'd come to know about this baby girl to unravel and become untrue.

Heavy with the gravity of the risk, I anchored my mind on trusting God for the best possible outcome. I remembered the steadiness of the child I was carrying and clung with white-knuckled faith to the hope that she was healthy and whole.

I quietly acknowledged the wisdom that had called me to nest early with my bags tucked neatly in the corner of our room, the house whisked into order, and meals prepared ahead. Lucas and Avie were with me already, and my doula was anticipating my call. I witnessed a refrain of gratitude rising from my heart.

When I called to tell Claudia, my doula, we were inducing, she let out a long breath she'd been holding all weekend. She knew it was time. She was a pillar of safety and security during childbirth. At 72, she'd delivered thousands of miracles and had the innate wisdom to match. She had seen babies in similar condition wait too long for delivery and not survive, and she knew the only safe environment for my baby's continued growth and development was outside the womb.

Had this happened only two days later, she would have been out of town on a family trip, and I would have been calling in the backup doula team I barely knew. The crisis had this redemption, then; the timing was perfect, and her grounding, faith-filled presence would be there.

As I settled into the delivery bed, the nurse covered preliminaries and jotted goals on the whiteboard that would become my spotting point in the hours to come. Along with the goal of pain management and something else I don't remember, she asked what we would like to add.

I said, "Peace."

Wrapped inside that deliberate word, I meant the encompassing, supernatural peace of God, peace in our hearts, peaceful labor, peaceful baby, and the peace that is complete wholeness of mind, body, and spirit.

They hooked me up to the labor-inducing Pitocin drip, notching up the dosage as the hours dragged on. By dinner time, contractions still hadn't progressed, so we sent Claudia home to wait for active labor and Avie to spend the night with friends.

As if waiting for the darkness of nightfall and the sacred quietness of being alone, labor lurched into gear about an hour later.

We called Claudia back. When she arrived about nine o'clock, I was already in painful, nonverbal labor that rumbled into a crashing cadence.

They turned the Pitocin down, but labor came so fast and intense that it was shocking to my body and the baby's.

"Turn over on your hands and knees!"

Ericka was the midwife on call that evening. With her experience and gentle wisdom, I was in good hands. But there was an uncharacteristic urgency in her tone. What I didn't know was that they had lost the baby's heartbeat.

I'd refused pain medication in the attempt to have as natural of a birth as possible. But that meant I bore the full force of every brutal Pitocin-filled contraction, with nothing to ease the jagged pain. The vicious waves assaulted my body, nearly knocking the wind out of me, and I only knew that I couldn't move.

In the fleeting rests between contractions and assisted by countless strong hands, I managed to turn.

Concern mounted as each minute crept on. We were racing time.

I couldn't last. I was only four centimeters just minutes ago, less than halfway to the ten required for delivery. It seemed like endless miles of dark tunnel left to grope through.

I felt like I was drowning, being smothered like the light I had was flickering out. I wanted to go back and turn off labor. Dying felt easier than going on.

"Who put this here?" I snapped at Claudia and flung the paperwork she'd been using to fan my face.

Somehow, one thought stood out through the chaos like a scarlet thread of salvation in the terrifying space. *If I can't go on, it must be nearly over.* I remembered Claudia coaching eight years earlier during my first childbirth class. *The point you feel like you absolutely can't do this, you're almost through.*

I gulped air and gathered hope. Courage. Strength. Resolve.

It didn't matter if all the boxes were checked and the professionals gave me permission. I knew she was tiny. Suddenly, I was fully inward, aware of nothing but submitting to the instinct of my body to birth my child.

The long tunnel I'd seen ahead was just forty-three excruciating minutes of active labor until the catapulting train suddenly broke through into open air. The jarring ceased, and time stopped as I bore her body into the world.

"Is she alive?" I dared to ask, choking on tears and trying hard to focus through the disorienting pain.

"Yes, she's alive," came the response.

Relief flooded my heart and caught in my throat. Yet, there was still urgency in the midwife's voice.

I couldn't see that she was tangled in the cord, listless and grey. They unwrapped her tiny body end over end.

"Can I cut the cord?" Lucas asked.

"Yes, but quickly."

We'd planned delayed cord clamping and immediate skin-to-skin contact, but at my first glimpse of her, she was across the room on the warmer.

I was delirious and drained but still tensed with uneasiness. A fragile minute passed while they lifted and dropped her hands before she rallied and let out her first cry. Then another four minutes before she was declared healthy.

And the color gushed back into the room.

Because of the escalation, the doctor had rushed in to deliver my baby. The unit was short-staffed, bustling with multiple deliveries all at once, and Dr. Golden had barely made it from another birth to be there in time. Then, she disappeared as quickly as she'd come to attend to another patient's emergency C-section.

They placed my baby's miraculously new and tiny body on my chest.

We were nearly settled on naming her Olivia, meaning *peace*, but hadn't fully committed. Yet, in that instant, even without words, I knew that we would.

She was the gift of peace I'd prayed for, materialized in my arms. Her giant almond eyes locked with mine as if to say, *Mommy, is everything going to be okay?*

My gaze reassured her, *Yes, all is well.*

But I barely had time to savor the moment.

Just as one crisis dissipated, another appeared like a harsh spotlight blaring its ugly heat straight down at me.

The contractions to deliver the placenta came as aftershocks only a slight step down from the force of delivery. Through those grimacing tremors, we realized something just wasn't right.

"Push!" directed the midwife.

I obeyed.

Repeatedly, for nearly an hour, I bore down against nothing, calling on deeper wells of effort than I could find.

The veins in my neck and forehead nearly popped, the strain stirring up a deafening headache.

Lucas and Claudia lifted my shoulders to help me push.

As if dragging a stubborn mule, the midwife pulled on the cord that was still firmly affixed to my uterine wall deep inside.

Waves of contorting pain coursed through me, and I collapsed into convulsive shivering.

She sent the nurse to bring Dr. Golden, but the doctor was still occupied in surgery.

"She can't come. She said you'll have to do a manual extraction."

Ericka's face was composed. Calling on her inner strength, she was rising to meet the challenge.

Yet at the moment, I knew this was a doctor's work. I studied her with a gaze that said, *I know you are terrified, and so am I, but we can do this.* And then her whole arm was inside my uterus, struggling desperately to pry the placenta loose.

After multiple failed attempts, as I cringed and shuddered in pain, Dr. Golden emerged and attempted the same procedure fruitlessly.

Earnestly, she breathed, "I'm not doing this anymore. We need to take her to the operating room."

Two anesthesiologists appeared and mercifully pushed the first pain reliever into my leg before wheeling me out of my baby's room to surgically remove my retained placenta. I saw the clock marking 10:45 p.m., Lucas cradling our baby girl, the doorframe, then the altered reality of a glimpse inside the sterile steel of the operating room where I was asked to move myself onto a narrow beam-like table.

During surgery, I took a sharp turn for the worst.

That's when, with my memory suspended, I truly hit rock bottom. Over the next four hours, my body plummeted harrowingly close to death as I faced one life-threatening complication after the next.

As soon as the placenta was scraped free, I hemorrhaged severely, losing at least two liters of blood. Then, my uterus refused to clamp to slow the blood flow. They placed a balloon into my uterus to add counterpressure, but the bleeding would not relent. They nearly resorted to an emergency hysterectomy.

Three hours later, as they rounded the corner, wheeling me out of surgery, I suddenly fell unconscious. They rushed me to ICU, unstable and in critical condition. At some point, the hospital loudspeakers blared with a medical alert, summoning a cross-disciplinary team of specialists, including a respiratory specialist and an intensive care specialist, among others.

I was facing a life-threatening emergency called DIC, with severe bleeding caused by an acute clotting disorder that arose because of complications in childbirth and surgery.

With this complication of platelets and hemoglobin, I slumped quickly with severe anemia, and my blood suddenly began forming small clots throughout my bloodstream. These clots were in danger of blocking small arteries and veins. Complicating matters, they used up platelets, depleting the clotting factor I needed to control the excessive bleeding.

I was unconscious, bleeding profusely and uncontrollably, with the risk of multiple organ failure and a fifty percent survival rate. My condition was desperate, and the prognosis was grim. If I pulled through this, there could likely be long-term damage to my brain, heart, liver, and kidneys.

My blood pressure tanked, refusing to stabilize. All the color seeped out of my body, even my lips, and my kidneys stopped producing urine.

I didn't look like I was going to make it.

This meant that my new baby girl nearly became motherless just hours after her birth. Lucas would have been left a single dad to raise two girls on his own.

What I couldn't see at the time was that moment nearly became the period at the end of my story. There would have been no closing chapter. No chance for editing. No tying together the loose ends. No saying all the things I'd planned to communicate over the coming years. Music, and then silence. All my good intentions, plans, and hopes for the future had almost been

10

snuffed out abruptly with no warning. In a matter of minutes, my life on this earth had almost vaporized.

That would have meant I wouldn't have been there to invest in my baby daughter's life with a relationship. I wouldn't have been there to nurture my girls as they grew into young women. My last piece of advice would have been spoken, my last hug to steady my girls and kiss their boo-boos, my last memory created together.

There I wavered on the brink of death, with no guarantee that anything would pull me out of the nosedive. The only way to try was to transfuse blood to restore the balance of my blood composition, but all the blood they gave me was just flowing right back out. My life hung from a thread that was a tiny red IV line trickling a massive blood transfusion. The seconds, minutes, and hours wore on as my doctors hoped beyond hope that it would work.

2

JOLTED AWAKE

How My Near-Death Experience Became the Catalyst of Our Legacy

. . . Instead of being superficial, death invites you to be a person of depth . . . the message of Ecclesiastes [is] an invitation to be a person who realizes that living a good life means preparing to die a good death.

Have you met people like this? They're actually fully alive, engaged with the world and their family and the goodness of creation because they know that they have it all on loan—it's a gift—and that one day God will simply call time, but when He does, they're ready to go.

—David Gibson, *Living Life Backward*

I was given a second chance at life, and the meaning of that incredible rescue was not lost on me.

I had been unconscious for forty-five minutes.

Then, as miraculously as cold embers reigniting, my eyelids fluttered open, and my vision found a place to land. Though fuzzy, I noticed the clock overhead first—almost 2:30.

2:30 what? Must be a.m.

It must have been nearly four hours since Lucas had last seen me, and he must be worried sick!

Again, my body shivered violently. This time, I felt the comforting heaviness of warmed blankets piled high. The tiny room was a glare of bright lights, and nine solemn faces circled tightly

13

around. Watching. Waiting. Witnessing. I drifted in and out of consciousness as the details slowly started to drop into place, like the color from a crayon deliberately rubbing a paper to life. There was Dr. Golden, the OBGYN I had last seen in the delivery room. Dr. Humphrey, who, just days ago, during a prenatal visit, had cleared me to go home. A man with a kind face, who I recalled asking to hold my hand for comfort as my fear had welled up—at a time, it seemed so long ago.

A simple, solitary feeling washed over me and pervaded the room: *I'm grateful to be alive.*

It started like the single pitch-perfect note at the very beginning of a song, subtly rising from the stillness, calling every fiber of my being to awaken, and rising to a crescendo that flooded the room.

My thoughts expanded.

God is good.

I knew He had been close and carried me.

Another several moments passed, and a new thought emerged into my awareness: *I am loved.*

I felt held by the highest in humanity. These scrubs-wearing staff huddled around—I knew their time, attention, and love had far eclipsed professional duty. They were working together for my health and my very life. I felt their depth of compassion and expert skill reviving me. Though the reasons were cloudy, every fiber of my being wanted to hug their necks and weep with gratitude.

These beautiful truths thudded softly and reverberated through my soul, weaving together like the strains of a melody. They coalesced, building and lifting me with the theme of a new song I couldn't place just yet.

And my baby?

Those deep, piercing eyes had gazed up at me with an otherworldly knowing, questioning if everything would be okay. My eyes had affirmed and confirmed that yes, darling, we are here, and everything is right in the world.

How was she? Where was she? Where was I? What had happened?

14

During those watery moments, I caught fragments.

"You lost a lot of blood . . . given lots of blood . . . ."

There had been a fight for my life. Substantial resources had been spent for me. There were many nameless donors whose blood now flowed through my veins and gave me life.

I breathed in worth.

"Very scary . . . you remember the worst situations in your career, and unfortunately, this will be a night I never forget."

"We're a low-risk hospital. We rarely see anything like this here . . . maybe less than once a year is there a postpartum case in ICU."

That's when I realized, deep down, that it could have ended another way. I may not have woken up to the oxygen of this world and the embrace of humanity.

Over the next two weeks, I assembled and connected snippets of conversation from eyewitness accounts of medical staff, Lucas, and Claudia. Even a year later, I'm still frenzied and wide-eyed Google searching to make the abstract medical terminology appallingly concrete. With each new revelation, I gape at just how close to the brink of death I had teetered, and how uncertain the outcome had looked over those four hours that my memory had erased.

For me, that changed everything. While I had to learn the details of this defining moment second-hand, the scars were immediately imprinted on my consciousness. I'd stared straight into the sickening jaws of death and almost hoisted the white flag of surrender. But I'd been plucked from its clutches. Death had relented, and I was astoundingly preserved.

First, I Recognized My Own Value.

In the rhythm of life, I'd become unaware of the gravity and meaning of my own moments. I'd planned and scheduled and coordinated and administrated and attended to the details *outside* of me. But I hadn't even noticed my own existence.

I'd seen what I *could do* but had failed to see *that I was*.

15

Now, simply *being alive* meant something grand enough to shake the foundations of my soul. I wasn't guaranteed the next minute, let alone hours, days, or years. Yet, here I was, living. That meant that God had deliberately granted my every shimmering moment, dropping them out intentionally and measuring them one by one.

That awareness of both the fragility and the weightiness of my own existence bid me to weep in awe and reverence.

NEXT, I FELT CALLED TO MAKE EVERY MOMENT COUNT THE MOST RIGHT NOW.

Instead of waking up to the life I'd left, my consciousness had ripped wide open, and each breath I drew felt spiked with a crisp hyper-awareness. Almost dying had jolted me completely awake.

As if I hadn't heard when the Creator of the universe had whispered me to life the first time, He'd thundered *a second time* that word that had called me alive, awake, and resurrected. The way I could shout back my thanks and make my voice carry to the heavens was to punctuate time by making my moments count.

Like you, my love for my children is like a rushing river—wide, deep, and endless, with a strong current that tumbles around any obstacle.

In all my work, my children have always been my deepest *why*. They are the ones closest I need to lead, model for, and make wise decisions for because they're following in my footsteps and wanting to be like me. More than anything, I want to raise the ceiling of their possibility and pave the way for their long-term wholeness.

Any way you cut it, this is a lifetime's work. My best chance of hitting the mark requires living out the relationship for decades to come.

I'm thirty-eight. Ideally, I'll live a full life over at least the next seventy-five or so years, age gracefully into a centenarian, and be healthy, vigorous, and strong to experience it all. But what if I didn't have all those years to invest into my kids' lives?

In all my dreams about growing our family, never once had I contemplated our family without me in it. As any normal mother, I worry about something happening to my kids. But I'd never considered that something could happen to me.

Now, my invincibility cloak had been revealed as the emperor's new clothes, and my eyes were opened to just how vulnerable I was, right now, in the prime of my life, pressed between my mortality and my potential. The only way to care for them profoundly and secure a vibrant life for them was to do the *most* today.

But how?

Right now, Olivia's only a toddler. While the first five years of life are the most formative, the memories are also the least conscious. Everything I do now means so much for her future, but I have no way to love enough now to make sure she'll even remember me.

Avalynn is ten. Lucas and I have laid a strong foundation, and most of her life is now squarely in the space that she'll have memory recall for the rest of her life. But we've barely scratched the surface of teaching the intangibles that will serve her for the rest of her adult life.

I knew I could never give enough kisses, embrace long enough, take enough pictures, say enough I love you's, or even invest enough quality time to guarantee a strong foundation for them to reach the heights. Even if I courageously said all the words that needed to be said, fulfilled my life mission, enjoyed life to the brim, and earned "well done," it wouldn't guarantee their success.

How could I bring my love into high definition to mean the most and make the greatest ripple effect in the years to come? What could I do right now to ensure they know who they are and have the tools, teaching, and belief in themselves to be successful and create the best in life? How could I give them opportunity in the future, knowing that my own next breath wasn't a guarantee?

I needed a way to know that my love could hold my children for all time, even if my arms couldn't. I had to condense my mattering into *right now*—the only time I was guaranteed—to make it last and hit the mark and be effective and make the biggest impact in the future. If the future arrived and I wasn't there, I needed my love to continue existing and supporting and guiding and lifting my girls.

How could I love with a love like that?

And here's what happened next. I realized that building my family meant so much more than adding humans to our nuclear unit. It meant investing profoundly in the team of our family right here to create a multigenerational legacy that could change the world.

3

CONSTRUCTION

Building a Family Legacy

S tretched over hundreds of conversations, we'd talked a lot about what we wanted for our family, our kids, and our life. We'd been on a wealth creation trajectory for years and were continually aligning the threads of our life to live out what was most important to us. We'd even done contingency planning to make sure our children would be cared for, and the money was in place if anything happened to us. But we'd only thought about it from a conceptual, arms-length point of view.

Now, we realized if we weren't here to build our legacy with our moment-by-moment experience of living life together, so much was left to chance.

We had no way of knowing if our desires would be fulfilled and that everything we hoped for our children would remain intact. We already had an estate plan in place, but we had nothing written down to guide our appointed decision-makers on how to raise our girls and invest all of who we are into those precious babies if that became a reality.

We had done the planning, but it lacked meaning!

Here's how we discovered what was missing . . .

I was finally stable five and a half hours after leaving Lucas at the threshold of the delivery room.

To my left, I glimpsed his reassuring frame, striding, running, seemingly floating towards my tiny glass room, and then

19

we melted into sobs in one another's arms. Gratitude swirled with relief and the pain of seeing each other go through what we were experiencing. I don't remember him leaving, but eventually, he was gone again, back upstairs to care for our baby girl.

I drifted in and out of sleep. My body felt heavy and distant. My legs didn't move all day. I didn't shift my position or sit up. Simply moving my arms took all my effort and energy.

In contrast with my stillness, the room was constantly awake.

In a constant chugging motor and whooshing of air, my compression socks inflated and deflated around my calves to prevent clots and deep vein thrombosis. My bed stirred with a massage at intervals for mobility therapy. The blood pressure cuff pleaded with my cardiovascular system to normalize, squeezing to life about every thirty minutes. The phlebotomist came incessantly to draw blood for frequent lab tests, and labor and delivery staff poked and prodded to check my fundal height.

And silently, the thin red line continued dripping life-giving blood components into my veins. Several times, two nurses arrived together to replace the empty bag of blood, meticulously cross-checking out loud the blood type and match.

In total, I was given an enormous transfusion of eight units of blood until nearly every drop of blood in my body had been replaced. To quench my outrageous thirst, finally, I was permitted ice, then water, and at last, ginger ale.

Miraculously, I felt no pain except for the fat lip and sore throat I had from being intubated during surgery. The emotional pain was much greater. I knew Lucas bore the crushing weight of being both mom and dad alone through the exhaustion of sleeplessness and the unbearable worry he'd endured. I was separated from my baby, feeling lifeless and helpless. My baby didn't have her mama to be the reassuring smell and voice that had carried her all those months. She needed a bottle instead of breastmilk, and my new mama arms, craving to hold my child, were starkly empty.

It wasn't supposed to be like this.

The hospital chaplain visited to ask how to announce my baby's birth, and I realized that in the commotion, we hadn't even named her. The sacred, holy moment of wrapping the intoxicating purity of a newborn baby in words they'll be called their whole life through—we'd somehow missed that step, and our precious girl was still nameless the day after her birth.

I called Lucas's room on the hospital phone, and together in the same medical complex but separated by corridors, flights of stairs, and thick brick walls that blocked our cell service, we chose her name.

Olivia. It means olive branch, peaceful, fruitful, dignity, beauty, and prosperity.

The chaplain announced her birth over the loudspeakers to the whole hospital, and I smiled as her name settled in and resonated. Such a strong, brave girl she was to overcome so much on her first day.

Late that morning, I brushed my teeth and took out the contact lenses I'd been wearing since the morning before. The nurse pulled back my rumpled hair and washed my face.

After making sure the ICU was free of communicable diseases, the nurse was able to clear Olivia to come to visit me for a beautiful forty minutes. Soon, I saw a caravan of Lucas and the nurse, with the hospital crib carrying Olivia like a sedan chair. I don't need to tell you that it was a welcome sight!

She was more perfect than I'd remembered from the tumultuous hour the night before. She was finally here, in my arms at last, and I felt whole. She needed me, and I needed her. Our family felt complete despite me being tethered by an extra measure of gravity and medical cords and Avie still with our friends. I drank in the moment, deeply grateful we'd made it this far.

That day I spent recovering in the ICU was the tipping point for making huge changes in our life and our family.

I honestly have no clue how Lucas would have navigated a world of parenting our daughters without me. Even more critically, we realized what we barely dared to say in quaking and hushed whispers. I became aware of how dependent the quality of their life was upon our livelihood, and I wasn't confident that our girls would have the best if something happened to *both* of us.

Months later, Lucas had several casual conversations after church with a friend who was an attorney, mulling over the concepts of customized estate planning. Then, we dug deep and poured over several books on family wealth and estate planning. In our quest, we became aware of what was possible, far beyond the scope of the planning we'd already done, and we knew there were several limitations in our first estate plan that would need to be updated or replaced.

Even more than doing the legal planning itself, however, we knew we needed to consider our trustee, power of attorney, and guardian choices and own the communication with them so they would know what to do if they were ever called to rise to that responsibility.

Then, we needed to share the most important values and purpose of our family so we could preserve and protect everything we stand for. That meant we had some important questions to answer. We needed to translate our desires into a language that would clarify and provide guidance so the meaning of our planning, gifts, and dreams for our girls would not be lost. The problem was that there was little to help us navigate this monumental task in a simple and straightforward way. It took almost six months of tense conversations, giving up every evening after the girls were asleep, and we had to fumble and find our way in the dark.

We were piecing together books we'd read, ideas we'd collected over years of work parallel to the estate planning realm, and personal experiences of losing grandparents over the years. We were leaning into the hardest, most emotional, and most vulnerable things to think about, much less speak aloud. It felt like a lot of guesswork, where there was no map, and we were sitting down for conversations to create what we couldn't necessarily even define.

What were our goals? What did we want to accomplish in our lifetime? In generations past us? What was the best way to do that? What relationships needed to be cultivated? Why was this work the most important work we could be putting our time into again? What even is the difference between a mission and a vision? And are we thinking of ourselves personally, our business, our nuclear family, or longer-range?

There were thousands of questions about what would be best for our children and how we could write a plan that works right now but still leave it fluid enough that we could update it along the way as we evolve and grow. It felt like we were tackling ghosts, putting concrete words and planning around moving targets that will probably and hopefully never happen.

It was about eight years from the date we'd first thought about estate planning when we finally locked in a plan that we felt settled about and communicated all the necessary things to all the people in our legacy team.

You saw this list in the preface, but it is important enough to remind you here of exacty what we worked to create after that pivotal moment.

Ultimately, here is what we created:

- A **love letter** for our girls to read if anything happened to us
- A new **estate plan**
- A *Memorandum of Trust* to guide our estate plan that spells out the purpose of our trust, our family values, vision, mission, goals, and how to use our money to fulfill those aims
- **Relationships and transparent communication** with a carefully selected trustee, guardian, power of attorney, and contingent relationships
- The **upgraded life insurance** that would provide the most payout to fund everything we hoped for our family

- An **organization system** for all our documents, accounts, and everything our trustees and heirs would need to move forward after we pass away

Creating this legacy was how I waged war against my mortality. I took away its power to mow down my dreams for my girls by creating a plan that would work *with or without me.* That freed me to live more fully and to lean into loving hard and chasing our goals with everything we've got.

> CREATING YOUR LEGACY
> IS HOW YOU WAGE WAR
> AGAINST YOUR MORTALITY.

When we completed this legacy planning, we asked our estate planning attorney how often he sees people do the deep work to pass on money and guidance for future generations to flourish.

His answer shocked us. We were the only ones.

Most people never do any planning at all, and those who do plan often miss the most important part of communicating the purpose of their gift. Lack of planning leads to all the problems with gifting money that make us shudder—like leaving those you love a sudden windfall that makes life worse instead of better or creating entitled trust-fund babies who vaporize an inheritance overnight in a way that would make you roll over in your grave.

One day, I looked over at Lucas and wondered, *Would the work we'd done to carve out our family's legacy be a repeatable process that anyone else could use to create a failsafe contingency plan?*

Would it help families to live more intentionally and create a fuller legacy with their days? Could it soften the blow of a monstrous catastrophe for just one child? Might this planning empower families to live freer lives and do the most good in their family forever? Is it possible that they could provide a pathway to raise the level of wealth and flourishing in the next generation? Would it expand the definition of a legacy to more than money and empower people to create it with their life, not just with their death? Could it be true that without this process, there would be limits to the good your plan can do?

So, we tested it. We coached families at all different life seasons to create their legacy plan—parents with teens, grandparents, and brand new parents. And we discovered that, yes, this process didn't just work for our legacy, but that everything we had done was a framework that anyone could use to make sure their loved ones had *everything* possible to prepare the best life for them while they were living. This process would create the best-case scenario to catch your family if the unthinkable happened to you. And it guarantees that your legacy isn't stopped, shrunk, or slowed down when you exit this earth.

I realized this same confidence, freedom, and peace are accessible to anyone—with the right thinking and the steps to put it in place. That's why I knew I couldn't stop with creating this legacy for our own family.

Now I am on a mission to help you courageously become a legacy creator in the most profound sense. As you do, you will provide for your children and extend the reach of your love past you. Your legacy will be the thread that pulls your family in close and helps you scale your mountains.

With this legacy, you will become the setting that holds the diamond of each child and grandchild that comes after you, allowing them to prosper and flourish. You'll be the inflection point of a multi-generation ripple effect that elevates each one beyond you. Your life work will grow wings and last forever, so you'll have the greatest impact for the longest time.

This three-step framework for creating a legacy of more than money that lasts for generations is what I'll teach you now:

- Pillar 1: The Meaning
- Pillar 2: The Mechanism
- Pillar 3: The Money

And rather than teaching theoretically, I'll step in close and show you exactly what we did.

First, I'll demonstrate how we wrote down our family guidance system, to clarify what was most important to our family.

Then, I'll walk you through our estate plan and how we determined the most effective boat to carry our legacy between generations.

And finally, I'll show you how we guaranteed that there will be an inheritance of financial resources to grant our children every opportunity we would have created with our lives.

But before I walk you through those steps, let me show you how these three pillars work together as three essential pieces of a multigenerational legacy.

WANT TO TALK?

Would you like us to help you through the process of designing multigenerational wealth and your legacy of more than money? Book a call here to get started.

https://sevengenerationslegacy.com/strategycall

4

SPARE ROOM

Ready Whenever You Need It

Your family legacy is important enough to spend the time building each of these pillars that will support it through the generations to come.

- Pillar 1: The Meaning
- Pillar 2: The Mechanism
- Pillar 3: The Money

With these three pillars in place, you ensure the coherence of your financial plans and the confidence that you're using your money to carry out your family mission and strengthen your family in the years ahead.

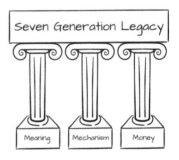

These three pillars calm my storming seas of worry about the unknown.

Each day, I'm reminded that I'm not invincible. I thank God for waking me up in the morning and letting me live to see another day. I step in to live to the fullest, draw out the most beauty, and make the moments matter. And each day, I can lean in, knowing that whenever my breath stops, there is a safety net to catch my family, carry forward the meaning of my life, and provide the funding to make it possible.

When you have these three pillars of your family legacy in place, it's like a spare room. Judging by the frequency of the foot traffic in your home, your spare room may seem to be the most non-essential part of your square footage. It's not as well-worn as your entry, as productive as the kitchen, as conversation-holding as the dinner table, or as loved as the playroom. Most of the time, it may seem like wasted space.

Your Generational Legacy Is Like a Spare Room

But a spare room is a *contingency plan* built into your house. Because of the spare room, you have the freedom to invite overnight guests, open your home to extended visitors, or consider foster care.

Just like a spare room, your legacy automatically builds a contingency plan into your life. It's always available, made up, and prepared, so you don't have to fear the unknown. And while I don't plan to befriend the unwelcome guest of death, if he arrives too soon, we have done all to prepare a life for our posterity and our posterity for a flourishing life.

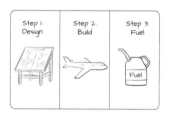

How to Create Your Legacy

Step 1: Design	Step 2: Build	Step 3: Fuel

PILLAR 1: THE MEANING—CREATING YOUR LEGACY

Before you can expect your legacy to fulfill all your hopes and intentions, you must define exactly what those are. This is the *WHY*. Why does your legacy matter? Why do you want to leave money to your children? What do you hope it will do for them and their children?

If you were going to design an aircraft, you must determine the *purpose* of inventing it in the first place. What would it carry? Where would it travel? How would it alter, improve upon, or transform previous designs to increase performance?

Without a *WHY*, you'll never know if you've succeeded. That's why the first step to crafting your legacy is to discover the meaning and write down your family's constitution. Your legacy starts with defining what makes your family a unit. This deep work becomes a rallying point for your family because it creates a shared meaning and culture. In fact, this step is the most often missed part of long-term planning, but it's the most important part of your legacy—far more significant than the money itself. That's because it provides the compass that directs the decisions, character, and stewardship of all your family's resources. The best way to raise your children with this compass is to walk through a lifelong relationship of guidance, mentorship, training, and character development. But if you don't get the chance to journey together or there isn't time to download everything you hoped to instill, creating this written guidance system is the single best substitute.

Step 1: Design

And as a bonus, it helps you be more aligned with everything important to you while you live out your everyday.

PILLAR 2: THE MECHANISM—CARRYING YOUR LEGACY

Once you have etched out the meaning you want to fulfill and experience on this earth, how do you guarantee that your death can't interrupt your life's work? You need to make sure the mechanism you choose to transport your legacy through time will serve its purpose, no matter when it's called upon. This is the *HOW*. How will you move your money and your memory through time across your relationships?

If you were designing and building the plane, this is where you'd build the physical structure and prepare everything necessary for flight. You'd order the parts, fasten every rivet, hire a crew, schedule flights, and sell tickets.

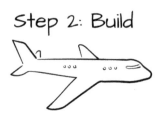

Step 2: Build

Like an airplane facilitates your travel, you need a mechanism to do the heavy lifting behind the scenes to hold and carry your legacy. During your lifetime, you direct your life, decisions, and assets. But after you're gone and can't continue directing the affairs of your own life, you need another agent to become an extension of you to take over your responsibilities, act as you would have, and *do* all the stuff of getting your values and your money to the next generation.

The best vehicle to transport your whole legacy from one generation to the next, one person to the next, or even from one person to a charity is an estate plan.

An estate plan accommodates the safe transport of your desires and wishes so that everything you dream and plan for your family beyond you will come to pass.

That means that the values, relationships, work, and production you set in motion will continue after your life across the widest range of economic and social climates.

In fact, even if you aren't married, don't have children, or don't have sizable assets today, putting an estate plan in place now allows you to decide who will handle your affairs and ensure your loved ones and legacy are set up for the future.

When passing the baton of your assets is done well, your legacy continues without getting interrupted or stopped because of your life event. Your money is available for your intended recipients without delay or shrinkage, and it's used to continue growing your family's whole wealth in each generation as you envisioned.

PILLAR 3: THE MONEY—FUNDING YOUR LEGACY

When you've fleshed out your family's purpose and guidance system and have set up a plan to transport your assets to continue that purpose past your own life, it's time to put your legacy in motion! Now we come to the *WHAT*. What will be the financial substance of your legacy? What determines how much good you can do and how long your legacy will last? It's how much fuel you put in!

Step 3: Fuel

Fuel

An airliner requires jet fuel to run its engines and propel it thousands of miles across the sky. Just how much fuel does it need? There are lots of dynamics at play here that influence fuel efficiency.[1] Those include the load weight and aerodynamics of lift, thrust, and drag, whether you're taking off or landing, and, not surprisingly, how much the fuel itself weighs.

I'm not an aviation engineer by any stretch of the imagination, but a little googling suggests that a commercial Boeing 747 at cruising altitude burns about a gallon of fuel per second.[2] That works out to about five gallons of fuel per mile of a flight.[3] So, to fly your aircraft the 3,000 miles from New York JFK to Los Angeles International Airport, you'd need approximately 15,000 gallons of jet fuel.

If that sounds like a lot, the 747 is capable of much more! Its fuel tanks can carry about 60,000 gallons, weighing over 400,000 pounds, and propelling almost sixteen hours of nonstop flight.

Your financial resources are the fuel that funds your legacy and determines its range. And the more money you have to propel your family vision and purpose, the further it will travel and the more impact it will have.

> YOUR FINANCIAL RESOURCES ARE THE FUEL THAT FUNDS YOUR LEGACY AND DETERMINES ITS RANGE.

But there are so many variables that are outside your control. How long will your money be invested? How long will you live? How much income will you need to use up each year along the way? How much can you turn your money into over time? How will taxes, inflation, and interest rates impact your whole financial world and your outcomes? Will you reach time and money freedom in your lifetime? And what will be left to leave to your children?

No one can answer these questions. While we wish we could see the future, it stays hidden backstage behind a curtain, leaving us to imagine what lies ahead. However, there is one way you can guarantee the best possible outcome across the widest range of circumstances.

It's by starting from the end.

STARTING FROM THE END

If you could restructure your finances, and doing so gave you the ability to do everything you're already doing even better, *plus* leave the greatest legacy possible, would you consider it?

The prevalent thinking about money is that it's a scarce resource in limited supply. From that perspective, everything is a tradeoff, which means increasing your financial legacy can seem like you must give up opportunities and experiences today. But the great news is that your money isn't a zero-sum game limited to the two options of spending today or spending later. Instead, focusing on how you can create more at the *end* means you do *both* better!

The way to have the most fuel to carry your family forward at the end of your life is to buy life insurance. No matter the size or complexity of your other assets, owning the best quality and most life insurance coverage possible gives you the perfect complement to your financial picture and ensures the greatest financial legacy at the end. And because you won't have low-grade anxiety about what will happen to your kids when you die, you will have more energy to dedicate to now. You'll be able to create more money in your lifetime and enjoy it more all along the way.

That's because when you gain sure-footed confidence from standing on unshakeable, solid ground, you'll begin to think differently and discover new solutions you couldn't see before. When you set your sights on the finish line of your life and work backward, that one inevitable event can bolster your family's financial footing rather than deplete it. And if you end well, you'll automatically improve everything else all along the way.

EVER READY

That's why—even while you're living out your regular life and it doesn't seem you have time to think ahead—creating a bulletproof contingency plan that's always ready to execute will help you live out your whole life better.

But rather than the one-dimensional planning of getting your money in order, you need all three pillars to leave a legacy with the most impact.

Here's the truth: you don't have to leave just money OR meaning.

> YOU DON'T HAVE TO LEAVE JUST MONEY OR MEANING.

With all three pillars of your family legacy in place, you don't have to settle for either/or. Instead, you can get both money and meaning, securing the best of both worlds and doing the most good for your family for generations to come.

That's because your legacy is complete when it is personal *and* financial, passing on the valuables *and* the values, the tangible *and* the intangible, the physical *and* the spiritual, the quantitative *and* the qualitative, the money *AND* the meaning.

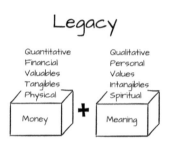

Legacy

Quantitative
Financial
Valuables
Tangibles
Physical

Money

+

Qualitative
Personal
Values
Intangibles
Spiritual

Meaning

For me, beyond securing substantial provision for generations to come, what I most want is to develop the kind of people who light up the world with their lives. Let me show you how this family legacy does just that.

HOW TO GET STARTED

The Wealth Creator's Seven Generation Legacy System

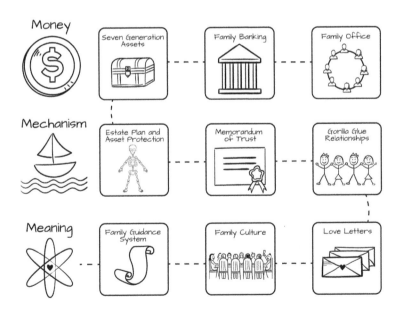

5

FIRST THINGS FIRST

The Definition of a Legacy

At the outset of any endeavor worth pursuing, we need a definition.

Definitions allow us to see clearly. It's like putting our stake in the ground and claiming that territory—something concrete, solid, and tangible that everything else hinges on. With clear definitions, we can know exactly what we're aiming for. Then, we can build a plan to get there.

The problem is that many things can muck up our definitions: our own experiences, what we've seen on TV, the story we've heard retold about Great Grandpa, the feelings our best friend shared in third grade. . . . Instead of having clear definitions, we walk around peering at the world through layers of everyone else's opinions, unaware that we aren't working with clear ideas.

What is your definition of the word *legacy*? Many people define a legacy as a financial inheritance, a windfall that you get when a relative dies, or the memory of a lost loved one. But these definitions aren't actionable. They don't have measurements, borders, or steps to achieve them. So, they get filed in our brains along with nice ideas we can't do anything about.

To bring your legacy out of the dark, forgotten corners of your mind, we need a bare-bones definition that makes sense and connects to our real lives like a Lego piece that snaps into place.

My definition of legacy is the character, values, and financial means to live life on your terms that are modeled, taught, stewarded, and given from one generation to the next.

Legacy

The character, values, and financial means to live life on your terms that's modeled, taught, stewarded, and given from one generation to the next.

To take it one step further, I define a perpetual family legacy as family wealth and flourishing that grows with each successive generation.

Your legacy is not about what happens when you die—it's about living your very best life and making sure that your impact is never interrupted by your absence.

While this may still seem a lot to wrap your mind around, it will provide that stake in the ground we need to begin building from—or toward. With this definition, you're headed in the right direction. Now, let's pack your bag with the two things you'll need to ensure the success of your journey.

Perpetual Legacy

Money and Flourishing Grow in Each Generation

Future Generations

Legacy Planning Check-In Exercise

Before we continue with the rest of the book, let's check in with what legacy means to you right now.

For each question below, rate yourself on a scale of 1–5, based on how true the statement is for you. If something is "not at all true," rank it a 1. If something is "most definitely true," rank it a 5.

When you've rated yourself for each statement, total up your scores, and use the Answer Key to find your next steps.

Legacy Planning Check-In Statement	Self-Rating
1. I want to leave a legacy for my children.	
2. I plan to leave a financial inheritance for my children.	
3. I have a systematic way to ensure the money I leave to my children will be a benefit to their lives, and I am not worried about them becoming handicapped, dependent, or feeling entitled to my wealth.	
4. I've equipped my children to use and steward money well, so it won't just benefit them personally—I trust that they will add to the monetary wealth for the next generations after them and train their children how to manage, grow, and steward money.	
5. TOTAL YOUR SCORE:	

What Your Score Really Means

Score 4–9
Time to Get a Healthy Relationship with Money

The bad news is that you and your family are missing out on the impact you could create. The benefit you could provide to your great grandchildren is limited because you've accepted cultural myths that money might corrupt your kids.

But it isn't your fault. We're bombarded with messages about the evils of money at every turn, making us feel guilty for our own success and production. Meanwhile, we also long to have the satisfaction of earning that allows us to access everything we need and desire out of life. It creates an internal conflict in which we condemn ourselves for the thing we've accomplished.

The good news is that everything you've created and learned during your lifetime could dramatically lift future generations of your family and equip them with a strong heritage and tools to flourish. But you need a healthy perspective of money in order to make peace with your own relationship to money before you can think about leaving a legacy.

Jump into the next section of the book, and pay special attention to Chapter 7 about the decision to create wealth, and why it's a necessary component of being able to create the impact you were meant for.

Score 10–15
Focus on What Your Legacy Means

You likely understand that you've created more assets and financial resources in your lifetime than you have the ability or desire to consume, and that something will be left behind to your children when you pass away. However, you might be concerned about how they will handle money, and whether it will be good for them.

The most important thing you can do here to improve the results your children achieve with their inheritance is to develop their character.

As you read on, you'll want to pay close attention to articulating and passing on the meaning of your legacy, including your values, which you'll read about in Pillar 1 and especially Chapter 11, on your family values.

Score 16+
Next Level Legacy Creation

You are now at a point in your family and wealth creation where you can add a greater degree of intentionality to your stewardship training by designing systems for your children to practice their financial management with increasing financial responsibility.

Here, each 1 percent of improvement you make will dramatically increase the benefit to your children and grandchildren. Because, when you know they'll handle money well, you'll feel really good about blessing them with financial capital to fuel their development and capabilities even further.

You're in the right place, because the Seven Generations Wealth and Legacy Formula will hand you practical tools to not only communicate the lessons your children need to be financially successful, but to practice their financial responsibility in an environment of increasing consequence.

You'll want to pay special attention to Pillar 3, especially Chapter 26 on family banking.

If you would like help to implement any of these steps quicker and faster, book a call with our team here:

https://sevengenerationslegacy.com/strategycall

6

CHOPSTICKS

The Two Requirements for Legacy Planning

L et's break down exactly what you need to have so that you can create a legacy that lasts for multiple generations. There are two components that must go hand-in-hand.

We'll call this pair of essentials you must pack for the journey, "chopsticks." And I'll go so far as to say that if you don't grab these chopsticks, you can't create a Seven Generation Legacy. One without the other will leave you frustrated and spinning in circles. But when you have both, you are armed with the tools to do most of the heavy lifting of building your legacy. In fact, with these two tools, you're already 80 percent of the way to leaving a multigenerational legacy, making absolutely everything about legacy planning easier and faster.

So, what exactly do chopsticks have to do with your legacy? Let me illustrate with a story.

I'll always remember the date with my mom to get Chinese food. I was probably about twelve, and we were likely leaving an orthodontist appointment during those awkward preteen years. It might have been one of our only dates with just the two of us, a rare occasion of undivided attention in a house bustling with kids.

One of the reasons I remember it so clearly is because someone a few tables over noticed me and gave me a compliment: *Wow, you're good with those chopsticks!*

I beamed with pride. It would have been easier to have used the fork, of course, but my parents had taught me an appreciation for Asian food—including how to use chopsticks to best enjoy it!

The thing about chopsticks is that they come in pairs and must be used together. One by itself is completely useless. But together, they have the powerful capacity to move things and accomplish a goal.

That's the way it is with a legacy. You need two crucial components to get you started and propel you forward:

1. A decision to create wealth, and
2. Seven-Generation glasses

These two requirements are the unseen motivation that you must have to achieve results. And they're both decisions available for anyone to choose.

In the next two chapters, let's unpack each of these two chopsticks.

Chopsticks

7

A DECISION TO CREATE WEALTH

The first chopstick you need to create a multi-generational legacy of more than money is a decision to create wealth.

To live the fullest life, reach the most people, and create the root system for a family tree that will continue thriving like a mighty oak for generations, you need the *most* money possible.

Not because having money makes you valuable. Not because happiness can be bought. And not because money itself is valuable.

In fact, if you fail to see your value *before* you make money, you'll never make money. If you wait to be happy until after you have money, joy will always evade you. And if you regard money as the ultimate prize, this lazy emotion will blind you from using it to the fullest.

Instead, here's why you need as much money as possible to create a legacy that lasts:

- First, money is *one of* the primary ingredients of wealth.
- Second, investing in your family with the best gifts and experiences takes money.

45

- But most importantly, the personal growth required to make money in the first place will give you the precise skillset you need to create a legacy.

To illustrate this, let me introduce you to our long-time family friends.

George and Sharon built their dream home on beautiful Lake Tapps overlooking Mount Rainier. They've spared no expense to make this space a welcoming place to build lifelong memories with their kids and grandkids. There's the wavemaker boat for surfing, tubing, and water skiing. There are paddleboards and kayaks for group excursions. They even have wetsuits in every size, so no one has to sit out. There's a gas fire pit for everyone to gather around for late-night dessert and conversation, a sandy beach area on the water for the kids to play endlessly, and a whole floor in their home with extra bedrooms and bunks for all the grandkids to stay. The space is complete with bins and hooks labeled for each child to hang their towels, and even extra toothbrushes in the spare bathrooms, so their kids don't have to plan much to get together when they visit multiple times a week. There's even an art room for the littles and a whole wall of pictures from the most recent photoshoot of the entire family.

It's so apparent that family means the world to them, and they're living out a beautiful legacy where each child knows they are loved and celebrated. One of the reasons they can spend so much time coaching and cheering on every child who tries and learns new water sports is that they have the money to prepare this environment for building relationships. See, without the ability to build the house and buy the boat, there would be far more limits on the quality of their memories.

George and Sharon would tell you that they didn't always have money. But what they created through their remodel business has improved their life by providing more of the tangible, physical things they wanted, so they can improve the quality of their life and relationships.

You, too, were meant to live full out, to experience the most out of life, to enjoy all that you're capable of, and to make the greatest impact possible. Fulfilling that requires the use of money.

PEOPLE AND MONEY IMPROVE EACH OTHER

With the most money possible, you can then pay for the greatest experiences, travel, and masterminds with people who have knowledge you want to learn. These experiences contribute to your growth and make you more valuable as a solution provider for others.

Next to money itself, this human potential is the second key ingredient of wealth.

Financial Capital × Relationship Capital = Wealth

James E. Hughes, renowned estate planning attorney and author of *Family Wealth*, says that complete wealth is made up of five kinds of capital, including human, intellectual, social, spiritual, and financial capital.[4] That means that increasing the intangible things like expanding your mind, relationships, and capabilities contributes to your overall wealth.

WEALTH IS HUMAN FLOURISHING

When you look at it through the lens of abundance, money and people have a symbiotic relationship. Investing in people increases financial capital, and financial capital can be used to develop people. And both increase wealth.

And that brings us to the true definition of wealth, which is *human flourishing*.

That's why, at the forefront of a decision to create the greatest legacy, you have to decide to create wealth. That means you're deciding to do the most good for others and

WEALTH = HUMAN FLOURISHING

invest the most in people. Money just so happens to support and elevate all the other components of human flourishing.

With that decision, we're ready to lay down the other rail, the second chopstick, so you can create your greatest legacy.

8

SEVEN-GENERATION GLASSES

The second chopstick you need to create a multigenerational legacy of more than money is the right perspective of Seven-Generation glasses.

Seven Generation Glasses

The glasses we wear determine what we see—and we're all wearing glasses when it comes to money. That means in your wealth creation, you need to choose the right glasses.

Growing up homeschooled, my family often found extra-curricular learning opportunities with homeschool groups. It was at one of these enrichment classes that I had squinched my eyes tight, straining to read the French words on the chalkboard so I could transcribe them in my notebook. Even though I was embarrassed to interrupt again, I whispered to the teacher's aide yet another time to ask what was written on the board. After class, the teacher quietly pulled my mom and me aside. A pit grew in my stomach as she gently expressed her concern that I might need glasses.

I was terrified at the idea of something being wrong with my eyes and looking weird in glasses. I dreaded the vision exam. I couldn't decide on frames.

But after I put on my purple and gold metal frames a few weeks later (hello, 90s!), everything changed in an instant. The carpet gained texture, and for the first time, I could see myself in the mirror across the room and know what I looked like! I started noticing individual blades of grass and saw that the forest had individual trees with individual leaves, with edges!

Just like that, our financial lens forms our perspective, and ultimately, our reality.

If your vision for your wealth creation is just about what you can personally do with it, you'll never create everything you're capable of. That's because it's a limited goal that requires only limited resources and only calls on your capabilities a little bit. But deciding to create the greatest impact will fuel endless development of your skillset, network, and production.

To make the greatest impact, you need to select the right viewpoint to inform your daily decision-making.

The Perspective With the Greatest Leverage Is the Longest-Range View

Our tendency is to think about right now. But short-term thinking can lead to making poor decisions because it's based on limited information.

If I think about right now, I eat the pizza I'm craving. If I think about tomorrow morning, I'll pass it up because it makes me bloated and sluggish. If I think about decades from today, I know my food choices are contributing to long-term mental health, longevity, a healthy heart, and a body that's agile and strong, and I choose to fuel my body with a diet congruent with my goals and values.

My choices get better and better the farther ahead I think. I'm able to be more strategic and accomplish my goals more successfully if I weigh the long-term impacts.

Looking long-term is like zooming out to get a better understanding of the big picture. Then you can see the lay of the land, note the destination, anticipate obstacles, gauge your progress, and choose what is aligned with your higher purpose.

Just how long should that vision be?

Proverbs 13:22 begins, "A good person leaves an inheritance to his grandchildren . . ."[5]

One of the marks of living well is having a vision of our wealth and resources that extends at least two generations beyond ourselves. It's no wonder we struggle with this responsibility, though. Generational thinking is almost entirely missing from the American definition of *family*.

OUR CULTURAL HANDICAP

In the United States, we praise bootstrapping and memorialize rags-to-riches stories. Fulfilling the American dream usually involves proving your worth by starting from nothing, with no one else's help, and rising by your own merit.

In western cultures, the family is the nuclear unit—a temporary living arrangement that exists until children are old enough to go out on their own. Then, they, too, will begin all over and see what they can make of themselves.

Embedded in that paradigm is the belief that you should not leave an inheritance or should leave very little money to your kids; otherwise, you are going to enable them to be dependent, lazy, and entitled. From that worldview, it would make sense that we should leave them nothing, so they can enter the struggle that will shape their identity. And naturally, since we don't want to have anything left when we die, we should consume our resources as the reward for our own accomplishments or, out of guilt, give it all away.

But what if companies thought this way? Imagine Coca-Cola, Boeing, Kellogg's, or UPS selling off the company and starting over from scratch every time a CEO retires. Rather, corporate giants that have stood for more than a hundred years have benefitted from their organizational memory, continuing to grow through multiple leadership transitions.[6]

What if we adopted the lens that family, like an enterprise, is meant to last through the generations? The leaders, like runners in a relay, would be replaced with the next generation, while the family line continues, gaining resources and increasing its contribution over time.

With a generational view of family, you look for the best use of resources for more than just now. The purpose of money is to contribute to making things better for the ones who come next in the family line, just as those before us would have done for us.

Multigenerational
Family Enterprise

Leaving an inheritance would raise the starting point for the next generation to continue building where the previous one left off.

I've never seen this more clearly than in ancient Iroquois tradition.

THE SEVENTH GENERATION PRINCIPLE: IROQUOIS TRADITIONAL WISDOM

I was wowed when I learned about the Iroquois' furthest-range view from the profound book *Complete Family Wealth*.[7] In the Great Law of the Haudenosaunee Confederacy, ratified in the 1700s, the Iroquois wrote about the *Seventh Generation Principle*, a value that dates way back to their ancient tradition as early as the twelfth century.

The tribal elders would begin a tribal council with something like these words, "*As we begin our sacred work of tribal decision-making, let us hope that our decisions today, as well as the care, deliberation, and wisdom we use in making those decisions, will be honored by and truly beneficial to the members of our tribe seven generations from today, as we honor the decisions made by our ancestors seven generations ago."[8]*

The Iroquois didn't think about just today, next month, the season, the year, the decade, or even a lifetime. During council meetings, they made governing decisions in light of the impacts *seven generations* ahead.

> THE IROQUOIS MADE GOVERNING DECISIONS BY CONSIDERING THE IMPACTS OF NOT MINUTES, MONTHS, SEASONS, YEARS, DECADES, OR EVEN LIFETIMES, BUT *SEVEN GENERATIONS* AHEAD.

They wanted to create what was best for their great-great-great-great grandchildren!

I don't know about you, but when I first heard this, I found it hard to wrap my brain around something so far in the future. I can easily imagine my grandchildren, but their great-great-grandchildren? It starts getting so distant from our present tense that it's barely comprehendible. It's far beyond the scope of our own lifetime.

And that's the point. A seven-generation lens makes me think way beyond myself. To put on the Seven-Generation glasses takes courage and a bit of research.

WHAT EXACTLY IS SEVEN GENERATIONS?

Thinking backward, seven generations before me goes back to my great-great-great-great-great grandparents—that's five greats, plus my grandparents and my parents.

Even with some family genealogy research, the stories have lasted about as far back as my great-grandparents, and those stories are sparse. I know my great-grandma Alberta on my dad's side had refined taste, taught etiquette and French in Berkeley Junior High, and traveled internationally. There's a green stained-glass lamp in my gram's guest room that was a wedding gift to my grandfather's great-grandmother, Eva Brown, when she married

Marcus CoyKendall in 1873, five generations before me and six generations before my children. One of my ancestors, Thomas McKean, signed the Declaration of Independence. And four generations back on my mom's side, my grandfather's granddad was a coal miner from Frankfort, Germany, who came through Ellis Island and settled in South Dakota to homestead in 1888, even before the territory became a state.

Generally, a generation is about twenty to thirty years. Seven generations averaged out would be about 200 years.

For me, born in 1984, seven generations prior turns back the clock to the year 1784. In American history, the Continental Congress was ratifying the Treaty of Paris, ending the American Revolution, and Britain formally recognized the thirteen colonies as the free and independent United States of America.

Seven generations back bridges me all the way to before anything I consider the "olden days." Over that time gap, the way we experience daily life has dramatically changed.

Over the span of the last 200 years, countries have risen and fallen, electricity, dynamite, radio, and television were invented, car and airplane travel became possible, and then space travel. Penicillin and x-rays brought significant advances to medical possibilities. And communication went from the newly invented Alexander Graham Bell telephone to smartphones and Apple watches, merging phones and computers that shrunk from filling rooms to slipping out of our hands.

Looking forward, seven generations ahead bridges me all the way forward by the same span to my great-great-great-great-great grandchildren, whom I'll never meet, to the year 2184. What will our geopolitical climate look like then? Will country borders have shifted? What will the educational model be? Will technology have made possible things we can't comprehend now? How long will human lifespans be? What is the future of science, medicine, agriculture, transportation, and money?

To create a legacy for people who will live in this unknown future environment, how do I best help them flourish and thrive?

If you want to carve out the ability for future generations to prosper and experience the most flourishing possible, try donning seven-generation glasses. They will give you a powerful new perspective.

A SEVEN-GENERATION LENS STRAIGHTENS MY PATH AND TELLS ME IMMEDIATELY WHEN I'M OFF COURSE.

Your family is a multigenerational organization—an enterprise that you're responsible for managing and equipping to handle the future beyond you.

When I look ahead seven generations, I realize that I want to model self-leadership, so I can create a culture of teaching my children to lead themselves. I want to become as resilient, adaptive, resourceful, and creative as possible and to normalize discovering solutions and creating value in the world.

When I think forward to seven generations ahead, I want to provide a value system that will guide my great-grandchildren like a rudder, be a model of remarkable character, and hold to a sound life philosophy. I want to stand in the hall of a long lineage of ancestors who knew who they were, made the most of themselves, cast their light to illuminate the world for others, and produced the capital to enjoy the best things in the world.

> YOUR FAMILY IS A MULTIGENERATIONAL ENTERPRISE THAT YOU'RE RESPONSIBLE FOR MANAGING AND EQUIPPING TO HANDLE THE FUTURE BEYOND YOU.

A seven-generation lens requires you to live your highest calling and noblest life. It's the perfect antidote to shrinking from hard things I just don't feel like doing, neglecting to share words of courage and love, or fumbling through life checking off menial to-do lists without ever rising to what matters most.

How would you live differently today if your objective became the flourishing of seven generations beyond you? What attitudes, learning, words, responses, activities, and events would you approach differently? Are there skills and wisdom you would develop? Which books would you read? Are there books you would write? What businesses would you start? Who would you coach? What clarity would you share with others? How would you invest?

With a seven-generation lens, you do today what will help those beyond you to prosper and flourish.

A SEVEN-GENERATION LENS GIVES YOUR ACTIONS MORE POWER AND MEANING.

For me, having a seven-generation perspective helps me parent my daughters more intentionally because I'm leading women who are leaders who will also choose to become wealth creators. That means my moment-by-moment actions are not only serving my future but my children's and their children's too. The seven-generation timeline also steers me to making better relationship, entrepreneurial, financial, social, health, and even spiritual decisions as well because I realize that the ripple effect of everything I do right now matters far beyond right now.

A seven-generation lens gives power to the moment and to the decisions you make right now. With a legacy, you're not just looking at the full scope of your life, but the full range of possibilities you are creating for your children and generations to come after them.

A LEGACY IS INVESTING IN A FUTURE YOU WON'T EVEN BE ABLE TO SEE AND TOUCH DURING YOUR LIFETIME.

I first heard about the copper beech tree from my read of *Complete Family Wealth.*[9] Hundreds of copper beech trees grace the landscape surrounding the Newport mansions in Rhode Island, built around the turn of the 20th century. These summer cottages were the destination of the wealthy, who built luxurious estates as getaways in the majestic landscape. They planted copper beech to become remarkable shade trees that would throw off the elegant and contrastive hues of deep purples, gold, and orange, reflective of the Gilded Age.

Copper Beech Tree

The estate owners who planted these trees knew that they might not live to see these beautiful trees come to maturity. That's because it takes at least thirty years and up to 70 to 100 years before these trees reach their full glory.[10, 11] But instead of only seeing how this landscaping would maximize their own enjoyment of the land, the estate owners looked ahead, planting trees that many generations beyond them would be able to enjoy and experience fully.

The true meaning of life is to plant trees under whose shade you do not expect to sit.
—Nelson Henderson

Seven-Generation glasses give you a future vision as clear as those who planted copper beech trees, knowing the beauty and remarkable future you're creating for those far ahead of you.

BOTH CHOPSTICKS ARE REQUIRED

The decision to create wealth *and* seven-generation glasses are the two chopsticks that go together, complementing and supplementing each other.

Each makes the other that much more potent and productive!

If my goal is that seven generations past me will flourish and thrive, I more naturally pick up the mantle to make the most of myself as a producer. And if I'm endeavoring to create the most money, I'll make more with the motivation not just to live well but to live so that my great-great-grandchildren gain opportunities as a result.

With just one chopstick, you'll have great ideas and intentions, but your action plan will be unbalanced and unsustainable. You may have the means to live however you choose but still be unfulfilled and unhappy. Or you may find a wedge splintering your family and driving you apart. Without *both* chopsticks, you can't lock in to do the work of building a legacy. That means that you'll be stuck in a perpetual state of wondering *what if something happens to me* but feeling powerless to do anything about it or make a difference.

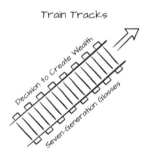

But with both pieces in place, you'll gain the full benefit of a tool that works for you. And you become the inflection point of a powerful legacy. These two elements—the decision to create wealth and the decision to put on Seven-Generation glasses—become like the two rails of a train track, giving you endless running room and infinite capacity to create a powerful legacy for generations.

BUT HERE'S "THE CATCH"

And now here's where the rubber meets the road, because most planning is estate and financial planning only, but it leaves out the added element of meaning.

Most successful families who have created tremendous wealth and care about their family are told that they need to do estate planning. You've likely tried that and either gave up because it was too complicated and overwhelming, or maybe you even overcame the trepidation and now have an estate plan, and probably a financial plan too.

But without meaning, all you have is a legal mechanism and money, which create a structure to transfer assets.

When you add in the component of meaning to your legacy planning, you can create a true inheritance that allows you to leave a gift with spirit and successfully pass the baton of stewardship to the next generation.

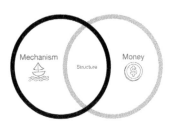

So, if you want to build a legacy, and not just an estate plan, you need to infuse it with meaning. And not in some intangible way that's hard to measure, but in a real, specific, practical way that's clear to you, your children, and the world exactly what your planning was for.

It's not your fault. Most people don't do this work to spell out the meaning of their legacy. Estate planning attorneys would love if everyone did it, but they don't have the time or fee structure to slow down so you can think this all through. However, it's no secret that it's the meaning of your legacy that matters most. How well you define and communicate this will make the difference between an inheritance that creates spoiled and entitled trust fund babies and one that empowers even your great-great grandchildren.

That's why the Seven Generations Wealth and Legacy Formula was created to deal with this specifically, helping you to work out the meaning of your legacy, so you can benefit your posterity for generations to come.

Now, come on, let me show you our first pillar!

Key Section Takeaways

- Legacy is more than a monetary inheritance. It is the character, values, and financial means to live life on your own terms that you pass down. And to do that, you have to model, teach, steward, and give the character, values, and financial resources to the next generation.
- Wealth is not just money. It is human flourishing, including personally, intellectually, socially, spiritually, and financially.
- You can do more than just leave a legacy to your children—you can create a legacy that benefits many generations after you by creating financial resources that expand in each generation because you've attended to and provided for human flourishing.
- To create a Seven Generations Legacy, you must make a personal decision to create wealth, and make decisions with a seven generation view. That means you must believe wealth creation is good, exercise it personally, teach your children to do it, and use the longest-range view in your decision making to consider how your choices will benefit those seven generations after you.

PILLAR 1

THE MEANING:
CREATING YOUR LEGACY

Meaning

9

FAMILY CONSTITUTION

Drafting Your Family Guidance System

The first critical step in the Seven Generations Wealth and Legacy Formula is to create your Family Guidance System. That's why we've dedicated the next five chapters to demonstrating and teaching you how to get that first step accomplished as quickly as possible, so you can have a quick win that moves the needle on your legacy planning.

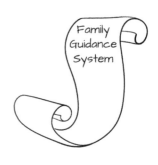

The first thing you need to know about designing your Family Guidance System is to lean into one solitary question: *If we lived our highest and fullest life and reached everything we wanted for our family, what would that look like?*

It was one thing to swoon over the sleeping faces of our children and promise to make the biggest difference for them and their future. But actually holding those whispered hopes long enough that they grow roots that sink down deep, so those promises come true—that is a whole 'nother story!

Lucas and I knew we would have to be clear, specific, and intentional about what we wanted if we were going to direct the course of our legacy. So we breathed deeply, then pulled our chairs together and opened our laptop.

It was time to pen the constitution of our family.

When we hear that word, naturally, we think about the United States Constitution. It begins with these hallowed words, "We the People of the United States, in Order to form a more perfect Union, establish Justice, insure domestic Tranquility, provide for the common defense, promote the general Welfare, and secure the Blessings of Liberty to ourselves and our Posterity, do ordain and establish this Constitution for the United States of America."[12]

Our nation's founders laid out the principles and philosophy that make up the bedrock of our government. But even more noteworthy is that they created this constitution as the single highest authority in our nation. That's because the constitution is what grants power and direction to every elected official sworn to uphold it. See, our nation's founders spelled out their intentions for this sovereign and independent nation. Then, they bound all future representatives to live up to these intentions. That means the U.S. Constitution not only *began* a sovereign country, but it also *determined the course of its future.*

And in the same way a constitution can establish and direct a country, it can also determine the course of a family's future.

You don't have to let your family decisions be selected by however you feel in the moment or the whim of the next generation. Instead, you can clearly articulate a family constitution that will become the guidance system to steer your family for the rest of time.

As we began this vital work, we knew that our family constitution would spell out our goals and dreams for our family and exactly how we would live to fulfill them.

It would be the guide rails to steer the direction of our family through our own lifetimes and through generations to come.

It would define our principles and give answers about how to approach any circumstance congruent with those principles.

It would define who we are, why we exist, and what it means to be part of our family.

To launch us into the process and gain momentum, we committed to writing it all down. That forced us to bring all our subconscious desires into our conscious brain and out of our mouths, to talk them through at length, and then to type them out and watch them become concrete as they streamed across the screen. Getting this out in the open took us one step closer to making them our reality.

See, being honest enough with yourself to commit to writing down what matters most to you awakens your truest self, which usually lies dormant. This articulated meaning of your life creates a magnetic pull back to the real you. That means you remember your highest values, hold them in conscious awareness, and gain the power to live them out.

In the process of creating our constitution, we created something that can speak *for* us, relaying the message of what matters to future generations, so it can be our mouthpiece even after we're gone. No amount of money and legal planning can do this for you. That's why starting to formulate your legacy with financials and legal structures can feel empty compared to the rich heritage you're creating with your actual life. And that's why it's up to you to communicate what matters and how you're going to do it and then put everything in place to support your convictions.

We felt like the forefathers of our country writing the Constitution of the United States of America. As they birthed the guidance system to govern a fledgling nation, the room was teeming with potential that often devolved into spirited debates about the best way to lay the rails.

> YOUR CONSTITUTION IS THE MOUTHPIECE THAT SPEAKS FOR YOU, RELAYING THE MESSAGE OF WHAT MATTERS TO FUTURE GENERATIONS, EVEN AFTER YOU'RE GONE.

What makes our family a unit? Why were we living? What are the characteristics and values that distinguish us as a family? If we died and left them money, why? What did we want them to use the money for? And how could we encapsulate all our intentions on just a few sheets of paper?

Cue our own cinematic music, dramatic lighting, and existential pondering.

By choosing to articulate what was important enough to spend the rest of our lives on, we had accepted the daunting responsibility of carving out our legacy.

This document would spell out everything we wanted in our lives and everything we wanted to continue at our death. It would include the values we hold dear and the intangibles that guide our decision-making. We knew that if we got this right, it could lift not only our family right here and now, but everyone born or chosen into the family for the rest of time.

If this sounds overwhelming right now, you're not alone. The ambiguity and the enormousness of the task are what keep most people from creating a legacy that lasts. That's why I want to lead the way and show you how we worked through this.

PICKING A STARTING POINT

Over the months we worked on our family guidance system, we pressed on by thinking not about what happens if we died young . . . but about what would happen if we lived? What if we achieved every goal and our family flourished to the fullest . . . what would that look like?

It was like writing out a full screenplay. Not only were we thinking through the character development of each of our family members, but what was required to achieve it. But this wasn't just about individual people; it was about the storyline of our family as a whole unit and how the whole of us would become our best.

To gain traction, we leaned on Simon Sinek's profoundly simple mantra, "Start with *WHY*." That's because the why of something is the central essence, the core, the *raison d'etre*. If we could really articulate the *why* of our existence, it would give us the foundation to build our legacy on.

SEPARATE PRINCIPLES FROM STRATEGIES

So, we organized our planning by mentally separating out the principles we live by from the strategies that we'll use to walk them out.

First, we needed to articulate our most important truths that are so central to everything we do that they're relevant across all our life contexts. They are the things we want to uphold in every area of our life. When questions would arise later about *what* to do and *how* to go about it, we could always come back to the *why* to get the clarity we would need to make decisions. That's because the *why* is the reason behind all the strategies and tactics.

Next, we laid out the strategies we'd use to live out our *why*. This is where we cast the vision and set the limits and boundaries that would make it possible. Here, we needed freedom, with responsibility and rules to ground them. We needed the running room to allow our family's full potential to flourish and the guidance to steer them away from self-destruction and disaster.

Before we got started, we deconstructed our *why* into four parts—our *IDEALS*, *VALUES*, *MISSION*, and *VISION*.

We gave each of these assignments a definition so we could stay focused as we worked through each one independently.

- Our family **IDEALS**: our family standards of the best, highest, and most noble within us
- Our family **CORE VALUES**: the character qualities we want to demonstrate by the consistent way we choose to show up every day

- Our family **MISSION**: is our place in the world now, and how we are improving it
- Our family **VISION**: the aspirations we want to accomplish in the future

Now, it was time to flesh everything out. First, we wrote out our ideals and core values. Next, we worked out our mission and our vision. Then, we articulated the strategies for how we would accomplish it all. And finally, the whole compilation became a *Memorandum of Trust*—a soulful document that would supplement, guide, and direct the legal component of our estate plan.

This process helped us take time to discover what was, at the core, *most* important to us. This important work would become our family guidance system to navigate the messiness of everyday life. It would elevate us by calling us to the highest within us. And with it, we defined what would give us clarity and direction in everything we do.

In these next chapters, I'll share parts of our family guidance system and outline exactly how we arrived at the words that spell out our family DNA, starting with ideals. Let me lead you up the mountain step by step so you don't have to procrastinate, get overwhelmed, or bushwhack your own path.

If you would like a shortcut to designing and building your own multigenerational family legacy, reach out to our team to get started here:

https://sevengenerationslegacy.com/strategycall

KEY CHAPTER TAKEAWAYS

- Your Family Guidance System is a document that will spell out everything you want in your lives and everything you wanted to continue at your death. It will include the values you hold dear and the intangibles that guide your decision-making. If you get this right, it could lift not only your family right here and now, but everyone born or chosen into your family for the rest of time.
- Your Family Guidance System should be written from the perspective of living the longest and fullest life possible and achieving everything in your heart. What would that look like?
- Your Family Guidance System includes your family's Ideals, Core Values, Mission, and Vision. Your Ideals are your family standards of the best, highest, and most noble principles within you. Your Core Values are the character qualities you want to demonstrate by the consistent way you choose to show up every day. Your Mission is your place in the world now, and how you are improving it. Your VISION is the aspirations you want to accomplish in the future.

10

ANTI-GRAVITY

Ideals

O ur family IDEALS are our family standards of the best, highest, and noblest within us.

Ideals

Think of the kinds of things that inspire us—the heroic, the courageous, the redemptive, the wise, the beautiful, the strong, the true. These are essential aspects of our reality, and when someone embodies them, whether it's an elite athlete, a world-class speaker, or a dialed-in dad, we feel like we're watching another human step into their highest and best self. It compels from us a reverential awe. That's because we know that the same capability resides inside of us.

But we don't always step into that higher plane of excellence. On most days, we slip down into our habits and tread somewhere in the murky middle of to-do lists, expectations, and the next thing that demands our attention. I think my sole disappointment when I live that way is that I know I'm meant for more—more joy, more centeredness, more connection, more presence, more vibrance, and more freedom. Perhaps you know it too.

There's a Greek word that best expresses this concept of moral virtue or living up to your full potential. It's called *arete* (pronounced *ahr eh TAY*).[13] It means excellence and goodness, or the ideal form of a good thing. Arete is a calling to live at our highest and best version of ourselves.

The sister word *arête (eh RAYT)* gives us a profound visual. It means a sharp mountain ridge.[14]

If your life were a mountainous landscape, living your ideals would be like finding the highest pathway through connected peaks.

The opposite would be slipping and falling into the lowest, basest posture of human existence—competition, struggling, self-preservation, fear, anger, and protection. Where gravity pulls you to your worst, your ideals become a force opposite gravity, drawing you toward your personal best.

> WHERE GRAVITY PULLS YOU TO YOUR WORST, YOUR IDEALS BECOME A FORCE OPPOSITE GRAVITY, DRAWING YOU TOWARD YOUR PERSONAL BEST.

Creating the best for your family requires you to step into and live from the best version of yourself. That's why it's critical to clarify, write down, and remind yourself of your ideals often. When you do, you train your mind how to think about yourself so that your actions can follow, and you can bring your vision to life.

I'm going to share our family's ideals with you here as an example for you to follow as you're creating your own. While you may find similarities or differences from your own philosophy and perspective, the important thing to note here is that ideals help you translate wishful thinking and optimism into a practical articulation of what it really looks like when you're thriving. It's a perspective transformer that you can read when things get off the rails to instantly set you back on course.

Our Family Ideals

Here's a look at our family's ideals and belief system.

THE FAMILY

We believe our family exists to serve each other. When everyone in our family fulfills their duties and obligations, i.e., when we serve each other, the result is a wonderful place where everyone has everything they could need or want.

We value and honor our ancestors. Taking pride in their achievements and what they have done to allow us to improve upon what they have given us, we strive to make their ceiling our floor and do the same for future generations. We are creating a multigenerational legacy of more than money.

> As we begin our sacred work of tribal decision-making, let us hope that our decisions today, as well as the care, deliberation, and wisdom we use in making those decisions, will be honored by and truly beneficial to the members of our tribe seven generations from today, as we honor the decisions made by our ancestors seven generations ago.
>
> —Iroquois 7 Generation Principle, spoken by tribal elders before starting a tribal council[8]

THE INDIVIDUAL

We believe that our family's true wealth resides in each individual member. For our family to be healthy and flourish, each individual must be healthy and flourishing. We encourage and celebrate each member's differentness. We value each member's freedom to establish their own sense of identity and pursue their own dreams.

THE TABLE

We believe the best tool our family has for connecting, building lifelong bonds, fostering conversations, and hospitality is through sharing meals together at our table.

MEETINGS & RHYTHMS

We believe that family is an enterprise and that to be successful, we must be an enterprising family. To that end, we have daily, weekly, and annual family meetings to plan, improve, and facilitate working together. We plan our days and weeks to create a rhythmic and systematic way of living that eliminates chaos and allows for a peaceful home.

TRAINING

We believe the parents' role is to coach their children to know how to act and be in the world so they can flourish. We help our kids discover who God uniquely created them to be and what they are capable of.

Proverbs 22:6
Train up a child in the way he should go,
Even when he grows older he will not abandon it.[15]

ATTITUDE

We believe your mindset determines your results. We value always being grateful and staying positive despite appearances. Have a growth mindset and focus on what is expanding and improving in the world.

SELF-IMPROVEMENT

We believe continuous improvement through reading, curiosity, learning, quality experiences, and travel makes you a better person. If it comes down to it, prioritize experiences over things.

RELATIONSHIPS

We believe being present, connected, and creating lasting memories with the people we love is extremely valuable. We respect the autonomy and liberty of others.

COMMUNICATION

We believe constantly improving our communication skills and offering love and encouragement everywhere we go is important to lift others to their personal best and to win friends and influence people.

SPIRITUAL

We value a relationship with Jesus Christ and faith in Him, not our works for salvation. We believe the Bible is the owner's manual for this life, and therefore we value reading and studying scripture by understanding what is being said in the original languages (word studies in Greek and Hebrew), understanding the context, viewing each scripture in light of all the others, and determining how to apply the Bible to our lives.

Galatians 5:22–23
But the fruit of the Spirit is love, joy, peace, patience, kindness, goodness, faithfulness, gentleness, self-control; against such things there is no law.[16]

CAREER

We value the ability to pursue life passion and maximize our unique ability to achieve profit.

HEALTH

We believe that peak performance and optimal effectiveness are our responsibility so we can enjoy all that life has to offer and fulfill our life's purpose. To that end, we value developing strength and mobility through exercise and nourishing our bodies through quality sleep and healthy eating.

WEALTH

We believe that financial success is a valuable and admirable accomplishment and that financial success is determined by the difficulty of the problems you solve, the amount of value you create, and the number of people you serve. True wealth is more than money, and it includes thriving in every category of your life (5 Fs: Faith, Family, Finances, Fitness, and Friendships). We believe generosity is key to creating sustainable wealth because it primes the pump of giving and receiving, reminding us that money isn't the means or the end goal—people are.

OUR PROCESS TO CREATE OUR IDEALS

Your ideals will look different than ours. But at the core, you may find some or many of our ideals to be true for you as well.

Let me walk you through our process of defining and refining our ideals so that you can create your own.

SIMPLIFY TO GET TO THE GOLD

The most important place to begin is to recognize that your ideals and beliefs list doesn't need to cover every strategy or how you walk it all out. Instead, think of it as the primary *why*, the thing behind all the other things. Once you look at what's important to you, ask why. Then ask why again. And again. And again. Do this until you've distilled the pure essence or motive behind everything important to you.

The challenge will often be to boil down and simplify your beliefs, not to expand them. You could likely write a thesis on each area of your life. For me, there's Christianity, Montessori, nutrition, Non-violent Communication, Growth Mindset . . . and that's only the tip of the iceberg!

Our goal in writing our ideals was always to say more by saying less and get to the root of each. To get down to the lowest common denominator, we continued to peel off the layers of the onion. When we got to the core belief we hold about what is valuable and worthy of our attention and effort, we knew we'd struck gold!

DESCRIBE YOUR IDEAL WAY OF BEING

To get this simple, compact, and comprehensive ideals list, we talked through our ideal *way of being*. It's important to realize that our ideals are *not* goals, achievements, or accomplishments. They are the ideal way we show up when we're at our best.

FIND COMMON GROUND

During this process, couples may differ in their viewpoint, approach, or experience. Instead of avoiding the topic or pushing each other into an agreement, use this time to open the dialogue and seek to understand your differences. Ask questions, stay curious, and lean into the discovery process. You're opening up about your deeply held values and discovering what it means to solidify the shared values that make you an indestructible team.

CREATE YOUR CATEGORIES

First, we came up with our categories. To do this, we thought through every context of our lives that was important for us to show up fully.

If areas were similar, we lumped them together.

For instance, we used one category to encompass our way of relating to other people, including in our marriage, parenting, friendships, business relationships, extended family, and even the people we've never met who enter our proximity. We called it *relationships*.

We separated out *communication* because it surfaces continually, especially in our most comfortable environment of being at home, as the one area that we need the most consistent reminder to show up with love.

The one that surprised us the most but also turned out to be one of our most important ideals was the value of the *individual.* At the center of building a family legacy and wealth, we knew we needed strong relationships to continue to grow together. To have strong relationships, we needed an extraordinary and committed marriage and kids who ultimately want to spend time in our lives even when they're grown. And to get that, we needed strong, healthy, and whole people who continued wanting to do life together as a unit, not by compulsion, obligation, or duty. That meant creating an environment that celebrated our uniqueness, respected differences, and praised individual expression.

DESCRIBE YOUR IDEALS IN EACH CATEGORY

Then, to articulate our highest ideals in each area, we asked these questions:

- What is the fundamental belief in this area that always allows me to live out the best version of myself?
- Is it always true? Is it ever not true?
- Why does this really matter?
- Does it work not just for me but also for my spouse, our children, and future generations?
- Is it bigger than personal preference or personality?
- Is this a way of being rather than a strategy or external achievement?

STAY CENTERED ON YOUR WHY, NOT HOW YOU WALK IT OUT

Sometimes, we found ourselves getting stuck in tactics or strategies. For instance, health is profoundly important to us. We are continually leveling up our performance by calibrating our sleep, water, exercise, nutrition, and supplementation. I usually sleep nine hours per day and find a way to move my body, sweat, drink at least a gallon of water, and take eight supplements daily. I also eat almost only vegetables and meat, with minimal grains, sugar, or processed food. We're sold on chiropractic care and blue light filters for devices before bed, and we've experimented with cold showers and intermittent fasting. We want our children and their children to take ownership of their health in the same way.

However, none of the strategies are our ideals. Rather, they point us to what matters. Our ideal that drives these choices is that we want to be the best stewards of our physical bodies so that we can fully experience and enjoy our lives.

NOW IT'S YOUR TURN!

Use our experience as a springboard to create your own family ideals.

Remember, simplicity is key. And while it appears to be easy, it can actually take more time and effort to encapsulate your ideals in fewer words, so you'll need to extend yourself some grace and patience as you work through this meaningful task.

Here's a quick list to get started:

1. Describe your ideal way of being
2. Find common ground
3. Create your categories
4. Describe your ideals in each category
5. Stay centered on your *why*, not the strategy of how you walk it out
6. Simplify to get to the gold

Pause here and grab a sheet of paper or a journal to jot down your broad stroke ideas as we close out this chapter. Since everything is fresh on your mind, take advantage of those ideas bubbling to the surface. You can come back and boil everything down later, but this will help you make progress on your own family ideals right away when your ideas are flowing and there's less friction.

Writing down your ideals requires raw honesty and a willingness to challenge your thinking. You'll need a posture of honoring yourself enough to dive into self-awareness and yet still hold on loosely enough to recognize that you'll probably update them many times as you continue to grow.

Then, once you're finished, the very next step of laying out your value system will take this work from theoretical to practical and tangible, so it can guide your actions when you're in the thick of real life. We'll do exactly that in the next chapter.

11

THE COMPASS

Values

Our family CORE VALUES are the character qualities we want to demonstrate by the consistent way we choose to show up every day.

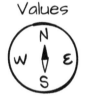

Values

We see our core values as our family's compass. They point us to our true north when we're in the dark woods of everyday life. That's when we most need something simple and constant to remind us of how to take the very next step.

Living our values helps us always be moving in the direction of our ideals.

For us, our values are our one-word reminders loaded with generous heaps of meaning.

For our family, our core value discovery really began about the time Avie was six. I'd had some not-so-proud moments of allowing her outbursts to trigger me. I just wanted *her* to be calm so we could solve the problem at hand.

> VALUES ARE ONE-WORD REMINDERS THAT KEEP YOU MOVING IN THE DIRECTION OF YOUR IDEALS.

We finally made progress when I realized that *I* was the one who needed to remain calm, so I could be her anchor to help her understand and process her needs and emotions and not have us both whirling round and round, caught up in each other's storms. I needed an easy reminder of how to show up in that instant.

At the time, *calm* was a word I could always find to remind me exactly how to act so that we could find the need, solve the problem, and live our ideals.

When we set up our family's values, we needed words to remind us *how to act*. So, we set up our values to address our foundational beliefs that we want to cultivate in each individual person in our family. These are character qualities that we want to instill in our children so that they'll influence everything we do and the character that distinguishes us as a family. This becomes a compass for our personal choices, our marriage relationship, our parenting, and the way we show up in friendships, business, and our social circles.

OUR FAMILY CORE VALUES

Our family's core values are actionable words. They are qualities or attributes we can demonstrate. Here's a look at our list:

1. **Freedom**—the power to think, speak, and act as you choose
2. **Responsibility**—owning the consequences of your choices and fulfilling your obligations
3. **Loving Mutual Respect**—honoring each other's uniqueness and treating all people with kindness
4. **Contribution**—serving others by creating value that improves their lives
5. **Gratitude**—being content, positive, and thankful for all things
6. **Growth**—expanding our capabilities through courage, curiosity, and continual learning
7. **Collaboration**—working together to multiply our efforts
8. **Trustworthiness**—dependable, reliable, honest, and truthful

SUPER SLEUTHING

The way we discovered and defined our core values was through a process I call "super sleuthing."

I first used this silly term as a super-mom move one day when I asked Avie what her favorite moment of her day was, and she stated simply, "Good." I asked what made her most happy. She said, "Everything." I asked if there was anything that made her angry. Sad? Proud? I still got one-word answers that felt vague and reluctant. As much as I wanted to connect, I just wasn't getting through.

So, I combined her love of all things detective and made it a game. I said we were going to use our super sleuth skills to figure it out. Then I started asking about who greeted her when she walked into school, where she put her backpack, and what happened next, and next, and next. She had fun following the clues to remember the events of her day. I'll admit, super sleuthing is corny, but it worked! I captured her attention, pierced through the shell, and opened the dialogue.

Super sleuthing your core values is looking for clues in the data we have available to us. It's a process of searching for and labeling the most important character qualities already present in your life that give you the most meaning. And it requires being gut-level honest with yourself.

As we turned over the clues to super sleuth our core values, we looked at our story, our resources of time and money, our past, ahead to the future we wanted to create, and both inside and outside the home.

For instance, in our house, we are constantly reminding our kids to have patience, choose a good attitude, and be respectful.

Those words are giant clues to your value system. Chances are, they're the things that will best help you create the environment, dynamics, and relationships you want in your home.

And spoiler alert: they're probably the exact same areas you need to do the most personal work on daily.

Oh, just me? Yeah, I didn't think so!

We were seeking clues about our values across every area of our life ... why we wake up when we do, read the books that we do, create family time, spend it on certain activities, how we choose to discipline our children, why we are building a business, why we resonate with specific thought leaders, how we approach challenges, and which activities refresh us that we want to spend more time doing.

Your values should show up and be true across every context of your life. They should make up the consistent character that is part of every area of life where you show up best in your marriage, parenting, social life, health, finances, career, leisure activities, and even in your intellectual, emotional, and spiritual life.

Then, once you've done some significant super sleuthing, it's time to write and organize your core values.

Consider Starting with a Values List

You might consider pulling up the Boy Scouts' values or a list of character qualities like the one in Andrew L. Howell and David R. York's book, *Riveted: 44 Values That Change the World.*

Whatever list you use, it can be helpful to start from something other than a blank slate. That way, you can get the juices flowing to jumpstart your brainstorming session. It's also a great check to make sure you don't forget about something deeply important to you.

Some Values Can Be More Important Than Others

For us, the first three of our eight values—*Freedom, Responsibility,* and *Mutual Respect*—are the most important. They're like a three-legged stool that holds up everything else. (And, in a pinch, it's easier to remember three words than all eight!)

We first heard them from Jon and Missy Butcher of Lifebook as they shared their family rules with us. We resonated so strongly with the same way of being that we adopted these rules as our own. We also felt that these were the three governing rules that we could use to align any action we ever take. If something met all three criteria, it was right.[17]

Freedom was the open-ended, sky's-the-limit emphasis on abundance.

Responsibility is the counterbalance, the check, boundary, and control on what kind of freedom should be celebrated.

And when our action also *respects* the individual and is covered with gracious love and a choice to be a cooperative whole, we know that it's going to produce the fruit we want in our life.

CREATE A DEFINITION FOR EACH VALUE

One of the most helpful things we did was define each core value as simply as we could while preserving the robust meaning. That helped us condense our list, which was, in all honesty, way too long.

The final five of our core values are the most simplified, yet comprehensive finished product. We had several others, like *love, stewardship, abundance, authenticity, leadership, kindness,* and *courage.* But when we defined each of them, the definitions gave us insight into which were really part of another value or maybe a description of how that one value shows up in a particular context.

PRINCIPLES, NOT JUST PREFERENCE

We also thought in terms of principles, not just preference. For instance, *collaboration* took a multi-hour conversation. It's more of a need for Lucas than for me. I prefer more independent work. However, I realized that collaboration is a way to be a cohesive team that functions together with separate roles, each part doing its unique part to accomplish more together. And that's something I can rally behind all day long.

THE ROLE OF FAITH

We wanted to point to Jesus, the source of our life who fills us with the power to recognize and live out our values in the first place. With this in mind, we felt that faith in the God of the Bible was greater than our core values, not part of them.

CAUSES, NOT RESULTS

Lastly, you should think of your values as a way of acting that you have sole responsibility for, not as something you get, contingent on someone else or a set of circumstances.

Then, you have the power to choose to act according to your value system.

ON DISPLAY

If you're going to use a compass to help you find your way through the brush and bramble to your destination, you can't keep it in your pocket. You've got to look at that thing regularly so you stay on course. That means it needs to be out in the open and visible so you can use it to guide your steps.

Our friend Richard Wilson strongly advocates doing this deep work on family values. In his work with family offices, he often consults ultra-high-net-worth families and their advisors on the importance of doing this work. Then, he says that you need to take it to the next level by displaying your values in a prominent location where your family can see and discuss them daily. Better yet, he leads by example, printing them to hang up on his wall.

Because family values are that important to keep front and center of your attention daily, we first kept them on the chalkboard wall that doubles as our family command center. Later, we had a custom sign made to display in our dining room.

If we see our values every day, we will be thinking about them and talking about them all the time. Then, they will work their way into our psyche, so they begin to make up the fabric and fruit of our lives.

If you want to display your values in your life, one of the quickest shortcuts to make that happen is to infuse your vision with them by displaying them where you'll see them all the time.

Now It's Your Turn!

Use our process to super sleuth your own family core values and display them prominently in your home. Even if you don't feel like you've really grasped them the first time around, you can see your core values as a work in progress. The good news is that you're growing more and more aware of the deep-down value system that runs your life.

If you'd like some questions to help you get started with this part of the Seven Generations Wealth and Legacy Formula, we've included them in the QUICK GUIDE: How to Get Started with Your Family Guidance System that you can find in the bonus resources provided along with this book. You'll also get our list of 170 core values to consider as a starting point for finding your family's core values. Flip over to the Resources section at the back of this book for access.

Next, you need a single mission that clarifies why your family exists to give a sense of shared meaning and purpose to your life and your moments. This group identity pulls everyone close like a family tribe while valuing each person's uniqueness and individual contribution. Stay tuned, because in the next chapter, we'll break this down in detail.

12

THE ASSIGNMENT AND THE DESTINATION

Mission and Vision

We had articulated the highest and best version of ourselves. And we had identified the values that make up our compass, pointing us toward the character qualities we need to choose moment by moment.

Next, we needed to define why it was all necessary. Where were we going? What was our mission today and the place we wanted to end up in the future? What was our calling and the assignment of not only our own lifetime but also generations after us?

To show you what I mean, I want to highlight a quick case study of a coaching client.

Through working with us, the Milas family got very clear on their mission. As a blended family, they recognized their choice to value the unique characteristics of others, and be accepting and inclusive. As a result, part of the mission they crystalized was that their family exists to be good citizens who contribute to society in ways that make a difference in the world, and at each stage of life, to mentor and shepherd others.

See, our family MISSION is our place in the world now and how we are improving it.

Then, our family VISION consists of the aspirations we want to accomplish in the future, and so should yours.

We believe that all people are created for a grand purpose and that honoring that purpose makes our souls come alive and sing. We believe that all the members of your family are not an accident but integral parts of a whole. As a team, we know that we have a key objective during our time here on earth. When we are living out this mission, we are truly fulfilled and our souls come alive.

The same is true of you. If you are here on this earth, you have a purpose. It's up to you to discover that assignment. It's the life work you're meant to do.

> OUR FAMILY MISSION TELLS US, OUR CHILDREN, AND FUTURE GENERATIONS WHAT WE LIVED FOR AND WHAT IT MEANT TO HAVE OUR FAMILY NAME.

Remember, our ultimate point in doing this strategic planning was to intentionally create our ideal life for our family, not just today, but for generations to come. This work wasn't just for our benefit. It would be the mouthpiece to tell our children and future generations what we lived for and what it meant to be a Marshall.

MISSION

It was time to clarify our family's mission. *What was the purpose or ultimate assignment of our family?* We wanted to spell out the family mission we've been called to right now. To do this, we simply needed to encapsulate the objectives and culture of our family today.

Mission

We wanted to create the path to choose best while we were living, teach our children, and give guidance to future generations in our absence.

Because your family is an enterprise, you can think of your family mission from a business perspective. *What is the organization's purpose? What do you do? Who do you serve? How do you serve them?*

Here is our family's mission:

> We exist to love God, love our lives and enjoy them fully, love and bless people uninhibitedly, honor our elders, build a life and business we love (do work that makes us come alive, provide the most value and do the most good in the world), and bless our family and others in and through our home and table, where we craft amazing experiences.

VISION

Vision

Next, our vision would be the long-range single objective that is most important for us to accomplish. It is our goal to live into and achieve in the future.

Here is our family's vision:

> Build a multigenerational family legacy of more than money— *a family team based on the biblical blueprint*—and help one million other families do the same.

With our family mission and vision, we put the capstone on our why. It would be the rallying point that we could always use to make sure everything we do is in alignment. It transcended individual strengths, vocation, and our current life as we see it.

Since we've recognized this calling to our family mission and vision, we've answered that call by choosing to embark on a path to fulfilling it. That means we're committed to overcoming every obstacle and challenge for the sake of making it true.

NOW IT'S YOUR TURN

Using our experience, work out today's mission and the long-range vision for why you exist as a family. Keep in mind that while it may fit your family today, both your family's mission and vision may change over time as your family grows and new members come and go.

If you'd like some quick questions to get started with your mission and vision, check out the Resources page to access the QUICK GUIDE: How to Get Started With Your Family Guidance System in the bonus content provided along with this book.

Or to get our support so you can speed up the process, hop on a call with our team here:

https://sevengenerationslegacy.com/strategycall

Now, it's time to flesh out how you are going to live up to your family's goals. Because it's not enough just to write down what you want, you need a strategy to make your vision a reality. Most people skip this step, but then their values lack teeth to make it into practical application. So, now that you've done the hardest work of getting clear on what matters to you, continue that momentum into the next chapter, where we'll talk about creating a strategy to bring your ideals, values, mission, and vision to life by growing your family's resources.

13

THE MAP

Strategy to Grow Family Resources

I f you want the plans you're designing to become a reality, you need to
be brave enough to step in close so
you can examine them in detail. If your
hopes and goals stay in concept mode,
they'll float around as fairytale wishes
more suited for children or utopian
dreams that rarely happen. But when

Strategy

you spell out how you'll execute your legacy in every area of your
life, you gain the power to make it happen. That's because when
you see clearly, you can create the strategy and steps to take action.

Let me illustrate with a quick story.

Lucas and I drove across the continent three times during the
summers of 2007 and 2008. First was a move from the University
of Idaho to Alexandria, Virginia, right outside the Washington
D.C. city limits for the summer. Then, we drove back to finish
our senior year of school. Finally, we drove to our new home in
Chesapeake, VA, where we had both landed full-time jobs.

This was before the days of smartphones with data plans,
good cameras, and built-in GPS. To plan our route, we used
MapQuest online to decide where we wanted to stop each night,
book hotels, or stay with friends or family we knew in that area,
and then printed out detailed directions for each day's travel.

We knew we were driving east, but to arrive at our destination, we needed more than a hand-wave gesture toward the horizon. We needed a plotted-out path that zoomed into the details so we could see the steps along the way.

It's the same with your legacy.

Clarity in your strategy is like a zoomed-in map to follow to your destination with highways, mile markers, individual turns, and the distances between them. It's what gives your brain and your posterity instructions on what to do so you can carry out your legacy in your lifetime and in generations to come.

The good news is that reaching this clarity isn't haphazard or lucky. Rather, it's a scientific, systematic process with a formula.

Let me show you how we're walking this out.

THE TWO MAP VIEWS YOU NEED

With a map, you can often toggle between satellite view and map view to get the best idea of the journey ahead. Similarly, when outlining your family's strategy for building your vision, there are two areas where you will need to draw out your detailed map:

- A strategy for growing money, and
- A strategy for growing people

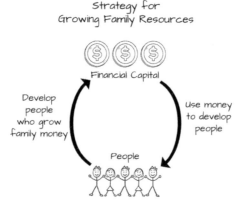

These two components will become the support beams of your mission and vision. That's because family wealth and human flourishing are inextricably linked as two sides of the same coin. With people and money contingent upon the other, you need to handle each in a way that lifts the other. You must have a clear plan for how you will secure your family's financial future so that it will benefit the people. *And* you'll want a guide for how to develop people who contribute to growing family money.

Our goal is to grow family money that improves people while, at the same time, building people who grow family money. If we do both well, our legacy will be unstoppable. That means that in both areas, we need a plan that we can execute. And then, we need to ensure that nothing interrupts or derails the plan we set in motion.

Our Strategy for Growing Money

Right now, Lucas and I are in the trenches of building the financial infrastructure that will serve as the trusses of multi-generational wealth. We are creating long-term sustainable wealth that's not just a high income, exorbitant returns, or a giant net worth.

Because here's the rock-bottom truth: A high income requires you to keep trading time for money. If you're living up to your means, you're always just one paycheck away from poverty. Striking it rich with a lucky investment is like winning the lottery. (Tell me how many casino millionaires stayed wealthy.) And net worth is a pile of cash. No matter how great the figure is, when you turn it into income, you can run out.

Instead, we are building financial freedom with cash-flowing assets that produce an ongoing stream of income, so we never have to worry about running out. And this income will continue to benefit our family today and in the future, giving us a foundation of confidence and the means to live the way we've dreamed.

Let's take a look at exactly how we're doing that.

OUR CASH FLOW SYSTEM

We've implemented a cash flow system to first keep as much of the money we make as possible, then secure and protect it, and then put our money to work so it will make more.

We first have a non-negotiable financial principle to pay ourselves first, at least 30 percent of our income every month.

Next, we're protecting the money we keep. We're suited up with the armor of insurance and legal protection to ensure that no life event can sweep in and rob the wealth we're building.

Then, we're focusing our investing in opportunities we know and control that leverage our unique abilities.

Today, our primary asset is our business, where we're creating intellectual assets, value ladders, and helping as many people keep and control as much of their money as possible, maximizing our profitability while we do so.

Because we want real assets that create cash flow, appreciation, tax advantages, and that don't rise and fall with the whims of the stock market, we are adding streams of income through real estate and alternative investments. While this has been our stance through both strong and tumultuous economic times, our strategy of real assets has proven especially relevant in today's unpredictable world.

And while our end goal isn't an income target, a dream house, or a bucket-list vacation, all those things will result from our plan. Rather than focusing just on more *spendable* income, we are creating more *investible* income, more cash-flowing assets, and more asset-based income. This is the foundation for wealth that stays in the family and continues to grow with each successive generation.

OUR STRATEGY FOR GROWING PEOPLE

That last part, *"wealth that continues to grow with each successive generation,"* is a massive undertaking. It's bigger than any person can singlehandedly do in a lifetime. Instead, this long-range goal requires me to develop other people who will carry it out. That means that I need to help my children reach their potential, so they can help their children reach theirs. And the crucial skill they need that underlies and facilitates this expansion is financial stewardship.

Financial stewardship is the ability and discipline to handle money responsibly, allocate it in alignment with your goals, invest well, and create more than you consume. And those who are excellent financial stewards do more than just protect and grow money; they create it in the first place.

That means they need to become producers who add value to the world and make money as a result. It means they hone their talents to benefit the world most and cultivate reciprocal relationships with other people who are shaping and advancing the world in their own unique way. When they do this well, they will always have the financial resources to increase their own and their children's enjoyment of life.

To ensure your legacy continues to travel through the generations, you need to start a chain reaction of financial stewardship so everyone in your family becomes wealth creators, not just consumers of wealth that someone else amassed. And that means you are responsible for helping your children develop financial stewardship.

Reproducing Wealth Creators

That's why our goal is to grow children and grandchildren who take up the mantle to become producers and contributors, profitably using their own unique abilities to solve problems for others. Then, they'll add to the family wealth,

> WHEN YOUR CHILDREN BECOME PRODUCERS AND CONTRIBUTORS, THEY'LL ADD TO FAMILY WEALTH, NOT BECOME CONSUMERS DEPENDENT ON FAMILY CAPITAL, WHO, CONSEQUENTLY, DISPERSE IT.

not become consumers dependent on family capital who, consequently, disperse it.

To grow this capacity, we choose to use our financial resources to provide access to the best education, opportunities that advance their natural talents, high-caliber relationships that challenge and improve them, travel that expands their horizons, and experiences that enrich their lives. But most importantly, we choose to invest time in teaching and mentoring the skill of making and growing money.

Even though our girls are currently eleven and three, we're involving them in our wealth creation and management as much as possible and giving them increasing opportunities to develop their own creative capacity.

Three Ways We're Mentoring Our Kids in Financial Stewardship

Here are three key ways we're mentoring our kids in financial stewardship:

First, We're Encouraging Their Own Production and Business Pursuits.

We look for the unique abilities in our children and coach them on using their gifts to bring products or services that give value to others. After all, that's the essence of all business.

Avie is creative, imaginative, and has an uncanny way of effortlessly stirring up conversation and connecting with anyone! We call her the "Fun Bringer" because she is always injecting an extra measure of silliness and excitement into any environment. And she is a natural-born communicator and sales queen.

Almost two years ago, she participated in a five-day business incubator with Kid Biz Launch and created a cookie club to combine her passions for baking and bringing joy to others. Since then, she's sold a membership-based fresh homemade cookie dough delivery service door to door in our neighborhood and online to our local community, and she has quite a following of delighted customers. With her profits, 40 percent goes into savings, 10 percent to giving, and 50 percent to spending on anything she wants.

This is just one of her first businesses, and she's gaining enormous skills on every front! She's making money and friends while learning business, math, profitability, sales, quality control, and customer service. She's realizing the value of developing her talents, experimenting in business, and we're instilling the responsibility of sound money management while giving her the freedom to make mistakes and learn.

SECOND, WE INCLUDE THEM IN FAMILY FINANCES.

Most people hold their financial choices close to the vest as personal and private. They're about as closed about their money as an oyster shell. But everything about your money, from your production to your management, reveals your deepest values. In fact, your money is the true window to your soul. Opening up about your financial choices allows your children to see more of the person you are, deepens the relationship, and provides greater accountability to make decisions consistent with your principles.

We discuss our own finances with Avie as well, giving her a window into our reality. We share what is age appropriate and make sure it is in a productive way where she can participate.

Today, we talk about our fun spending plan that we use for dates, eating out, and fun activities, and we include Avie in deciding how to use that cash. This gives us the opportunity to talk about the tradeoff and opportunity cost. For instance, she helps us decide whether we go to a concert or get waterpark passes. Or we can have five stops to Chick-fil-A vs. one outing to a nice sit-down restaurant.

That means she's more committed to what we do with our money because she has some say in the matter. She can voice her opinions and share what's important to her. And she's aware of why we turned down other activities as well, so she feels less sense of unfairness when we say no. She knows why there's a cap on how much we spend in any one area and why we plan ahead rather than spending on a whim.

She also knows that if she wants something that's not accounted for in our family spending plan, she can save up her spending money to buy it herself. This gives the opportunity to understand how much work is involved in creating the money to make a desired purchase and starts the conversation about how valuable something is to us based on how much joy it brings or how long we worked to pay for that purchase.

Eventually, we'll have our children sit in the conversations as we make investing and major capital decisions to observe the process. The exposure will put them light years ahead of textbook theory to understand real-world analysis and evaluate performance against goals and expected outcomes.

THIRD, WE HAVE ESTABLISHED A FAMILY BANK.

To teach financial responsibility and encourage productive endeavors, we've created a family bank. That means we're warehousing our capital in the best vault we've found. Then, we're deploying our capital strategically to increase the family's cash flow.

Creating a family bank is easier to do than you think. My team and I are here to help you make it happen should you want support.

A FAMILY BANK IS THE BEST TOOL TO TEACH FINANCIAL RESPONSIBILITY AND ENCOURAGE PRODUCTIVE ENDEAVORS.

When our children are adults, they will be responsible for their own welfare, but they'll always have access to family resources through loans. So instead of using our family money to subsidize or gift future generations, our capital is available for loans that will increase the family balance sheet. That means we're not enabling one-way transactions like an ATM, but instead we're providing an opportunity to access *and* replenish capital.

A family bank will provide the resources to our children to start businesses, attend college, buy a home, invest, or enhance their knowledge and capabilities. To get a loan, they'll need to present their case for why the loan should be granted, as well as their plan for repayment. So, when they make a withdrawal from the family banking system, it will come with checks and balances, plus the accountability to add back more than they withdrew to pay forward the same opportunity to future generations.

KIDS WHO CAN USE FAMILY MONEY BECAUSE THEY WON'T NEED IT

The reason we're so acutely focused on developing financial stewardship in our children is that it's the foundation for literally everything else we want to enjoy together.

Our vision shows exactly how we develop people who grow wealth and how to use wealth to grow people. This vision of creating wealth *and* wealth creators is how we will fulfill our why.

This vision allows you to use the seven-generation lens to empower future generations of wealth creators.

This will mean children and grandchildren will be able to liberally *use* family money because they won't be dependent, entitled, or *need* the money. Instead, each one can enjoy life the most and develop their capabilities to the greatest degree. And we'll create this opportunity by living out our mission, rising to our ideals, and demonstrating the consistent character of our values. The result is that we'll influence the character of future generations so that they can do the most good.

That's why your vision drills down even further into how your family operates in the fabric of everyday life. When you have a clear vision, it can become the script to direct and produce your lives right now so you can fulfill your role as the stewards of your life. And it's the map that the next stewards of your family resources can pick up to carry on right where you leave off without missing a beat.

CHILDREN AND GRANDCHILDREN WHO BECOME FINANCIAL STEWARDS CAN *USE* FAMILY MONEY BECAUSE THEY WON'T BE DEPENDENT, ENTITLED, OR *NEED* THE MONEY.

In this way, our vision helps us live out our very best life and ensures that our impact is never interrupted by our absence. Remember, the definition of legacy is *the character, values, and financial means to live life on your terms that are modeled, taught, stewarded, and given from one generation to the next.*

The most important part of your legacy is the way you improve the people who come after you.

In my experience, you can't be intentional about something you don't put into words. But when you take everything you hope, dream, desire, and long to create with your life and press it into words, you're charting a course that your whole life can line up with.

Once we completed our family vision, we added it to a *Memorandum of Trust* that supplements our estate plan. You'll get a look at our vision in greater detail when I discuss estate planning in the next pillar.

NOW IT'S YOUR TURN!

From where you stand today, sketch out the map of how you'll execute your family's *why*. Pay close attention to both your plan for building long-term financial wealth and your plan for using money to build people.

102

Check out the Resources page at the back of the book, where you can find the QUICK GUIDE: How to Get Started with Your Family Guidance System among the bonus resources provided along with this book.

Or, if you'd like a fast pass to getting this done for your family, hop on a call to see how our team can help you: https://sevengenerationslegacy.com/strategycall

You'll work this out more fully in the next section, so it's okay if you don't feel like you've nailed it completely here. The important thing is that your brain is already working on the question. Chances are, you already know more of this than you'd dare to admit—it's just time to bring it through the layers from your subconscious out into the open to tell yourself what you already think.

Notice, there's no destination. There's no arriving, completing this mission, or mastering your core values. You'll always feel a tension between the idealistic meaning you've carved out and the fact that you're not completely aligned today. You'll never fully express this meaning on paper, never quite capture everything perfectly, and you won't measure up to your values and ideals all the time. But the point is that you're constantly improving. And with every step you take to progress, you'll become more because of the decision.

Don't wait until things are perfect first. Start where you are today and tend to the meaning of your legacy along the way.

Now, let me show you the four benefits you will get immediately when you finish this work.

14

ENDORPHINS

The Immediate Advantages of Legacy Planning

B efore we dig into the four biggest benefits of completing your Family Guidance System, especially getting clear your ideals, I want to share a quick story.

I was sluggish, unfocused, and generally moody and blah. The last thing I wanted to do was to put on my running shoes. It was hot out, there were toys all over the floor, dinner needed to be made, and I was already feeling behind on my goals for the workday. If I went running, it would further delay everything else and pile on the defeat, I reasoned.

But there's one thing about exercise. It's that when you do it, all the rest of the time in your day seems increased. You have more energy and everything seems easier and gets done faster.

It had been a while since I'd hit the pavement, but I knew this little sweat fest would be the best thing to jump-start my motivation. Three miles later, I was red-faced and salty as I wheeled the stroller back into the garage and parked it. I tackled dinner with joy and welcomed the new insights that helped me easily organize the rest of my day to make time for what mattered.

See, we all know exercise is fantastic for long-term health benefits like reducing your risk of heart disease, stroke, diabetes, and cancer, strengthening your heart, bones, and muscles, improving brain function, balance, and coordination, and maintaining a healthy weight. But there's something magical about the way exercise immediately makes you feel good! That's because the flood of endorphins changes your brain chemistry.

Just like exercising gives you an immediate boost, so does completing your family constitution. The long-term benefits are profound, but the immediate benefits are even more interesting to me. One of the immediate benefits of doing this planning and solidifying the meaning of your family is a little happiness boost, just like the endorphins that allow you to do everything else easier.

1. YOU'LL GAIN AUTOMATIC ACCOUNTABILITY.

When I look back on my childhood, my family culture had sound morals, discipline, and internal consistency. The four of us kids knew what was expected. If you asked each of us what our family valued, however, we would probably all come up with our own list. That's because we didn't articulate our mission, values, and ideals in a way that created a *shared language* we could all rally around.

Without language, everything most important to you stays a locked secret. If I keep my ideals a secret, it's easy to hide through life and hope no one notices the ways I self-sabotage and under-perform. But with a standard that's clear as day, you can no longer allow your mind to wobble around and choose the path of least resistance. You won't be able to make excuses, blame your circumstances, or resign yourself to a way of being that you must constantly apologize for.

When you create language to articulate your family ideals, now everyone can see whether you're living up to them or not. I can't ask my children to choose well but then let myself off the hook. I've opened the floodgates of accountability—from the most unlikely place, these tiny humans who look up to me. They hold me to my best as much as I do for them because we've created a culture around our ideals and normalized talking about their application regularly.

As if writing down our family ideals wasn't enough for me, I've now shared them publicly right here with you. I feel like I've just accepted the greatest responsibility to live excellently because I've invited you to witness how well we walk out our intentions and beliefs. That's a little intimidating because you now have next-level expectations of our character, and you will know if we don't go all in and live them out to the best of our ability! While you don't have to broadcast your ideals to gain the benefits, writing them down is an act that, by itself, makes it possible to show up that way more consistently.

2. YOU LIVE OUT A BEAUTIFUL GIFT.

Far from creating pressure to perform or demand perfection, sharing your ideals is more like a gift. That's because articulating, owning, and stepping into your best is risky and vulnerable. When you choose vulnerability, that courageous act means others can depend on and trust you more, which creates safety for them to also take the risk of rising.

In that way, one person owning their ideals becomes like a candle in the dark that ignites others. The more consistently you share your full, authentic self with others, the more you'll elevate everyone within your reach. Because, wherever you're at now, even if your family is disjointed, disconnected, or damaged, all it takes is for one brave soul to verbalize their ideals to begin to lift the trajectory of your whole family.

3. YOU'LL FIND THE HIGHER-LEVEL GUIDANCE TO ANSWER EVERY QUESTION.

Because your ideals are your way of showing up as the most excellent version of yourself, they answer all of life's most difficult questions. After all, it's far easier to orient your life towards something well-defined than just rising to the occasion—or not—depending on how you're feeling in the moment.

For instance, Lucas and I are always navigating this tension between respecting the individuality of our children and supporting their freedom while also guiding them to make wise choices.

Recently, we updated our family rules on eating candy. For years, we've been minimalistic and true to our health code. First, it was no candy at all, then one piece per day, then only after dinner, and it always required permission. But that had created a trophy-like aura around this forbidden fruit. Whenever our oldest was with friends or at school, she'd conveniently forget the rules and eat any candy she could. Thankfully, truthfulness remained intact, and she'd always admit it, but it worried me when she'd forget to eat meals and chow down any sugar she could when we weren't there to object. We want her to be healthy, but more than that, we want her to grow into an adult who makes her own healthy choices, not just be a begrudgingly obedient kid. At nine, we figured it was finally time for her to choose her own sugar rations if she finished her dinner. Thankfully, she's exercised some moderation, and to my pure relief, she didn't eat the whole bucket!

In this case, our *health* ideal was challenged by our *individual* ideal. Health could be forced. The individual ideal asked us to respect our daughter's maturing ability to decide what was best for her and let go of control in that area.

See, your ideals act as an anchor. They fix your focus on your end goals so you don't get caught up in micromanaging behavior. For us, that means we're teaching character and disciplines that will last a lifetime, not just make life easiest right now.

WHEN YOU LIVE FROM YOUR IDEALS, YOU SERVE YOUR END GOALS INSTEAD OF JUST MAKING LIFE EASIEST RIGHT NOW.

4. YOU'LL GAIN THE POWER AND CAPACITY TO LIVE AT YOUR BEST.

So, does declaring our ideals mean that we always demonstrate them perfectly? Absolutely not! In fact, I'll admit our ideals challenge me. And they should!

We so commonly live distant from who we are designed to be. And the one thing that will bar you from living your *arete* is believing it's not really you! You may feel that you can't create and live up to your highest code of conduct because of the frustration, guilt, and even shame or anger for the ways you've acted out of alignment with your ideals. After all, the evidence proves we are less than our ideals—we yelled, rushed, ignored the needs of others, avoided a challenge, or acted callous and indifferent. And whether it was years ago or within the hour, these incongruencies taunt and jeer that we are not and cannot ever be excellent. When you let yourself down, it can be the heaviest weight to lift your eyes back to your ideals and truly believe that's who you are.

But when you paint a vivid picture of yourself and your family at your best and share it, it's like you've staked a claim and said, *This is who I am, who we are.* It starts a chain reaction—first, you lift your mind, then your actions, then your family. That first step literally pulls you upward into alignment. It's like an imaginary string lifting a dancer's crown to the ceiling. It elongates their spine, raises their carriage, and allows them to gracefully defy gravity.

While your ideals are who you really are, they should stay above how you're consistently living right now. They should stretch you and pull you higher. Your ideals should be above your habitual thoughts and behaviors. Then they will become the very thing that helps you elevate your normal way of being. Remember, your ideal life is the one you're not fully at home in just yet. But it's the highest and best version of you that you choose to live *toward.*

THE MEANING IS THE MOST IMPORTANT PART OF YOUR LEGACY

Now I've walked you through building the first pillar of your multigenerational legacy of more than money. You've penned your family guidance system and defined what it means to be a family. With it, you've articulated your *why*—your *ideals* that defy the gravity of human nature and pull you into alignment with your best and your *core values* that are the compass pointing to your true north of character and stewardship. You've documented your *mission* as the greatest assignment of your family today and your *vision*—the long-range goal you're aiming for. And you've sketched the map that shows how you will build all of your family resources during your lifetime.

By completing this work, you've captured the *meaning*—the most critical piece of your legacy. This is the element that makes your legacy *yours*. It's what passes on your story, with the rich lessons and the wisdom gained. It unites each family member into a team by defining what it means to be a part of your family. And it lays the foundation of your children's character—the one thing that no one can ever take away from them—that becomes their greatest strength to help them the most. And you've laid the foundation for your family culture—the rhythms, routines, customs, celebrations, and expectations that you live out every day. A common mantra in the management consulting space is that "culture eats strategy for breakfast," and it applies in the family as greatly as in the workplace. What you do day in and day out writes your family story and forges your relationships. And the bonds formed through your culture will ultimately trump any of the legal and financial work you do in the next two pillars.

Family Culture

In Pillar 1, you've written a family guidance system to remind you of what matters and become your mouthpiece to direct your family for generations to come. You've given them the training and tools to create, grow, and steward wealth well.

Now, because you've prepared your children, you can take the next steps of putting legal and financial tools in place to leave a great inheritance in good conscience, knowing that more money will improve your children's lives.

You've drafted the architectural design. Now, it's time to build your airplane, rivets and all, staff it, and start booking passengers. In the next pillar, I'll walk you through how to guarantee that your death can't interrupt your life's work. Here, I'll give you the grand tour of our estate plan that we've customized to carry our legacy most effectively through the generations.

WANT TO GO DEEPER?

At this point, you may have questions about anything we've covered so far, or maybe you'd like support in how to start mapping out Pillar 1. If so, you can jump on a call with our team here:
https://sevengenerationslegacy.com/strategycall

KEY SECTION TAKEAWAYS

- Your ideals are like anti-gravity. Where gravity pulls you to your worst, your ideals become a force opposite to gravity, drawing you toward your personal best. These are your life categories with descriptions for how you show up in each area when you are most satisfied and fulfilled. Creating your family ideals requires simplifying to get to the gold, describing your ideal way of being, finding common ground, creating your categories, and staying centered on your why (not how you walk it out).
- Your core values are like a compass—one-word reminders that keep you moving in the direction of your ideas. To discover yours, you can "super sleuth" your story, your resources of time and money, your past, the future you

want to create, and objectives both inside and outside the home. Articulate principles over preferences, create a definition for each, and then, when you're finished, put them on display as a centerpiece in your home.

- Your mission is your assignment today, and your vision is the aspirations you would like to accomplish as a family in the future. Both help you prioritize how to spend time as a family, and remind you what it means to be a part of your family.

- Then, you need a strategy to grow family resources. This includes both a plan for growing money that improves people and also, at the same time, a plan for growing and developing people who grow family money. To do this, mentor your children in financial stewardship by encouraging their own production, include them in family finances, and establish a family bank.

- When you complete this Family Guidance system, you gain a shared language that increases accountability, so you increase your capacity to live at your best.

PILLAR 2

THE MECHANISM: CARRYING YOUR LEGACY

Mechanism

15

OVERHAUL

Why We Updated Our Estate Plan

Before we dig into Pillar 2 in the next eight chapters, I wanted to take a minute to explain why it's so important. See, we wanted to live out our Family Guidance System, not only during our own lifetimes, but also in the generations to come. That meant we needed to preserve our family values, continue growing wealth, and advance the flourishing of each person in our family through the generations. To do this, we needed a mechanism, or a "boat" to carry our mission across the water of an unknown future, intact.

The solution was an estate plan.

And although we'd already done this once before, the original plan wouldn't be adequate to accomplish our goals.

The last time we'd sat in an attorney's office, two-year-old Avie bounced around in her yellow tulle dress, with the handmade blush pink peony hair flower holding her curls out of her eyes and precocious pearls draped around her neck. We'd wanted to include her in the estate planning process, so we'd brought her to the document signing with crayons and crackers in tow. She even decided, with an air of sophisticated mischief, that she wanted to grow up to become an "a-tow-nee." I'd felt like we were doing grown-up and responsible things, planning for who would take care of her if we couldn't and who would handle our health and financial choices.

At the time, we selected a close friend as a trustee who would manage our money in our absence. Then, we tucked away the important-looking binder. There were a few sheets of paper we were supposed to fill out with demographic details like our parents, siblings, Social Security numbers, account numbers, etc. Those papers stared blankly at us from their perch on the desk in the office nearly every day for years, but we never found the time to complete them. We started over a few date nights when we were first pregnant with Olivia, but let's face it, there's nothing that more quickly kills the mood than talking about your wishes at your death.

Over the years, we'd made a few adjustments. The friend we thought knew how to manage money well was indicted for running a Ponzi scheme. While we weren't impacted directly, we quickly removed them from the role of stewarding our assets. In fact, this became a tipping point for Lucas and me to discover the real foundations of building long-term wealth.

And now that we had another child, we needed to confirm that those we'd listed as guardians would still be comfortable raising both girls if we weren't here. We wanted to make changes to our trustees again. And that brought up questions of how family assets would be used to benefit both of our children if we died. Would we split everything equally between them or keep the money together to benefit them both? And would we distribute money straight to their bank account when they were a certain age or continue to keep it in a trust? How would we manage the trust and direct how our money was used after we were gone?

We followed these questions, and they led us to a complete overhaul of our original trust.

Now Olivia was about a year old, and it was during the COVID lockdown. We crouched on our bedroom floor, the only place safe for our adventuring climber to play quietly but unobstructed. Eight-year-old Avie listened in as we put our attorney on speaker and talked openly about what would happen if Lucas and I were no longer living.

WHAT HAPPENS WITHOUT A PLAN?

While you're mentally competent and able-bodied, you make your own decisions about what to do with your money, how to raise your children, and how to line up your life with your priorities.

But without any kind of planning, the moment you cannot make your own decisions, your life can fly off its hinges.

Your accounts can be tied up in probate, exposed to the public eye, and shaved down by court-appointed attorneys. Assets you acquired for cash flow and income may have to be liquidated to be distributed. Controversy can arise over your wishes, creating family rivalry and feuding as each demands their share. Creditors of you or your children stake their claim and get the first right to any inheritance. Children may enter the custody of a family member who will take them, even if you didn't see eye to eye on matters of education, religion, or discipline. If your kids are still minors, even the life insurance you faithfully paid for can't go to them directly but must use a court-appointed guardian as an overseer. Without written guidance, everything you wanted may come crumbling down.

In this next pillar of building your multigenerational legacy of more than money, I'll show you how we did the legal work with an attorney to draft our estate plan.

16

BOAT SHOPPING

Selecting the Legal Structure to Transport Your Legacy

S tay with me . . . we're going to talk boats in this chapter, because it illustrates the purposes of an estate plan to carry family assets from one generation to another.

When I talked with my friend George about his boat, he beamed with pride. Of thousands of boats to choose from, they had found their perfect match. But how did they narrow down their options and shop for the one that suited them best?

First, they decided what they wanted their boat to do.

Since George and Sharon had lived on the lake for a few years, they'd had time to observe boats and watersport enthusiasts from afar. And during that time, they were keenly drawn to the challenge and thrill of wake surfing. George found out that wake surfing could give even diehard surfers more surf time than traditional surfing in the open ocean. And with that time, you could keep refining your technique and never get bored!

To do this, you needed a wake surfing boat with a special mechanism to take a few thousand pounds of water into the hull. This would weigh down the boat, so it would displace more water and then churn out a beautifully curled wave as the engine roared. This special boat would need more horsepower than similar boats, but it wouldn't travel as fast.

For George, that was a fair tradeoff. Although the fingers of Lake Tapps are extensive, they're also intricate, with mazelike channels. Even on the widest inlets and longest stretches, you can only open the throttle for a few minutes. He thought you don't really need the extra five miles per hour anyway.

Next, they were ready to narrow down by brand. A friend suggested a Mastercraft, and word-of-mouth from other happy boat owners confirmed the decision.

Finally, when they decided on the specific make and model, they attended a boat show, where they were able to order the perfect boat in a crisp white that wouldn't ever go out of style, snagging a great deal at the same time.

An estate plan is a lot like a boat. That's because it carries everything you own across the expanse from one generation to the next, the same way a boat transports its cargo across the water. And just as a boat may have to navigate layers of unknowns during its passage, an estate plan will keep your legacy afloat across social, political, environmental, and economic unknowns.

So, that's why you should think of setting up your estate plan just like boat shopping. Instead of being overwhelmed with the options, the first thing you need to do is determine what you want your boat to *do*.

> TO SELECT AN ESTATE PLAN THAT CARRIES EVERYTHING YOU OWN FROM ONE GENERATION TO THE NEXT, FIRST DECIDE WHAT YOU WANT IT TO *DO*.

While I've never purchased a boat myself, I've paddled a canoe leisurely through underbrush around Lake Anna during a camping trip with another couple. I've also set sail from Puerto Rico on a cruise ship for a week-long island-hopping excursion in the Caribbean with thousands of strangers. I've watched whales in British Columbia from a skiff that bounced on top of the water, ridden the ferry past the Statue of Liberty, and cycled the churning pedals of a paddleboat on numerous family adventures. And

I've even tried to surf behind George's wake surfing boat. (Seven tries is a valiant attempt when you're being waterboarded!)

In every case, I traversed the water, but each boat provided a very different experience. That's why there are so many different styles of boats to meet wide-ranging needs. You may need to select a flat-bottomed barge for river transport or a tugboat with the power to propel it, a cargo ship to handle the transoceanic transport of imported and exported freight, an ocean liner for distance, or a cruise vessel for island hopping closer to the coast. You might need a wind-propelled sailboat or bowrider for speed and handling rough water, a yacht for luxury, and a bass boat, kayak, pontoon, or trawler for fishing, depending on whether you're fishing in freshwater, in a river, small lake, or on the open ocean.

Like selecting a boat, there are many options for your estate plan. That's why before establishing your estate plan, you first want to know what you want it to do, so you can hone in on which type to consider. Then the decision becomes a matter of preference, price, performance, and proximity.

And exactly like boat shopping, there's no such thing as a one-size-fits-all.

What Is an Estate Plan?

So, what exactly is an estate plan?

An estate plan is a big word that's like a wrapper around a plan for everything you own when you die.

Here's the essence of what it does:

Behind the legal terminology, the bare bones of estate planning are that you've planned and written

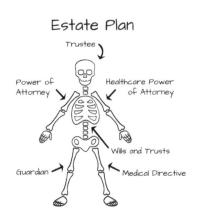

Estate Plan

down what happens when you can't make decisions anymore and what happens to all your stuff—including your children, your house, your money, your investments, and your businesses—when you are gone.

From person to person, the ideal estate plan that serves your goals and assets will look completely different.

Your plan could include a will, trust, power of attorney, medical directive, and healthcare power of attorney. Your process could range from filling out a template online to sitting down in an attorney's office. And then, the law firm you employ could range from providing a basic cookie-cutter estate plan to a comprehensive asset protection strategy with multiple trusts and entities.

OUR FAMILY'S ESTATE PLAN

Our estate plan is a mammoth binder full of legalese. I promise it would do you no good for me to share it here. You wouldn't benefit from reading it cover to cover, and even an excerpt would probably put you to sleep. More important than showing you the actual estate plan itself, I want to tell you what's included and why.

The main thing we wanted our estate plan to do was to provide funding to take care of our children if we couldn't and ensure we carried out our family mission into our posterity. We wanted our kids to remember our why, walk out our vision, and execute our plan to grow wealth in each generation and use the family money to create the best life for each member. And it would infuse character to build true success because if our kids are successful, they'll better enjoy and steward the resources.

Our estate plan:

1. Appoints proxies to make health and financial decisions for us and gives them instructions on what to do, so they can stand in the gap for us if we are unable.

2. It includes a treasure chest that owns and holds all our stuff for our benefit and designates a shepherd to watch over our assets in our absence, just like we did.

3. And it sets up someone to raise and care for our children the way we would have.

We want the boat of our legacy to sail without the delays, costs, and publicity of probate court. And we want to pass our assets in a trust, meaning that they won't cause a taxable event for our kids, and they can't be taken in a lawsuit. And most of all, our estate plan ensures the state won't decide who will care for our children or place them as wards of the court in the foster care system if we passed away, veering off on a detour that derails the strength of our family and the thrust of our legacy. It means we have charted out a contingency plan to continue their life as we had intended with them, with as little interruption and upheaval as possible, and pre-arranged someone to manage their financial resources to pay for it all until they can do so on their own.

We've gone to great lengths to set up a customized estate plan. This includes:

- A *Revocable Living Trust* to protect our privacy, minimize estate taxes, and avoid probate
- A *Power of Attorney* to make legal decisions on our behalf
- A *Healthcare Power of Attorney* to make health decisions on our behalf
- A *Medical Directive* to clarify what kind of lifesaving care we want
- A *Pour-Over Will* to transfer assets into our trust that we haven't already assigned
- *Guardians* we've selected to raise our children
- and *Trustees* to manage the family assets

But even more important than the legal structure itself, we've outlined our express written instructions for how to use and grow wealth over time and have invested in the relationships that will carry it out.

WHY ESTATE PLANS ARE FOR EVERYONE

You might think, Rachel, it sounds like you're planning to die!

Well, by golly, you're right because I know that I will! And for me, being prepared for whenever that day comes gives me the confidence to hug my precious children and know that nothing can snatch away the impact of my love.

Or maybe you think estate planning is only for rich people. The problem is that most people's definition of rich is "more than I have." Most people don't think of themselves as wealthy. But most people also need a plan, and most people have done far less planning than they need to.

You might also be turned off because estate planning sounds expensive, time-consuming, and extraordinarily boring. But here's what you need to know. First, the cost of setting up a good estate plan is far less than the court costs and fees of 2–5 percent of the estate assets you'll rack up in probate. Second, it's not as hard as it sounds if you dive in and get started. And finally, sure, no one wants to do this end-of-life planning, but I guarantee no one else wants to sort it out for you after you're gone.

Or maybe you're one of the few who have already done your estate planning. I encourage you to stay with me because while the initial plan is crucial, so is keeping it current so that it fulfills your intended purpose.

Lucas and I have a very specific way we want our life, endeavors, and money to benefit those who come after us. We wanted control over how our money is used, without everyone getting a front seat to our affairs and without getting stuck in the time-consuming and expensive probate process.

Will your plan look exactly like mine? Probably not. You may be at another stage of life or wealth creation. You may need more complexity or less to accomplish your objectives.

Sometimes, Simple Works

My mom's father passed away about three years ago. Having lived in Selby, South Dakota for over eight decades, Ed Lemler was a pillar of his town. He'd volunteered at the local nutrition site, a senior center that served meals to the community, raised the flag with honor every day, and delivered dinners to each person like they were nobility. Everyone knew him by his ready smile beneath his ballcap brim and the punctuated sound of his cowboy boots.

He died with a simple will that directed everything to be divided equally between his two daughters, who were both listed as Personal Representatives. My mom and her sister worked through his affairs together as efficiently as possible, with no contest or disagreement. Her sister handled all the medical power of attorney decisions during his last days, and my mom took responsibility for all financial matters as executor of the estate.

They made several day-long trips to South Dakota to clean out the property, organize an estate sale, do minor repairs, find a buyer for his thirty-four-year-old trailer home, pay off his medical bills and final expenses, and divide the remaining belongings and assets. Because they did a lot of the legal accounting themselves, they reduced the bill for the probate attorney. In all, it took about three months to finish all the work, and finally, about a year later, they received the final sign-off to close probate. This was nearly as quick, clean, and efficient as it could have been. That's because it was a small estate with no minor children and no disagreements between heirs in a small community in a state with a streamlined probate process.[18]

In my grandfather's case, a trust ended up not being necessary. But in most cases, the stars don't align so perfectly. The point is that he had a plan, and any plan is better than no plan.

REASONS TO CONSIDER A TRUST

One of the primary reasons to do estate planning is that if you don't, your state will step in and implement their own plan for your stuff. This process is called probate—the messy, lengthy, public, and expensive court-determined process for validating your will and distributing your estate. And the worst part is that you don't get a say. I don't know anyone who wants to give up control like that.

A trust helps you pass on assets in a way that avoids probate, saves time and court fees, and minimizes estate tax. It tucks your assets into a treasure chest for your benefit while you're living. And it allows you to pass down that treasure chest to your beneficiaries and direct rules for distribution. However, even more importantly, it forms relationships among the trust creators, trustees, and beneficiaries.

The Trust Is a
Treasure Chest

Although it's highly unlikely, it's possible to avoid probate without a trust. In the slim chance that you have a small estate, all your beneficiaries are adults with perfectly copacetic relationships, you had a will and painstakingly titled all your assets precisely correct, and no unforeseen factors arise that upset the balance, you might be able to circumvent the probate process *sans* a trust.

But chances are, you're building extraordinary wealth, you have clarity on how you want your financial wealth to benefit those after you, and you want the highest chance of success for your posterity across the widest spectrum of future events.

With who you are, what you want, and where you're going, a full estate plan with a living trust is the boat that fits best to accomplish your goals.

There are several reasons to use a full estate plan, including a trust.

1. You have minor children
2. You want the pot of money you leave to be used in a certain way
3. You have a large or complex estate, including any business or real estate investments
4. Not everyone in your family gets along
5. You or your children have gone or could go through a divorce
6. Your or your heirs have or could have creditors or lawsuits
7. You're in a state that requires inheritance tax to be paid by those who receive your estate
8. You have a child with special needs
9. There's potential for disagreements about the distribution
10. You have assets held across multiple states
11. Your state has a typical, non-streamlined probate process
12. You want to protect your cash from being used up for your own long-term care

See, even if things seem okay now, there are so many factors outside your control.

First, and most notably, estate taxes could change. In 2022, estates over $24.12 million as a couple—and $12.06 million for a single person—paid estate taxes.[19] That's because those numbers are today's current threshold of the federal estate and gift tax exemption—the size an estate must reach before it's subject to tax.

So, just how much tax will these estates pay? After using up your exemption and having a stair-step marginal tax rate on the next $1M, your remaining estate will be taxed at forty percent. This means that if your family's estate is $100M today, you could end up paying the IRS $35.12 million—over a third of your estate—in taxes![20]

Does this mean that if you have an estate smaller than the exemption, you're home free? Sure, but only today. That's because, just like with any taxes, both the tax rates *and* the thresholds of those tax brackets can be changed in an instant with a legislative vote. That means that even though most people are excluded from paying today's estate tax, and you may fall under the threshold yourself, there's no promise estate taxes will stay out of your corner.

If you look back about twenty years ago, in 2002, the estate tax exemption was just one million, at a whopping 50 percent tax rate.[21] That means that a significantly higher portion of the population was lassoed into giving up almost half of their estates. While estate tax exemptions have been on the rise for decades due to legislative changes across administrations of both parties, it shows that exemptions and tax rates are the furthest thing from steady and predictable. Even if they don't affect you today, you have no control over whether they could shave off half your estate in the future.

Next, if your kids are successful, an inheritance from you may push their own estate over the exemption amount, inviting more IRS meddling than they want.

Additionally, creditors or lawsuits could crop up for you or your children. Divorcing spouses can lay claim to what they see to be their fair share. And everyone's definition of rightful fair share can clash in a battle of the ages. In the words of estate planning attorney Andy Weinhauss,[22] "In-laws can become outlaws." Often the rivalry isn't malicious. When individuals with different perspectives stand up for what is best for themselves and their families, disputes can result.

> TO NAVIGATE AROUND THE SINKHOLES OF PROBATE, TAXES, RECKLESS SPENDING, AND FAMILY FEUDING, YOU NEED AN ESTATE PLAN THAT'S CUSTOM-DESIGNED FOR YOUR FAMILY.

This may sound overwhelming, but there are so many unknowns in your future. That's why it's best to make a plan that works in the widest range of circumstances, not just if everything works out perfectly.

One thing is certain: all the meaning in the world won't help generations after you if you don't have a mechanism to transport family money and the wisdom to grow it through the generations. That's because probate, taxes, reckless spending, and family feuds can squander and dry up family resources, and it can take years to settle an estate. To navigate around these sinkholes, you need an estate plan custom-designed for your family.

NOW IT'S YOUR TURN

So, don the Sperrys, roll up your sleeves, and untuck your shirt-tails! We're going boat shopping!

With our clients, we always recommend talking with an attorney directly. Just like it's hard to buy a boat online if you've never been in the boating world before, it's impossible to know exactly what you need from an estate planning perspective if you aren't an attorney.

Whether you have never done an estate plan or already have one in place, it's time to evaluate where you can improve. Maybe reading through what we've done in our family has been like peeking in through the window to get your bearings in the foreign world of estate planning and what it means to put your affairs in order. And hopefully, that means what might have seemed too scary now feels just a little bit more doable. The first step is to start thinking through what exactly you want to happen when you are gone or no longer able to make decisions.

Take two minutes right now and carve out some time to start this process. Pull out your calendar and schedule an hour to talk with your spouse to start the heart-to-heart conversation. If you don't, you'll never find the time.

For a quick list of questions to get started on your estate planning, grab the QUICK GUIDE: How to Get Started with Your Estate Planning that you can find in the book bonuses you received along with purchasing this book.

You'll find access to this tool in the Resources section at the back of this book.

Right now, you don't need to worry about finding the right attorney; just focus on being mentally prepared for the conversation by getting a clear idea of what you want it to do for you. That's because, just like a great boat, an estate plan is a means to an end. Rather than being a point of interest itself, it helps you solve a problem and do more because of it.

Narrowing in on the right structure and exactly what to put in just depends on what you want and need to happen.

My estate plan gives me the confidence that everything is in place to bring my multigenerational legacy of more than money to pass. Come hell or high water (pun intended).

In the next chapter, I'm diving deeper into how we made our estate plan specific to our unique family, not just good for the generic family. And I'm pulling back the curtain on why we're not giving an inheritance outright.

Key Chapter Takeaways

- Probate is the public, lengthy, and expensive, default process plan for the transfer of your estate when you pass away. One of the main goals of estate planning is to minimize or prevent your assets from going through probate, moving them from one generation to another safely and intact.
- At a minimum, your estate plan should do the following: 1) appoint proxies to make health and financial decisions for you and give them instructions on what to do, so they can stand in the gap for you if you are unable. 2) include a treasure chest that owns and holds all your stuff for your benefit and designates a shepherd to watch over your assets in your absence, just like you did, and 3) set up someone to raise and care for your children the way you would have.

- To accomplish those goals, an estate plan should include a trust, power of attorney, healthcare power of attorney, medical directive, pour-over will, guardians, and trustees.
- There are many reasons to set up a trust, including having minor children, owning businesses or real estate investments, not wanting your children's estates to be subject to estate tax, and protecting your children from creditors and lawsuits.

17

UNINTENDED CONSEQUENCES

Why We're Not Giving an Inheritance Outright

The best way to explain why we're NOT giving an inheritance outright is because we want to avoid the flaws in most estate planning that you'll discover as you read on.

I'm not a fan of big government. There, I've said it. Agree or disagree, we can still be friends. But hear me out.

It seems to me that no matter who is in office, our nation keeps spending. Another billion here, another trillion there, even if it's for things that I like and consider to be good things, it all has unintended consequences. Every time we ask the government to do more, it increases the US national debt—currently sitting at about $29 Trillion—in an insanely reckless and irresponsible way, like a car blazing through a residential area at 120 miles per hour.[23] We're digging a deeper and deeper hole of insolvency, indebtedness, and inflation that our kids and grandkids will be left to solve. I think reveling in the benefits we enjoy today without a glance at the unintended consequences is hamstringing our children's generation. Frankly, I believe it's immoral!

It's shortsighted and unsustainable to consider only immediate results and ignore the trailing effects.

This same logic has me turning to natural medicine over and over again. I don't want to Band-Aid one set of symptoms to end up creating side effects that need a vicious cycle of more

Band-Aids with more side effects. Rather, I want to solve root causes and get maximum long-term health.

So how do you avoid creating unintended consequences more lethal than the problem you set out to solve? You have to step back and zoom out to look long term. Long-term thinking requires strategy. And often, the best move isn't the most obvious or direct. It can seem completely backward or counterintuitive.

With most estate planning, you gingerly protect your assets while you're building your wealth but leave the gate wide open to risk the moment it's time to grant the inheritance. That's because it's common to put assets in trust during your lifetime, but then when you die, the assets are distributed directly into the beneficiaries' bank accounts.

It's as if you carefully wrapped all your belongings in a trunk and stowed them safely inside a shipping vessel. They stay neatly packaged during the voyage across the sea, bypass probate court, and arrive at your intended destination intact. But as soon as they're offloaded, someone dumps the trunk over, and everything spills out on the dock. Now, your recipients have to gather everything in their arms and try to carry it safely home through a dangerous back alley.

Maybe one beneficiary spends his new fortune quickly in the city and finds himself a bitter and penniless peasant within three months' time. Another faces a lawsuit, and the lengthy process is expensive, drying up the inheritance even before the case reaches settlement. The third was facing bankruptcy, so creditors used a bank account levy to freeze his accounts and legally take the funds to cover the debt. The fourth owned a thriving dental practice. She discovered that now the inheritance had pushed her estate over the estate tax exemption, impacting the inheritance she'd pass on to her children.

That's dramatic, maybe, but the point is that the gift you intend for good may barely be delivered and can quickly invite the unintended consequences of ruin, injustice, disproportional taxation, and heartache.

My mother would have fallen prey to these unintended consequences had my grandpa passed even a few years earlier. You see, my parents had divorced, and my mom was personally responsible for some prior IRS tax obligations. She was able to work out an offer in compromise which, through a stringent set of requirements over multiple years, settled her debt. If the tax debt had still been outstanding at the time of receiving the inheritance from her father, every penny would have been garnished instead of benefiting her life in any way.

That's because when an inheritance hits your beneficiary's bank account, it becomes *their* property. It can now be attached to their creditors, claimants, lawsuits, or flagrant spending sprees.

THE FLAW IN MOST ESTATE PLANNING

The flaw in most estate planning is that it dumps money straight into the possession of a person. And for kids, this inheritance has usually been pre-selected to drop at an arbitrary age. While a minor child cannot directly receive a monetary inheritance, they can receive all the money when they turn eighteen. Or you can designate distributions of, say, 50 percent at age eighteen and the remaining 50 percent at age twenty-five.

> THE FLAW IN MOST ESTATE PLANNING IS THAT IT DUMPS MONEY STRAIGHT INTO THE POSSESSION OF A PERSON.

While, at first, this windfall seems like a dream come true, it comes with some pretty ugly side effects. Their property is now exposed to tremendous risk. That's because there's no guarantee they'll be responsible and mature enough to handle it well. Creditors or lawsuits can stalk the inheritance like a predator and consume it. Or a gift can push your successful children over the estate tax exemption, auctioning off the assets to the IRS involuntarily.

That's why it's not enough to slap together the quickest and cheapest estate plan you can find just to check off this box and say your estate planning is complete. Instead, you need to carefully weigh how you disperse your estate to ensure your gift lives up to its full potential.

With our estate planning, Lucas and I had to grapple with the tension of wanting to do the most for our kids but not wreck them with excess like a casino junkie who wins the lottery. We wanted them to be able to use the money but not invite others to dip their hands in the pot and meddle with their money by flattery, trickery, or theft.

This is why we are not giving our children an inheritance outright.

So, what are we doing instead to avoid the pitfalls? We're keeping their inheritance in trust.

Holding an Estate "In Trust"

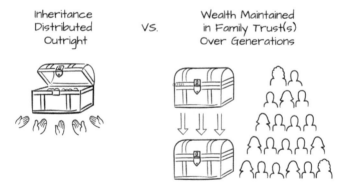

Inheritance Distributed Outright   VS.   Wealth Maintained in Family Trust(s) Over Generations

Let's break down exactly what it means to hold your estate "in trust" and how it helps us accomplish our goals. Instead of carving a channel for our assets to flow straight down into their hands, our family money will stay in a reservoir, moving from our current trust to trusts for each of our children. Our children will have access to use the trust assets according to the rules that we've set up in advance.

That means our children will receive the benefits of the family assets but not *own* the money outright.

This is the counterintuitive strength of the strategy. Because our kids won't possess the money directly, it's protected from sly or malicious threats. That includes *internal* threats of underdeveloped responsibility and *external* threats like theft, lawsuits, or exorbitant taxation that could whittle down family wealth.

And because our loved ones won't own the money directly, we have assigned that responsibility to someone we trust greatly to oversee and steward it instead. This trustee will serve as the gatekeeper to uphold the intent, vision, and rules of the trust. They'll have the authority to act on behalf of the trust, so they can manage assets for the benefit of our family.

In this way, we accomplish our top two priorities:

1. to grow family wealth for generations, and
2. to use it to maximize human flourishing.

And if the date comes early for us to part from our earthly stewardship, our children will have a wise mentor to finish the task of equipping them to steward family wealth, picking up right where we left off.

YOUR TURN!

To shatter the power of unintended consequences that threatens and disperses wealth, consider holding your estate in trust rather than forking over an outright distribution. When you do, you'll preserve the treasure chest for the next generation. In this way, someone else can hold the key for your children, charities, or whoever you leave your estate to, and you can set the rules for distribution.

Use these questions to think through your decision to hold assets in trust:

1. Is your family's wealth protected now? Will it be protected after you're gone?
2. What are some of the challenges you need to prevent with your estate planning?

Wealth can't grow unless it's protected. Holding wealth in trust maximizes creditor protection and asset protection for your children, so that family wealth can continue multiplying.

> WEALTH CAN'T GROW
> UNLESS IT'S PROTECTED.

Now, I won't tell you that holding wealth in trust is simple or easy. What's *easy* is leaving the next generation to figure it out. What's *simple* is removing the inconvenience, cost, and administrative duties of managing a trust and just going with the default distribution by giving money directly.

But our goals are to give our children the moon while making sure they're responsible enough to handle it. We want to demonstrate our trust in them but steer them to use their inheritance wisely. Our long-range vision is to equip each of our family members to be a conduit to continue the legacy of growing family wealth and enjoying the most wonderful things. What's *not easy* is setting up a system that serves these goals best.

The strategy of holding wealth in trust raises so many questions, like it did for us. These challenges aren't unique to your family situation. In fact, these are the epic and monumental challenges that each legacy creator must overcome. Usually, these tensions stay hidden in the shadows, lurking around the corner and giving us a sense of unease that raises the hair on the back of our necks.

In the next chapter, we're going to address head-on the concerns of keeping wealth in trust. And, we'll reveal the answers that will help you navigate those challenges to bring about greater communication and stronger family trust.

18

"IN TRUST"

Overcoming the Three Challenges of In-Trust Wealth

The reason we balk at the idea of wealth retained in a trust is that it seems like it could go sideways, but we don't often put language to our fears so we can dialogue about them openly.

When I was about eight, I took swimming lessons at a local indoor pool. Our class was ready to jump off the diving board for the first time. We all stood shivering and dripping wet as we waited our turn.

All too soon, I was next, and suddenly, each foot was heavier than lead. I climbed the stairs and inched my way out over the water below. My instructor waited beneath the diving board. Time stopped. I could feel everyone watching me. I flushed. I couldn't budge. The bottom of the pool bowed down like a crater below, and I just knew I'd sink to the depths. There were hot tears of fear, embarrassment, and frustration. My heart pounded, and my ears rang.

Finally, the lifeguard walked out with me and lowered me down into the waiting arms of my instructors below. It took the gentle firmness of someone helping me do what I couldn't do on my own to let me experience for myself that it would be okay. Within a short time, I was running over that same diving board and springing off the edge.

Just like my first diving board apprehensions, the reason these tensions of holding wealth in trust are scary is that they stay vague and unnamed.

But, instead of letting the fear of difficulty or the unknown paralyze us, let's turn on the lights and dive straight in. We'll confront these tensions directly by calling them exactly what they are. Then, we'll have the ammunition of clarity to defeat these foes and navigate the turbulent waters of estate planning so it can serve your intended purposes.

The three tensions of in-trust wealth are:

1. Crumbling the assets by subdivision
2. Mistrusting the trustee
3. Rigidity that defeats your values

CRUMBLING FAMILY ASSETS BY SUBDIVISION

One of the things that destroys family wealth is parceling it out and separating it rather than keeping it all together.

Right now, we have two children. Theoretically, each will get 50 percent of our estate. If they each have four children, each of their portions will be divided into 25 percent apiece, and each of those grandchildren will now have an eighth of the family wealth.

If you're thinking of family wealth as the finite quantity of your generation's wealth getting split up and chunked down, you can imagine this will shrink each person's wealth over time. By the time you reach seven generations out, even if the initial wealth was staggering, the inheritance each receives is microscopic.

But if I leave the money together in one family trust, how will I ensure each person has equal access? Will it be based on exactly equivalent dollar amounts distributed to each child? What if one has greater financial need than the other? What if one becomes independently wealthy, and the other becomes a missionary with very little financial compensation?

So, if I'm going to hold family assets in a trust, do we divide the assets and direct them into two separate trusts, one for each of them, or do I leave money all together in one family trust? Ultimately, we want to grow total family wealth over the generations.

Given the current ages of our children and the state of our business and investments, we decided what worked best was to divide our estate equally between them and at our passing, to establish separate trusts for each child. But instead of thinking of this money as a finite sum, we've given instructions for how to steward and grow these resources for themselves and future generations. In this way, our estate is the seed of infinite wealth creation, not the total of everything they'll ever have.

MISTRUSTING THE TRUSTEE

Another big problem with keeping assets in a trust is that inheriting children can feel that the benefactor didn't trust them enough. They can see the trust and the trustee as guards and gatekeepers to keep them from their money. The result is a power struggle and contempt for the trustee and the parents who established this protective mechanism in wisdom.

> IF CHILDREN SEE THE TRUST AND TRUSTEE AS GUARDS AND GATEKEEPERS TO KEEP THEM FROM THEIR MONEY, IT CAN CREATE A POWER STRUGGLE WITH THE TRUSTEE AND CONTEMPT FOR THEIR PARENTS.

If children are left in the dark about your wishes and the only thing guiding the distribution of money is the trustee, who supposedly knows what the parents wanted, there's a lot of room for emotions and personal perspectives to color the interpretation of what should be done. Perhaps one child is in their seventh year of an undeclared major at Harvard, feeling entitled to endless tuition coverage because that's what they think their parents wanted, and seeing the trustee who sets a limit as withholding their rightful share. This creates lots of room for doubt and distrust to settle in. And those emotions make wounds that erode the strength of the family and each person's confidence in each other.

Reality check: These unintended consequences are the opposite of everything we were working to create.

Seeing the potential for the problem of power struggles and misinterpretation to crop up, we needed to be intentional about providing for a trusting and respectful relationship between our children and a trustee. But how?

We decided the best way to plant, water, and nurture a healthy relationship with our successor trustee in advance was to carefully hand-select them, maintain a healthy relationship, communicate our vision and goals, and provide for our children to have a healthy relationship with the trustee while we are living. Then, we needed to communicate our intentions plainly all along so nothing would come as a shock and surprise to our children if the event ever arose.

Again, due to our children's young ages, we needed to communicate with our everyday life and words, as well as formally in writing. That way, anything we didn't have the chance to communicate directly wouldn't be lost in translation.

RIGIDITY THAT DEFEATS YOUR VALUES

Then finally, if we were going to spell out everything, how would we be plain enough to leave instructions to follow with no gray area but not undermine our children's freedom and autonomy? After all, our core values list is topped with freedom and responsibility. Tying the hands of our kids or the trustee would inhibit rather than facilitate their freedom.

For instance, if we accounted for $25,000 per year to be spent on college tuition for up to four years, what if the best school costs more? What if inflation brought the cost of education at that time above what we'd foreseen? What if tuition was covered but not a provision for housing and that prevented them from studying in their field? What if additional years of study were required for the work they felt called to do or because they were studying part-time while they worked and raised a family? So, how could we give freedom and flexibility to the trustee to change the method, based on factors we couldn't have predicted, to achieve the ideal outcome?

We decided to formalize our guidance for how to use family wealth into a supplement to our trust, toeing the line between being expressly descriptive but not overly restrictive. Then, we gave full authority to our trustee to use their discretion to adapt our guidelines to the situation to achieve the purpose of the trust in the first place: family wealth that grows with each generation and people who thrive and enjoy life to the fullest.

YOUR TURN!

For a quick list of questions to start thinking about how you'll deliver wealth and assets to your children, see the QUICK GUIDE: How to Get Started with Your Estate Planning in the bonus resource included with your purchase of this book. For access, flip to the Resources page in the back.

Next, if you hold your estate in trust, you'll need to navigate the tensions of in-trust wealth personally and strategically. That means creating an environment that grows wealth rather than shrinks it, a symbiotic relationship between your children and their trustee rather than a suspicious and resentful one, and guidelines that empower rather than restrict.

Our answer was to write out a *Memorandum of Trust*. This ancillary document not only solves the tensions of keeping money in trust, but it embodies the spirit our trust and estate plan need to carry on a multigenerational legacy of more than money.

Over the next three chapters, I'll show you how.

19

THE SPIRIT

How Supplementing the Trust Makes It Come Alive

Then the Lord God formed a man from the dust of the ground and breathed into his nostrils the breath of life, and the man became a living being.

—Genesis 2:7

Your estate plan needs the breath and soul that make it come alive. While your legal compilation of documents might be functional and technically complete on its own, it will still be a lifeless corpse. That's because, by itself, it's unable to carry your story, transfer your values, and bestow the wisdom of your stewardship.

Let me illustrate.

Of all the intensely beautiful and poetic scenes throughout time, this one captures me most. The infinite and vastly incomprehensible God stoops low, scoops together the rubble and clay, and artfully fashions every curve, angle, and hair of the human frame. He overlooks no detail, weaving nerves, muscles, bones, joints, arteries, a beating heart, and lungs with delicately branching airways waiting to hold breath that will exchange a perfect ratio of oxygen to fuel the body. He works with purpose and intensity. Of all of the Master's creations, this one is the crowning masterpiece.

His eyes sparkle as He adds the finishing touches. He sculpts rods and cones inside the retina of the eye to scan and absorb the wonders all around, the neurons and synapses in the motor of the brain to assemble and organize millions of pieces of data, and distinctive fingerprints to mirror the uniqueness of the Creator himself. He chisels the jawline and steps back to admire his handiwork. Just one last thing.

And then he leans down again, this time to breathe his own breath, his nature, into the nostrils of the finished form. The breath comes tumbling through every passageway and fills the lungs. Adam inhales the exhale of God's Spirit, and with the infusion, he gasps to life, a whole, thinking, feeling, purposeful person.

Estate Plan
and Asset Protection

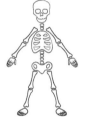

The word *breath* used here is the Hebrew word *neshamah*, which means *wind, vital breath, divine inspiration, intellect, soul, and spirit.*[24, 25] This breath was the Spirit of God—the breath that brought a lump of dirt to life. Without this divine breath infusing us with a soul beyond our physical flesh, we would be nothing more than a human-shaped animal or an exquisite human statue.

It's the same with your estate plan.

Most people who put together an estate plan do so because the task seems like the necessary, important, and responsible adult thing to do. But once they attended the ceremonial document signing, they check off the box and never think about their estate plan again.

YOUR LEGAL COMPILATION OF DOCUMENTS MIGHT BE FUNCTIONAL AND TECHNICALLY COMPLETE ON ITS OWN YET STILL BE A LIFELESS CORPSE—UNABLE TO CARRY YOUR STORY, TRANSFER YOUR VALUES, AND BESTOW THE WISDOM OF YOUR STEWARDSHIP.

That's where we left off with our first estate plan. While it would have worked legally in a mechanical and robotic kind of way, it would have fallen far short of doing the most good in our family.

For your estate plan to fulfill your intended purpose of transporting your family's legacy of more than money across multiple generations and accomplish all your grandest hopes and secret dreams, you need to bring it to life with the *spirit* of your family's *meaning*.

Complete Estate Plan

Legal Structure is the Bones ✛ Memorandum of Trust is the Spirit

That's why, as we launched into updating our estate plan, we needed two components:

1. The legal documents of our estate plan, and
2. Our *Memorandum of Trust*

Our attorney drew up the formal, legal documents that make up the bones of our estate plan—our revocable living trust, power of attorney documents, and pour-over will. But what brought our estate plan to life and made it our own was the *Memorandum of Trust*.

Memorandum of Trust

This document would communicate the heart of why we'd set up everything the way we had and infuse our family with a sense of identity and purpose. And it would guide our children, trustees, and future generations in exactly how to use our trust.

Once complete, this document was 100 percent our own, as unique to our family as a fingerprint. It was the words to communicate the *meaning* of our family and the *guidance system* for how

147

to use the money in our trust to fulfill everything we'd hoped and dreamed for our family.

You *could* think of a *Memorandum of Trust* as a supplement. Like the optional walnuts in the chocolate chip cookie recipe, the sidecar next to a motorcycle, or the garnish on your charcuterie board. But when you think of your memorandum as extra credit, you dull the precision and power of your impact.

Instead of being an afterthought, supplementing your trust literally infuses it with the *spirit* that makes your legacy come alive! That's because this memorandum holds all the weighty, important

Memorandum of Trust
= Spirit of Legacy Planning

> INSTEAD OF BEING AN AFTERTHOUGHT, SUPPLEMENTING YOUR TRUST LITERALLY INFUSES IT WITH THE *SPIRIT* THAT MAKES YOUR LEGACY COME ALIVE!

things that reveal the meaning of your legacy and give it wings.

With the work to construct our family guidance system, we'd been assembling the pieces of our *Memorandum of Trust*. So far, it included our:

1. Ideals
2. Values
3. Mission
4. Vision

But this document was missing two critical pieces:

1. The purpose of why the trust existed in the first place, and
2. The fine print detail about how to spend, manage, and grow the money handed down

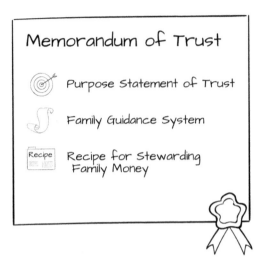

So, here's how we tackled these parts. We imagined step-ping forward into whatever time it was that our children were receiving their inheritance. They'd be sitting in our attorney's office, hearts sliced through with grief. Hopefully, they would now be grayed with age and wrinkles and have grandchildren of their own. Hopefully, we'd journeyed together and shared with them exactly what this moment would be like. Hopefully, they'd already caught the vision and had already contributed greatly to family wealth. Hopefully, they were already the wise stewards of this legacy, and the things about to commence were of no surprise at all. Hopefully, they'd already weathered years of teaching their own children and grandchildren.

But if they were younger and fewer years had passed, and they were about to learn about their inheritance and how exactly they would be able to use it, we needed to set the stage so every-one in the room could hear our immense love resounding like the ring of a bell.

Legal structures and terminology would never accomplish this. That's why we needed to write the words *now* to communi-cate hope and life *then*.

Not Legally Binding

Before I share with you these most important words in our estate planning, I first want to tell you that they are not legally enforceable.

"What?!!" I can hear you ask in astonishment. Why would I do all this work to write instructions necessary to lift our legacy off the ground and then make it optional for our posterity to follow the manual?

We could have supplemented the trust with an addendum that would be legally enforceable, just like the trust. But what kind of hands-tied obligation fosters connection and trust?

Even the God of the universe didn't force his way by creating humans who must meticulously do his bidding. Now, if He did, the world would be exactly right, and we'd be perfect . . . robots!

Instead, he created humankind capable of free will, with the ability to really mess things up. Why?

Because people are only capable of love and relationship when they are free to decide for themselves. In fact, you might think that God is exhausted by people who constantly disobey and choose what hurts themselves and others. But throughout all of time, God has never stopped pursuing people. He is relentlessly for us, desires communion with us, has always gone to the greatest lengths to demonstrate His love, and continually longs for us to choose Him.

The point is this: relationships must be mutually chosen, not forced. If we forced our will, it would destroy our family and the legacy we were creating. We'd create rebels that balked at the heavy-handed requirements of a controlling great-grandma and grandpa ruling from the grave and imposing their own way.

No, we couldn't *force* our legacy to work. Instead, we had to build the opportunity, equip our children, and then invite them to own the responsibility of growing family wealth. Only then could we raise future generations who flourish.

To scale this incredible feat, we needed to respect each family member's autonomy and provide each the power to choose their own path. That's why our *Memorandum of Trust* stands as the most important component of our estate plan. Yet, at the same time, instead of corralling, prodding, and forcing, it gently leads generations after us.

Stay tuned as I show you in the next chapter how we dug in deep, but with open hands, to this delicate task.

20

NO SURPRISE

Statement of Purpose

When you set up an estate plan, you want to tell your children exactly *why* you've planned this way so they can hear your heart, not just discover the plan. Since explaining legalese to young children wouldn't suffice, we successfully communicated the point of our planning in our trust's memorandum.

Trust's Statement of Purpose

Planning surprises is so much fun for me! Lucas likes predictability so much that he can sniff out any attempt at a surprise, but catching Avalynn off guard and overwhelming her with what she could never have expected has become quite an art form. We recently surprised her with a puppy for her birthday, so there was a whole world I had to keep under wraps. And, to make matters a bit trickier, I couldn't mention anything in front of Olivia, our two-year-old budding conversationalist, because she would surely have given away the whole game.

However, when creating your *Trust's Statement of Purpose*, you don't want any surprises. Instead, you can think of the Statement of Purpose as a toddler who blurts out the obvious and spoils the surprise. This section of your *Memorandum of Trust* is supposed to spill the beans on exactly why the trust exists in the first place and why you went through all the hoops to set it up.

For us, being in life insurance and financial services for nearly a decade gave us a keen advantage because we have had the opportunity to rub shoulders with and learn from industry experts and thought leaders. One of those sources of inspiration came from our friend Andrew Howell,[26] one of the most brilliant leaders in this space and a third-generation estate planning attorney whose grandfather had created Walt Disney's estate plan.

We started with a sample portion of a *Memorandum of Trust* that he used for one of his clients. The sample included a statement of purpose for why a family trust had been created and what the family's values were. The idea was that if your loved ones were becoming the recipients of family wealth, they should be reminded of the reason the wealth was created in the first place. The part of the memorandum we saw resonated with what we wanted to create, so we rewrote it in our own words and used it as the starting point to think through our own values and purpose.

Our Family Trust Statement of Purpose

Here are some of the most telling excerpts from the beginning of our own *Memorandum of Trust*. You'll notice that they outline the reason we were motivated to do this extensive planning.

> We (Lucas and Rachel Marshall) are establishing this trust for our benefit during our lifetime and for our children and generations to come, for as long as there are assets available in the trust.
>
> Our trust is a gift of love.

That phrase, "Our trust is a gift of love" was borrowed from the vast wisdom of James E. Hughes, Jr., who co-authored *Complete Family Wealth*.[27]

This was the single sentiment that we wanted to blanket every step of our legacy, from the initial creation of a trust to the transfer of assets in trust to our children, to who and how we designated a trustee and contingent trustee to manage family assets, to how we asked for family money to be spent and used.

OUR TRUST IS A GIFT OF LOVE.

These are the standards we wish to be upheld by this trust.

Notice that we didn't say, "must be upheld." This delicate phrasing points out that we want our beneficiaries to hear our heart and our hopes in these words but not read them as law with infractions bringing penalty and punishment.

> It is our intention that this trust provides the means for future generations to live their best lives, pursue their passions and dreams, be free to find and fulfill their purposes in life, and to find meaning and fulfillment in life.

> We value human freedom and liberty and want our posterity to be free. To that end, we recognize that it is impossible for us to plan for every future contingency and situation that may arise in our descendants' lives, and we do not want to be so limiting that we unintentionally prevent the freedom and liberty we value so much. Therefore, we are leaving significant discretion in the hands of the Trustees of this trust.

The heart of all our planning is love and freedom that creates flourishing in the lives of each of our family members. That's why we're not dictating or tying the hands of our trustees.

> Trustees are free to make distributions to benefit and provide opportunities for our descendants to flourish in life, business, vocation, relationships, health, personal growth and self-development pursuits, and spiritual and emotional well-being.

If anything conflicts in the trust and this letter, the trust governs.

And there it is—not legally binding. The trust dictates, then the trustee has discretion. The memorandum is a guide.

> While this trust will provide substantial financial resources, it is our belief that the greatest value we have to offer our future descendants is found in our experiences, principles, and values.

> In the event we are not here to pass on these values or for our future descendants we do not have the opportunity to meet during our lifetimes, we have created this *Memorandum of Trust* and family mission statement. It is our hope to convey the principles that guide us and the values we hold dear. We are outlining our views and attitudes on life as a guide in the administration of this trust, as it is our intent that whenever possible, the administration of benefits to beneficiaries of this trust is done in alignment with our stated purposes as described below, with the objective to maintain the incentive for our heirs to lead productive lives.

Ultimately, we want our money to facilitate the freedom and productivity of each person who comes after us. With our words, we communicated that even though there are things we can't see ahead, we're outlining the spirit we want to transfer to each next generation of wealth builders.

Next, to finish writing our memorandum, we needed to outline exactly how to spend, manage, and invest trust assets so that the money we leave will facilitate the long-term prosperity of our family, propelling our legacy into the future.

We'll outline the recipe to do just that in the next chapter.

21

THE RECIPE

Instructions to Steward Family Money

J ust like a recipe spells out everything you need to make a culinary masterpiece—which ingredients to use, how much, how to combine them, and the timing of everything—you need clear instructions that spell out how to allocate family resources. This is especially true if you want to give the formula to someone else so they can replicate and continue on your results. And instead of planning for your death, you need to plan for your life that lives into your family's mission and vision. Get ready to dive into exactly how, and why this matters.

First, let's step into my real-life kitchen to illustrate.

I've grown to love cooking! When I've had time to feed my creativity by bingeing Pinterest, I've found joy in making authentic cultural dishes—everything from Greek butterflied lamb leg to Panang curry, Chicken Tikka Masala, and Pad Thai.

Mastering a new recipe is an artful process of coordinating the right ingredients, the right heat, the right order, and the right timing. For a recipe to turn out well, you have to follow the recipe. Sometimes, my lack of preparation, or trying to follow all the steps with a potty-training, hungry, mess-making toddler underfoot while supervising fifth-grade math, or trying to cram a workout in while the food is on simmer can cause me to miss steps. The embarrassing result: too much burned food, forgotten salt, or mushy noodles and a meal that is less than appealing.

Like cooking, we needed to provide specific instructions for how to use family money whenever we pass away and our assets transfer to our children's control. That's why we'll spell it out in the next section of the *Memorandum of Trust*.

You can think of these instructions as a recipe because they are instructions for how to strategically spend financial resources so that you can live on mission and fulfill your vision.

Back in Chapter 13, we discussed that the map you need to lay out would address how you will build money and how you will concurrently build people. Both flourishing people and increasing wealth are needed to propel your legacy. Since both are interdependent, money can be used to contribute to the well-being of everyone and strengthen the family. At the same time, people who become wealth creators build the financial strength of the family.

The recipe we're outlining today gives instructions for how we'll use our family finances to improve our children so we can live out our family why and grow family wealth over time, even if Lucas and I are gone.

TIMELESS AND IMMEDIATE

It was important for our *Memorandum of Trust* to be timeless so it would be relevant and apply to *any moment* it was called upon. But one of the greatest tensions we encountered was how to make it true across the generations of our family to come while also applying to our *right now*. While we needed to maintain a long-range, seven-generation perspective, this document would be the map to instruct the most immediate, worst-case scenario of what happens if we both died tomorrow.

DEALING WITH BIG EMOTIONS WHEN IT'S SAFE

There would still be tragedy, pain, fear, and emotions I can barely fathom. But amid the mess, there would be a safety net. That's because the biggest questions of *what happens next* would already have been accounted for.

Avie is old enough for us to talk about this. She understands that we have planned for her and her sister to be taken care of, down to every detail, if something happened to us. It's a scary topic for sure, but we'd rather help her navigate and process the scary with us while it's safe than leave her to deal with all the questions, worries, and emotions on her own if it happened.

Similarly, on a perfectly sunny and normal day, we planned for how to handle a house fire. We purchased fire ladders, installed them in both of our upstairs bedrooms, and practiced exactly how to use them. While it made our hands shake a bit to practice, we'd rather deal with all that fear now in the daylight when the sun is shining and we're all relaxed and smiling.

ANSWERING QUESTIONS AHEAD OF TIME

To complete these instructions, Lucas and I asked each other: *What would our children experience if our lives suddenly stopped?* If Lucas and I were both gone too soon with our children still young, what would happen then? What would be important enough to have written down so that everyone has what they need and our legacy continues without interruption? Would they and our trustees have the tools to continue making the financial choices we were already making today so that they could continue living out our family why and growing family wealth over time?

How exactly would we want the trust assets to be used as they grow up, get their education, get married, buy houses, and invest? How do we want them to spend money to enjoy life fully and maximize their flourishing in a responsible rather than wasteful way? And just how do we expect them to preserve and grow their monetary wealth AND grow themselves as people, expanding their intellectual, social, spiritual, and financial capabilities?

These big questions needed tackling within the safety of right now, so we didn't offload the responsibility onto our kids of figuring everything out on their own. After all, it would be completely unfair to leave them a high calling and then withhold the directions to lay hold of it.

So, we left the safety of the rosy and optimistic, big-picture legacy creation and drilled down into the small-picture details of caring for the immediate financial needs of our children.

THE INSTRUCTIONS TO CONTINUE DAILY LIVING

Here's where the rubber met the road. We needed to connect the dots between the life we were choosing in real-time right now and the one our trustees and guardians would build where we left off.

We simplified this entire discussion by asking the opposite question: *What are we already creating together?* Instead of figuring out how to continue everyday living if we passed on, we spelled out the ultimate dreams, goals, and plans in every category of our life that we plan to experience together in this life. We wrote down exactly how we were already spending money to make this happen and how we expected to continue spending money as our family grew.

Then, instead of planning for our death, we were planning for our life! This one shift planted our feet firmly in today and helped us flesh out everything needed to continue the fabric of daily living. No matter *what* happened to us. And no matter *when*.

INSTEAD OF PLANNING FOR YOUR DEATH, PLAN FOR YOUR LIFE!

That's how we created the instruction manual with micro details for someone else to pick up where we left off building our life and legacy.

Creating these spending instructions quickly gave us clarity in two areas:

1. IT ILLUMINATED OUR CURRENT PRIORITIES.

Today, we've paid for our children's private schooling and bilingual nannies. We feel that both are providing a skillset and way of thinking that will give our children access to infinitely more opportunities in the future. But look at my home décor, and you'll see instantly by my floral couch from the 80s that it's taken a laughably lesser priority. It's important to me, just not *as* important.

Clarifying my spending priorities today illuminates how I'm contributing to my legacy right now.

2. IT SHOWED US HOW TO STRETCH OUR PRIORITIES OUT INTO THE FUTURE WITH CLEAR BOUNDARIES AND EXPECTATIONS.

How will we pay for cars, college education, first houses, and weddings? It might seem a little early to tackle these things if your kids are just toddlers now, but I promise you that it's easier than relinquishing control to chance. Or worse yet, going down a default path you never wanted, with no off-ramp and no emergency brakes.

You can spend years paying for your kids' insurance, cell phone, car, car insurance, and college (with who knows how many declared major changes), only to wake up and realize that your kids are adults, but you're still paying for all the things and don't know how to get them off your payroll. This happens more often than you'd think, and it's a major heartburn that can break up families.

Through a friend, I once heard of a couple's marriage being on the line because what they'd started as a nice gesture turned into what felt like a tourniquet. He'd agreed to pay for college for his three kids, but now they were all grown, established in successful careers, and made more than he did. His wife wanted to cut the kids off, but he felt obligated to continue making payments on their college debt to maintain the relationships and keep the peace.

Knowing your boundaries ahead of time means you can have open and honest communication with your spouse and kids about what is expected of them financially. That means you can have real relationships based on trust, not a sense of obligation. And that means that you're not creating entitled kids who are disincentivized to develop themselves because you're their money dispenser. Instead, you teach them to use money responsibly and create it for themselves—hitting the ultimate target of creating flourishing individuals and a flourishing family.

OUR FINANCIAL INSTRUCTIONS

I'll share some of the key excerpts from the financial instruction section of our *Memorandum of Trust* here. As you step into my life for a minute, notice the level of detail, but that we've written out these instructions so they wouldn't be overly restrictive.

EDUCATION

One of the key drivers of helping our children develop their own understanding, organization, and self-leadership, as well as aiding the discovery process of how they think and do things, is education.

> We want to give both Avalynn and Olivia every opportunity to be successful. For that purpose, we want them to be educated to their highest capacity in an environment where they personally own their learning path on their own heroes' journey.

> Grade School

> We are currently paying for, and it is our desire, that both girls would be homeschooled or attend private school at an Acton

Academy through the completion of grade school. If one is not available, we want them to be educated at a Montessori school or a similar private school that models the educational philosophy as appropriate for each individual child.

We fully encourage our children to earn a two-year college degree at an accredited school (while in high school) that would transfer to a university/college.

Extracurricular Pursuits and Skill Development

We want Avalynn and Olivia to develop their passions with as many extracurricular opportunities as possible, cultivate a wide range of skills, and discover what they love, including but not limited to dance, horseback riding, summer camps, sports, and music.

Higher Education

We do not believe that higher education is always the ideal path unless it is required for their chosen vocation. Education is an investment that ideally would produce returns greater than the cost of the investment.

If either or both girls would like to attend college, they should have a declared major, a clear purpose, a plan for completing a degree, and a commitment to pay it forward. When these requirements are in place, funding is allocated for tuition and living expenses.

We are still leaving full discretion to the trustee due to aptitude, ability, desire, goal-setting, and economic and environmental factors beyond our ability to see now.

We don't believe there's one prescribed path for everyone, and we think college is optional. Looking at the pure economics of it, we don't want our kids going to college for the friends and the experience if they don't know what they want to major in or whether their life path requires a degree. College is an investment that should pay returns and improve the family's financial situation, not deplete it. If they would like to attend college, we want our children to use the family fund to pay for school and then repay the loan to replenish the capital so it can be used for other opportunities.

In addition, we recognize many other valuable learning opportunities besides formal college.

Industry Conferences, Programs, Consulting, Training and Mentorship, and Lifelong Learning

There are many ways to enhance knowledge and skills outside of a typical classroom environment, and we would like the funds to enable broad lifelong learning.

If either or both girls would like to pursue business, entrepreneurship, investing, or expand their capabilities, we would like them to invest in themselves and learn all they are capable of to maximize the value they can provide. Before committing to any industry conference, program, consulting arrangement, training, or mentorship, we ask that there is a clear purpose and stated goals.

Business and Entrepreneurship

We hope that our descendants will use trust assets for the purpose of investing for profit or gain, whether for new start-up businesses or ventures or as a source of capital for existing business interests.

Starting and growing a business is one of the most rewarding and transformative life missions.

We have found these principles to be our guiding star in all business and investment endeavors.

- Dollars follow value

- People have intrinsic value; money does not
- You are your greatest asset and investment
- How much you value others is limited only by how much you value yourself

Read books, attend trainings, and hire a mentor.

Before going into business with a partner, ensure they share your principles, values, work ethic, and vision.

Before making business decisions, seek wise council.

Before starting a business, hire the following: Business coach/mentor, CPA, attorney, and insurance agent, and have someone(s) you meet with regularly to hold you accountable.

Books to read: *Rich Dad Poor Dad, The Cashflow Quadrant, Richest Man in Babylon, The Go-Giver, DotCom Secrets, Expert Secrets, Traffic Secrets, Dream100 Playbook, Profit First, The E-Myth*

Car

If you have your driver's license and a reason to drive, whether for school or work, the trust will provide a suitable car for up to $XX,XXX (in 2020 dollars).

We leave it to the discretion of the trustee to alter the amount as the situation warrants.

Home

We wish to design our home to be a sanctuary of the soul that we love spending time in and that is a welcome gathering place for family and friends.

We believe that your house payment should be less than 25 percent of your post-tax monthly income and should not be a detriment to your personal ability to save and invest.

If Avalynn or Olivia want to purchase a home, we would like to provide whatever is reasonable to help get them into a home.

We also want to make it possible (purchase home and/or property) for extended family to live or visit together as they want or need to. If we are still living, we envision having a home large enough to allow our parents to live with us either in our home or on our property. Additionally, this could be multiple dwellings on the same property or in close proximity, allowing for multiple families to live near each other.

Remember, these are guidelines, not laws. Your ultimate goal is to strengthen your family with how you pass on wealth so that you facilitate freedom and personal responsibility.

To do that and maintain alignment with our trust's purpose, we've given ultimate discretion to the trustee. This means we've given express permission for the trustee to color outside the lines if their assessment of the situation and judgment warrants achieving our ultimate objectives in another way.

> YOUR *MEMORANDUM OF TRUST* IS GUIDELINES, NOT LAWS.

NOW IT'S YOUR TURN!

Your *Memorandum of Trust* will be the key that brings your estate plan to life. It will infuse dry legal documents with the spirit necessary for them to bear the legacy you're scripting.

As you write out this portion of your vision, it's important to make it one hundred percent relevant to your *immediate* financial needs. When you do, you create the smoothest transition with as little disruption and upheaval as possible if their world were ever to be turned upside down. Over time, as your family grows, as your children age, and as you add investments and build businesses, you can update your estate plan and your *Memorandum of*

Trust to reflect that evolution. To complete this step, you'll have to leave the safety of the *someday* and talk about *today*.

If you'd like help working through your *Memorandum of Trust*, we can help! Book a call here to talk with our team: https://sevengenerationslegacy.com/strategycall

Either way, take some time now to jot down some notes for your own family. Pull out the calendar and schedule a time when you have a couple of hours to talk with your spouse and finalize your plans.

Done? Do you have your time blocked on the calendar? Okay, good.

Because now, without taking a rest break at all, I need to immediately tell you about the next piece of your estate plan, a piece that is, in fact, the primary active ingredient. You'll need to dedicate your full attention to this next piece; it's that serious. But you'll be relieved to know that you've already been working on this for your whole life. It's the one thing that will make everything else possible. That's why we call it "Gorilla Glue."

Key Section Takeaways

- When defining the passing of your assets to your heirs, you can designate distributions as outright or discretionary. Outright distributions can become a flaw in most estate planning, because the inheritance adds directly to the estate of your heirs, potentially triggering unintended consequences, including unrestrained spending or being sequestered by creditors, claimants, lawsuits, or even sudden "friends" wanting handouts.
- Discretionary distributions are accomplished by holding assets in-trust after your passing, protecting the money so you can grow family wealth for generations, and use it for your goal of maximizing human flourishing. Because these distributions are overseen and approved by a trustee,

this arrangement can also spark challenges. Most importantly, the trustee must know what you wanted, so you must communicate your wishes effectively to the trustee, clearly and specifically, but without rigidity that defeats your values. And to prevent heirs from seeing a trustee as the enemy keeping them from their money, you must lay the foundation for a healthy relationship of trust.

- Your trust is a lifeless document unless you communicate its purpose to your heirs. This is done best in a *Memorandum of Trust* that supports the trust, but is not legally binding. In that way, you can clearly communicate to both your trustees and your heirs the purpose of your legal planning and your specific intentions of how family money should be handled to live out your ideal life.

22

GORILLA GLUE

The Relationships That Hold Everything Together

If you want your legacy to accomplish everything you hope and dream, you can't possibly do it by yourself. That's why you need Gorilla Glue relationships.

Relationships

The ping of ceramic clattering to the floor made me cringe. I knew too well that sound of yet another ornament meeting its death on the hardwood. Peering around the Christmas tree, I saw the fragments. It was one of my shiny reindeer from 2006, a gift from my grandparents the year Lucas and I were married. I groaned, and my MacGyver skills went into reaction mode fast.

I grabbed the hot glue gun. Surely, I would be able to reattach the golden antlers. I don't know about you, but when it comes to mechanical stuff, I'm prone to find the quickest workaround in a pinch. It may not be the right or best solution, but it usually works to cobble the thing together and keep moving. I have no patience for the proper, slow-drying, clamp-requiring ceramic glue that I'd have to go to the store to obtain before even beginning to fix the thing. Elmer's is usually the quickest in reach, but it's messy and takes too long to dry. That's why the hot glue gun has been known to fix a few more things in my house than its inventors intended. But in this case, hot glue just wouldn't suffice. The bond was weak, and the application was too gloppy to restore Rudolph's headpiece.

I peeled off the hardened clumps of hot glue and remembered that we had some Gorilla Glue in the garage. Day saved! A dab, a few seconds to set, and the sweet ornament my grandma had given me had been salvaged, although sporting a few visible scars. From that day forward, Gorilla Glue has become my go-to favorite because of the quick-dry bond that's as strong as cement!

Your estate plan requires another intangible thing to hold together all the pieces so that your legacy is strong and indestructible—it's *relationships*! Every single dream you write down, every fragment of your vision, and every minute your legacy endures rely completely on *other people*. More specifically, your legacy depends on the depth of your bond with the other humans in your life.

YOUR DREAMS, VISION, AND LEGACY DEPEND ON OTHER PEOPLE.

If everything goes according to plan, your impact depends on the strength of your marriage and the connection and trust between you and your children and grandchildren. And if at any juncture, the people you've designated to make decisions for you, raise your children, and manage your money are called upon to step in, they will rise to the caliber of your *relationship* with them.

That's why your legacy needs *Gorilla Glue* relationships—the kind you can lean on heavily and trust to bear your weight. See, the success of your plans for a multigenerational legacy of more than money depends on *relationships*, not on perfectly crafted words. You could have an impeccable fortress of an estate plan that maximizes asset protection. You could even have the most eloquent and well-thought-out memorandum that fully details everything needed to pick up the baton of your legacy.

Gorilla Glue Relationships

170

But precision without a relationship will cripple your legacy. You need deeply committed relationships for this to work.

That's why it's most helpful to think of estate planning as the process of forming relationships among you, those whose lives will be improved by your plans, and anyone else who will support these primary relationships.

> PRECISION IN YOUR PLANNING WITHOUT THE DEPTH OF RELATIONSHIPS WILL CRIPPLE YOUR LEGACY.

MY MOMENT OF TRUTH

We're going to go deep and get gut-level vulnerable for a minute. It's risky, but I promise it's worth it.

I'm an achiever who likes to accomplish, be at the top of my game, feel great, and have everyone see only the strong side of me. But in truth, I've lived most of my life feeling weak, struggling, and exhausting myself trying to keep up the appearance that I had it all together.

For years, it was the suit and perfectly done-up hair, the spotless house, and all the answers. I remember the day I walked across the campus of a would-be employer to my first interview, clicking along in my pumps, trying to hide my insecurity, my sweating hands, and the limp from an awful ingrown toenail.

This visage extended to my relationships too. I wanted people to see a cute family with no issues. It seemed I was always trying to hide from others and even from myself. My figure, my prematurely graying hair, my imperfections, my needs, my emotions. Too much makeup caked thick, too much hairspray controlling every wisp, too much padding in some areas, and always covered with too many layers of clothes or the structured box of a suit jacket.

Every time I spoke up in a small group, it was always with raging heart palpitations. Networking, with friends, at a Bible study, it was all the same. Even though I'm an external processor who needs to talk to think, I stifled myself by overthinking my comments beforehand because I couldn't bear to risk saying something others might disagree with. Then, I would drift off at the end without any real conclusions or opinions.

I was working hard on my mindset, which at the time meant that I could justify an overly optimistic explanation for everything and never admit a struggle or weakness.

I also swing towards extroversion. I was always adding guests to any list. I felt safer knowing there wouldn't be deep, intimate, or revealing conversations. I could flit and float from conversation to conversation and leave feeling wonderful. I worried that with too much time with one person, I'd run out of things to talk about. Our culture celebrates extroversion, so it was okay for me that I had lots of friends. But there was a nagging emptiness that none were close friends. Although I didn't see it, I didn't value investing in relationships that no one else could see.

Then, my parents divorced. Even though I was an adult and thought I could handle it, it was devastatingly painful and shook me to the core. Deep down, I was scared it could happen to me too.

On top of that, one day, Lucas sat me down and tried to get through to me that I was always focused on everyone else and not on valuing the intimate relationships within my own family. I was looking outside of me for everything big and exciting and beautiful and successful, and everything inside my home was a constant reminder that I wasn't there yet.

About the same time, one of my best friends and I had drifted apart; it had been years since we'd really talked. She wondered if I had moved on because I no longer felt that we shared as much in common.

I cried tears of frustration, longing desperately to dance in soul-filling friendship and the musical sound of laughter. But it was a pool, and I didn't know how to step in or swim, and I was afraid I would drown. My strategy had imprisoned me; I'd become a stilted, stifled perfectionist walled off from being known and loved. And while I kept up the fake confidence on the outside, the relationship quadrant of my life suffered a depressing emptiness. I shrugged it off, telling myself that everything else was a higher priority and that I could build relationships later, crying on the inside because of the loneliness and isolation.

Everything hinged on courage, but I was hanging back in the shadows of what was safe. I barely knew myself, and from this position, I wasn't capable of forging deeply committed relationships. In fact, if I had tried to create a legacy years ago, it would have been hollow lip service, reaching for something I didn't believe I could actually do.

That's because I didn't have the eyes to see the value of true relationships at all. Instead, I'd settled for a cheap version of self-protective people-pleasing. If I'd stayed there, I wouldn't have been able to feel the great love and admiration for each of the infinitely precious members of my family or care about nurturing their capabilities and whispering their potential to life. And this book would have been a dry and boring instruction manual that revealed nothing of real substance, and you would have thrown it in the heap of books you never finish a long time ago.

I certainly never would have seen that relationships are like mortar that glues every piece together, making every individual brick into what they could never be individually. But now, because I've slowly stepped free of the clunky version of me who didn't believe in myself enough to create real relationships, I'm swimming with all my might out here in the open water, living out fully everything I'm showing and sharing with you. It's from this vantage point that I implore you to stop everything you are doing right now and launch yourself fully into the business of building relationships. There is no other opportunity as profound and lifesaving as this one.

You need—as a categorical imperative—the kind of relationships that hold you, cry with you, believe in you, and help you build what you can't do alone. And at the fountainhead of these relationships, you need to be the person who lives out in real life everything you've penned in your family guidance system. You need to be the one leading your own life so excellently that others want to be a part of it. You can't fake this, and there are no shortcuts.

Let's dig deeper into what Gorilla Glue relationships you need and the strategy for fostering these deeply committed relationships.

THE SEVEN CRITICAL RELATIONSHIPS YOU NEED

1) THE FIRST RELATIONSHIP YOU NEED TO INVEST IN IS THE ONE WITH YOURSELF.

You are the only person you'll travel your entire life with. You'll carry yourself with you through every quiet moment alone, the grandstand ones, the tumultuous ones, and the ones that you make every infinitesimal decision with. You'll only create as much as you believe you're capable of. So, when you look deep into every nook and cranny of the soul, you'd better like what you see.

2) NEXT, YOU NEED TO BE RIGHT WITH GOD.

There's no other source of peace, hope, and confidence than your Maker, who already knows you fully and loves you completely. It's not only the most unconditional and pervasive relationship you'll ever know, but turning your attention to loving Him back sets you up for an exhilarating journey that brings meaning and fulfillment to every other area of your life, too.

3) THEN, IF YOU ARE MARRIED, YOU NEED TO BE DEEPLY COMMITTED TO EACH OTHER.

You can't design something to last generations if the founding relationship is shaky or insecure. If you try, you'll spend so much energy on finding faults or repairing problems that you won't have the capacity to forge something strong and beautiful together.

That's why you need to be able to trust the other human you're building alongside. The core of your family is the two of you, hopefully, two independently healthy people with a healthy relationship that's as solid as bedrock. So, that vow to cherish until death do us part isn't naïve or utopian; it's a commitment with a running track that continues past the horizon. Because the head-waters of your legacy start here, strength in your most intimate relationship will overflow to strength in every other relationship.

4) AND YOU NEED TO BE COMMITTED TO YOUR CHILDREN.

You need a tenacious love for your children to compel you to do what is truly for their good, not just what's comfortable. If they're young and you're wasting every day annoyed by their quirks, messes, and kid-ness where they haven't yet mastered the art of living, you can soon see them as an impediment to every-thing, ignoring their needs and working your tail off trying to manage behavior. Or you can feel exasperated and helpless at the clumsiness of parenting, negotiating about everything that's not important, being permissive where you should be firm, and too forceful where you need to extend more grace.

As your children grow up, you need to create relationships of trust and closeness that they want to keep choosing, even when they no longer need you. Only then will you be able to raise up stewards who propel the legacy you began.

5) IF YOUR CHILDREN ARE MINORS, YOU NEED A DEEPLY COMMITTED RELATIONSHIP WITH THOSE YOU CHOOSE AS GUARDIANS.

If, at any point, you aren't here to care for your children, you need another person who will spontaneously step in and wear that mammoth mantle of responsibility. They'll need to love your infinitely valuable and precious children as their own and pro-vide a similar environment to grow that you had. That means

175

that you're handing over the reason for your own sleepless nights and ponderings over what to do and how to handle their hearts through every taxing struggle, to raise healthy, independent, confident, well-adjusted kids who reach their full potential.

And you'd be wise to have a backup guardian as well, which means you need *two* of these relationships with the ability to fully depend on either of them if the need arises.

6) YOU NEED DEEPLY COMMITTED RELATIONSHIPS WITH THOSE YOU CHOOSE AS TRUSTEES OR A BOARD OF DIRECTORS.

If you're gone, you also need someone you can trust completely and who's willing to pick up the thousand frayed edges of your financial life. This will be someone else who will administrate, manage, steward, grow, and use your money with the same thought and diligence you had. You'll need to count on them to approach it with your vision and goals, assess and take risks wisely, and discern the appropriate manner of spending your money to line up with the life you wanted to create.

Here, also, whether you select a contingent trustee or establish a board of directors, this role will be filled with more than one person.

7) FINALLY, YOU NEED ADDITIONAL PERIPHERAL RELATIONSHIPS.

In addition, you'll need to rely on one or more Powers of Attorney who will act in your stead and manage your current assets if you're incapacitated. You'll need a Healthcare Power of Attorney and contingent who will make the best decisions about your health at your most fragile moments if you can't make them yourself. And you may want to set up a Trust Protector who can override the decisions of any of your chosen proxies who make decisions outside your intent.

{A PAUSE}

I want to take a breather for a minute and acknowledge this conversation about relationships may be a place of deep pain or grief for you.

If you were getting a massage, this might be the deep tissue that is bound in excruciating knots, making you hold your breath. You may have had terrible relationship models or suffered abuse. These words may be tainted because you're struggling under the weight of losing a relationship you thought was indestructible or the hopelessness of a failing marriage. You may be dealing with infertility or just miscarried. You may have a child with special needs or an unfathomable illness. You may have tried everything to reconcile with a wayward child. You may have had to walk away from an unhealthy relationship. You may be twenty-five years into waiting for the right one and feeling that there must be something inherently wrong with who you are that repels others from committing to you. You might feel estranged from God. You may have lost a spouse or a child.

If building these seven key relationships feels exhausting and utterly impossible, I just want to pause to acknowledge your pain. Building these life-giving, sustaining relationships is the hardest, most vulnerable work you'll ever do. And you may need to pause before you're ready to go on.

No matter where you are right now, you are not too far gone. Even if there's a long line of broken relationships and broken promises, heartache, resentment, and years of walls and bitterness, you are not irreparable. You are capable of deeply fulfilling relationships, hope, and redemption.

Maybe you're like I was, and on the surface, everything seems pristine and ironed out, but underneath, you know that there's a part of your heart that's self-protecting and afraid of the unknown, a part that needs to step into unabashed courage so you can build these important legacy relationships.

You have everything it takes, and you've already been working on these relationships since before you were born.

I'm certainly not a relationship expert, but when you're ready to resume, I'd like to offer you some practical guidance I've used to build these resilient relationships. (You can find more about the four secrets to building resilient relationships in the bonuses you received along with this book. The access link is in the Resources section at the back of this book.)

We've chosen to go first, leaning into self-discovery and recognizing our own value. Then, we've used this same posture of discovery to search for the uniqueness in others. Instead of waiting for an invitation, we've initiated relationships. And, front and center, we've studied and practiced healthy communication—sharing about ourselves and disclosing our own feelings, desires, and needs instead of making statements and judgments about and demands of others. That means we've courageously stepped into a place of authenticity and openness, inviting others into that safe space to share what matters to them.

Then, we've scheduled and held regular family meetings to discuss our values, priorities, goals, or problem-solving to communicate, reiterate, build upon what we've established, and remind everyone of what's important.

Our Gorilla Glue Relationships

Practicing these skills over the years has helped us strengthen, repair, and forge our own Gorilla Glue relationships. We've done this deep work of penning our family guidance system, establishing our estate plan, and writing out a *Memorandum of Trust*. But it's not just tucked away in the back of the closet; it's at the front and center of all our relationships and communication. We're aware of how we're living in the day-to-day, so our choices, conversation, and activities display the things that are important to us for all to see.

Deep down, I know that this work could only come from the me who was reborn. Stepping into those waters of vulnerability churned out the highest yield returns I've ever seen.

Lucas and I have realized that we're about as opposite as fire and water, but rather than hoping we stay together, we're building together in lockstep. He celebrates my strength, and I lean on his consistency. Over the seasons, each of us has exchanged the role of leading the way, serving each other, our family, and our goals as a team. I'm finally honest about what I want, and we both love spending time together!

I have that friend who listens while I externally process everything I need to work out. I thrive on our Marco Polo chats about whatever challenges or inspires us—teaching methods to help students love learning, strategies for drinking more water, our progress on our top priorities, and the reformative and birthing process of writing this book.

I find so much joy in the standing monthly Facetime call with my siblings spread out across four different states, none closer than a ten hours drive from each other. We get to see each others' kids grow up, share silly stories, and find out about the home remodel statuses. We're sharing life and regularly investing time in talking about what is important to us. I love the laughter, the bond that's only growing stronger the older we get, and the childhood experiences that we revisit and see in a new way, like the hours we played in the woods of our Minnesota farm, building teepees, scouting trails, and naming the *Swamp of Everlasting No-Come-Back*, and how that experience of free, unstructured, and unsupervised outdoor play has informed our independence, problem-solving, and creative ingenuity.

Two of my siblings are named as guardians should our children ever require an adoptive family, and they know us by more than Facebook, our address on a Christmas card, and worn-out memories.

Our primary trustee is our business partner, Bruce Wehner. Our relationship started with me spilling my guts through sobs some five years ago about how hard it had been to build a business alone, with no guidance. Then, we started a podcast together, spending hours in strategic discussions that demanded the best of both of us to help wealth creators understand money and get in financial control. We were practicing building our trust in each other immensely. We've had our share of direct, no-holds-barred, iron-sharpening conversations required to propel our business forward over the past several years. He manages our advisor team, whom we trust to lead clients to create time and money freedom systematically and strategically.

Now he is our trustee that we are confident understands the nuances of our financial vision, has the administrative capacity, educational experience, and interpersonal wisdom to equip, challenge, and refine our children to fulfill their calling as wealth creators if we run out of time before the task is complete.

Another of our advisors, Ryley Smith, is our contingent trustee, who will step in if Bruce is not able. Over several years, we have grown to know and trust each other's mindsets and values.

And our attorney is a like-minded dear friend, Stephen Haynes, who has read and provided guidance on every single word of our *Memorandum of Trust*.

When we asked someone to fill a role in our estate plan, we did so thoughtfully and prayerfully. Because here's the tension of family leadership: those you lean on must *choose* to take up the responsibility.

We've shared the words of our *Memorandum of Trust* with every crucial relationship outside our home. The communication of these living, breathing, real-time relationships, along with the written guidance in our *Memorandum of Trust*, solidify the glue, giving us all the confidence needed to transfer control. We have the confidence to release and give over control, and *they* have the confidence to pick it up and move forward if called upon.

> THE TENSION OF FAMILY LEADERSHIP IS THAT THOSE YOU LEAN ON MUST *CHOOSE* TO TAKE UP THE RESPONSIBILITY.

Now It's Your Turn!

It's time to evaluate the strength of your critical relationships. Which ones have been through battle and stood the test of time? Do you need to work on any specific relationships to build a deep commitment as strong as Gorilla Glue?

Make a list of people you need to connect with—whether to invite over for dinner and share major life updates, invest in finding out their uniqueness, communicate an important piece of your estate plan, or all three.

And to make it less overwhelming, remember, this is a lifetime's work. You won't ever reach complete on this step, especially not overnight. Just take the one next step. The following step will be easier once you're already in motion.

With that underway, now it's time to put some fuel in this aircraft. We're ready to discuss the money that propels your legacy with more than good intentions. Remember, our definition of legacy is *the character, values, and financial means to live life on your terms that are modeled, taught, stewarded, and given from one generation to the next.*

There it is. Money, right at the start of the definition. It's the hinge that swings the door of your impact. We've left the money until the end for a very important reason. That's because most people would think that *legacy* is code for a *windfall* or an *inheritance*. They put all the emphasis on this flashy stuff because it's the only tangible part of the equation.

But money without the first two pillars of meaning and a mechanism to transfer it well will vanish like a vapor of smoke. That's why I've left it until last. For your money to do any good at all, your first two pillars must be as strong as steel.

So, now that we've built Pillar 1 by digging deep and chiseling the meaning of your legacy with your family guidance system of mission, vision, ideals, and values . . .

And now, in Pillar 2, we've worked through the legal structure that will bear your legacy through the generations, infused it with the spirit of your gift with a *Memorandum of Trust*, and bonded everything together with relationships that will support the weight of this precious cargo . . .

We're finally ready to talk about the fuel that will drive your legacy forward through the ages.

In the next chapter, whatever your net worth, we're going to talk about how to get the most mileage out of every dollar so it keeps on pouring through the generations and increasing in strength, volume, and impact as it travels.

WANT HELP GETTING STARTED?

If you have questions or need clarification or support on anything we've covered so far, reach out to our team here:

https://sevengenerationslegacy.com/strategycall

KEY SECTION TAKEAWAYS

- Your legacy depends on strong, dependable, and trusting relationships with other people.
- There are seven key relationships in which you need to cultivate deep commitment in order for your estate and legacy planning to work: yourself, God, your spouse, your children, the guardians, trustees, and powers of attorney you select to step in and make decisions on your behalf when you no longer can.
- Your *Memorandum of Trust* should be shared with every key relationship to communicate everything that matters most to you.

PILLAR 3

THE MONEY: FUNDING
YOUR LEGACY

Money

23

THE ULTIMATE LOVE LETTER

How Life Insurance Is the Greatest Gift

Love Letters

Life insurance extends the ultimate gift to your family, because with it, you offer the provision that ensures they will never have to worry about money if anything happens to you. But rather than it being a closet decision, tell your family about the gift and why you're preparing it for them with an ultimate love letter.

One of my most prized possessions is the cardboard box with trundle handles and riveted corners on our nightstand. On top, there's the fist-sized piece of coral Lucas and I smuggled off the beach of Frederiksted, St. Croix, that holds in the brimming contents. And inside are the love letters we exchanged during our long-distance courtship, the cheeky lunch notes from our first married year in college, Valentine's and birthday cards, and special messages we've shared and saved over the past sixteen-plus years.

These letters mean so much because they hold weighty words. These words remind us of the bedrock of our love, make our memories tangible, and convey a thread of consistency that's run the length of our whole relationship.

That's why when our lives lift off from this earth, we want to leave a letter filled with words that will slice through the murkiness of grief. Those words won't be empty; they'll be chock full of the deep love we have for our children *and* the financial means to fulfill everything we'd dreamed of together.

Even if that moment is far sooner than we hope, our children will feel the warm embrace of a financial deposit that will make them whole. They'll see that, even if we aren't here to provide for them, they will never have to worry about money. They won't have to wonder if they can afford living expenses or pay for college or a wedding. They won't have to forgo the travel that will shape their sense of self and understanding of the world. They won't have to start from ground zero, finding a job to make money, save, and then incrementally build up enough to invest.

Instead, they'll still have everything we wanted for them. That's because we know that our deaths will trigger a wealth transfer of everything we would ever earn for the rest of our lives. How?

No matter where our life project leaves off, we know they'll get a life insurance check for the most insurance we could purchase. And that check will fulfill our wishes, fully provide everything they'll ever need, and jump-start perpetual wealth that expands with every generation.

> OUR LIFE INSURANCE CHECK WILL FULFILL OUR WISHES, PROVIDE EVERYTHING OUR CHILDREN WILL EVER NEED, AND JUMP-START PERPETUAL WEALTH THAT EXPANDS WITH EVERY GENERATION.

Life insurance is how we're guaranteeing that we'll *end with the most*. And that means we have rock-solid certainty to speak about what they will receive on that day with confidence. When our assets jump into the ship and depart our hands destined for our children's, all our money will arrive on their shores in those packaged boxes. On top, we've tucked in a letter they'll see first so that our words pave the way, set the tone, and wrap them in a hug as warm as a down comforter.

186

If your legacy is like an aircraft, so far, we've designed and built it with meaning by writing out your family guidance system. Then, we staffed it and scheduled the routes with the most efficient mechanism of an estate plan. But we haven't yet talked about the fuel that will propel the length and impact of your legacy: your money.

With the most financial provision possible, you'll add the fuel to ignite the engine of your children's future. And because you unlock the gate of access to every opportunity you want for them and provide the means to develop their character, gifts, and stewardship, you lift generations after you.

Just like a stool that needs three legs to hold you, having all three pillars of your legacy ensures your work will be steady, stable, and last as the foundation for future generations to stand on.

Now, your financial situation will look completely unique to you. You may have a business with an eight-figure revenue, hundreds of properties, or you may just be starting out. Wherever you find yourself right now, life insurance is the one simple tool that's the greatest safety net to give your family the most resources and peace of mind you possibly can.

Let me tell you how I know.

ALMOST LOSING A SPOUSE

While I was in surgery, blissfully unaware of my crisis, Lucas suffered the worst night of his life. He paced the floor, cradling his moments-old baby girl. The lights were bright, blood was everywhere, and the room still seemed to be spinning. But along with me, the whole slew of medical professionals had vanished, and he was eerily alone.

His dad instincts shifted into autopilot, feeding Olivia and changing diapers numbly. He tried to enjoy these precious new moments, but all he could think about was his wife in surgery. It had been almost three hours since he'd seen my bed wheeled out of the room. And that was the last time he knew what was happening.

As each minute seemed to stretch on for eternity, his mind was a war zone. Worries screeched here and there like missiles and grenades, and yet, he felt paralyzingly powerless.

Finally, at 1:30 a.m., the door opened, and the doctor came in. But the tiniest hope was pierced like the jarring pop of a balloon as she gravely reported that they had removed my placenta but couldn't stop the bleeding. A lump caught in his throat, and his chest tightened. Then, he was alone again.

Terrified, he could do nothing. He was exhausted, but there was no way he could sleep with the suffocating weight of a crisis he couldn't fix.

It was another hour and a half of tensed shoulders and frantic thoughts . . . *What if I never see my wife again? Will she pull out of this? What will they do? What will I do?* He choked back tears. Groping for his own comfort, he reassured his baby girl, "Everything is going to be okay. Mommy is going to be okay. Mommy is going to make it because she is strong." Through the agonizing torment, he pleaded with God for a miracle.

It was 3:00 when the doctor returned again with news. But this time, it was a jumbled string of medical terminology that he couldn't interpret. *Stopped the bleeding . . . problem with platelets and hemoglobin . . . called in specialists.*

"Is it better or worse?" he grimaced, hoping for a translation that would quell his trembling fears.

"Worse. We're doing everything we can, but it doesn't look good."

His mind nearly redlined. Right there, in the hospital room, Lucas wanted to scream to wake up from his nightmare. Will I become a single father of a newborn baby? What if Rachel doesn't make it? What if she doesn't come home to be the mother of these girls? Through tears, he fought for the strength to be mom and dad to our kids. How could he tell his seven-year-old, Avalynn, that her mom was . . . dead?

He wrestled with focusing his thoughts on me being okay and seeing me again. "She's not dead; she's not going to die," he played on repeat, trying to turn the tide. "We've created a beautiful life together and have big plans and dreams ahead. It's not her time yet."

At some point during the sleepless hours, he distinctly remembers thinking, *Thank God we have life insurance.* It didn't take the pain away. He knew that nothing could replace me, his wife of almost thirteen years, business partner, best friend, and co-pilot through all of life's moments. But at least there was one thing he wouldn't have to flail to figure out. He knew he wouldn't have to worry about working to provide financially and trying to raise two girls on his own at the same time. It was the only lifeline of peace in that tenuous space.

Our life insurance journey started back when we were newlyweds in college. Lucas bought a little $50,000 policy that we felt was sufficient at the time. It would have been enough to bury him if anything had happened in the short term, we thought. And because I wasn't planning to be a breadwinner, we reasoned that I didn't need any coverage.

But later, after we became parents, we grew to value our individual contributions to our family. At the time, even though I didn't have much of an income from the time I dedicated to our fledgling business, I also managed the household, cooked, handled the laundry and cleaning, and raised and tutored the children. If I weren't here, Lucas would have needed someone else to handle all those things, and all these roles would have a price tag attached. So, while I wasn't being paid for these mom and wife duties, they were extremely valuable to our family. Maybe he could manage on his own, but we didn't ever want to be forced into the smallest life with only bare necessities.

Rather, we wanted to pave the way for everything we wanted. So, about five years prior, we had purchased as much life insurance as we could get on both Lucas and me. This is called insuring your *human life economic value.*

We realized that if something happened to us, there would be a financial hole amounting to everything we would have contributed financially to the well-being of our family for the rest of all time. If we were gone, so would our income-earning power be from that date forward for eternity. The maximum life insurance patched that hole . . . just in case something happened. We'd planned for a *what if* situation that had seemed almost irrelevant. At the time, we never thought for a minute that we might come this close to *needing* our life insurance.

> WHEN WE PURCHASED OUR LIFE INSURANCE, WE'D PLANNED FOR A *WHAT IF* SITUATION, BUT WE NEVER THOUGHT FOR A MINUTE THAT WE MIGHT COME THIS CLOSE TO *USING* OUR LIFE INSURANCE.

Finally, at 4:15 on Tuesday morning, after the longest and darkest night of his life, Dr. Golden brought the news that put Lucas's fears to rest. I was finally stable, and he could come to see me. His heart lurched with relief.

THE ULTIMATE GIFT OF LOVE

Now, as someone who's toed the brink of death and almost tripped over the edge, I know the reality that life insurance isn't just for an unlikely statistical probability. It's the very real bandage to cover an amputation that could happen to any of us at any time, even if we are vibrantly healthy and doing everything right. There are things that remain outside the grip of our own control, and our own mortality is one of those things.

Life Insurance Is the Greatest Gift of Love

My life insurance isn't just a piece of paper that demonstrates my acknowledgment of that fact. Instead, it's the ultimate gift of love to my family and loved ones who outlive me.

If anything happened to either of us earlier than expected, there would be as much money as possible to carry our family through. That means that instead of being forced into the debilitating fog of grief and the responsibility of raising children and earning an income, there would be a lifeline that could provide freedom to recover emotionally.

A check could never erase the pain, but it could hold the space for a spouse to collect themselves and clear their head. Instead of having to rush brashly into huge decisions, they'd have the freedom to slow down. Perhaps they could take years off work or even quit their job or hire a full-time nanny to cope with the upheaval.

And if our children ever lost both parents, they have the guarantee that financially, everything will be covered. They'll have more than enough for food, shelter, education, and travel. And the way we would have paid for weddings and helped them buy their first house would be accounted for, and they'd even know there is the seed capital to launch their vetted business ventures at exactly the right time.

We had peace of mind that even during a crisis, the financial category of our life was a pillar of strength. That meant we would always have options, and we wouldn't have to make choices because of a lack of money. No one would have to downsize, sell the house, move, pull kids out of school, or cause any more disruption than would already exist. There would be time to wait for grief to run its course.

That's because life insurance guarantees the capital to fulfill your wishes. With life insurance, whenever that fateful day is along the continuum of time, you'll be financially prepared to meet it.

One Part of Your Wealth That Makes Everything Better

But you might be wondering if I'm implying that life insurance should be your *only* tool.

Absolutely not! Rather, life insurance is just one small part of the wealth you're already building. If you have built a financial empire, it will add on like a supplement and make everything else better. And if you have no assets other than the life insurance itself, you'll still give a legacy great enough to satisfy everything you'd hoped to create together.

That means that life insurance helps you maximize your financial capabilities and do the *most* good you can. So, whether we've reached time and money freedom, or even if all our investments completely fall apart, we know there will be the most money to maximize our legacy.

That's because life insurance has the capacity to deposit money into the next generation. And whether you live a long and full life or are gone too soon, life insurance guarantees that even the worst possible life event would make your family financially whole. It guarantees the maximum fuel in your tank *at the end.*

But far from benefiting only your family after you graduate, it can also radically improve your life while you live. And having that kind of peace of mind frees us to lean into our best life now because we know that no matter what, we've done the most that we possibly can. With it, you can guarantee that the money will be there to facilitate the wealth of human flourishing well past your time.

Our Love Letter

In the year after delivering Olivia, we were face to face with a new reality. Because we'd experienced a brush with death close enough that we could feel its icy tentacles, we knew our life insurance wasn't just an "oh, by the way."

Rather, we recognized that buying our policies had been one of the most meaningful and loving things we could have done. In the moment of our family's deepest grief, there would be a financial safety net to catch them. But rather than just leaving a gift of money, we wanted to tell them the meaning of this gift by wrapping it with words that would last for all time.

And so, as we finished building and securing this third pillar of our legacy by maximizing the money we'd leave our loved ones, we chose to write a very personal letter to our children to commemorate everything we see in them, believe about them, want them to know forever, and to tell them exactly why we were giving them this money.

Here's our love letter that they would receive when our assets and the life insurance check are poured into trusts for them:

Dear Avalynn and Olivia,

Ever since the day that we found out we were pregnant with you, we have been overwhelmingly grateful for the opportunity to be your parents. We love you, believe the best in you, and feel that our life's greatest calling and ambition is to raise you well.

You are each precious, treasured, and valuable. You are beautiful, significant, important, intelligent, smart, kind, brave, confident, courageous, offer love and encouragement everywhere you go, win friends and influence people, successful, wealthy, rich, loved, and all these things are true.

As you grow, the years seem like barely enough time to share all of this with you, but Lord willing, we will have all that time and will do our best to share everything with you in person as we instruct you and build our relationship with you throughout this lifetime.

If we are not granted the ability to have the years to share this all with you, it is very important for us to pass on this legacy, and we will do our best to share it in this letter and in our *Memorandum of Trust* for you.

We want to share our values, wisdom, knowledge, and spiritual formation with you that we have gained through our lifetime so you will have everything that we are as your foundation to stand on and reach higher in this life.

The most important thing you need to know in this life is that God is for you. He is good, He will protect you, He will never leave you, and His love and faithfulness are greater than you can possibly fathom.

Dig into the Word and find the promises of God for you personally in your life. They will be a strength to you.

As we learn who you are, these are the strengths we see in you.

Avalynn, you are a beautiful bird, a breath of life, who lives free and gives freedom to all. You are gentle and kind, nurturing, and bring joy and laughter to others.

Olivia, you are peaceful prosperity, noble strength, and brave as a bear. You are purposeful, focused, and wise.

Be all that God has called you to be, make the greatest difference in this world, walk with confidence, knowing that you are seated in heavenly places.

Every day we pray over you: *I thank You that their minds are thinking about what is good, pleasing, perfect, admirable, desirable, excellent, praiseworthy, and of good report. I thank You that they are taking every thought captive to the knowledge of You and fixing their mind on things from above. I thank You that their heart is covered in righteousness, and they know that You love them and that nothing can ever take away Your love. I thank You that they are brave, strong, and courageous and have a faith that moves mountains. I thank You that they walk in the power of the Holy Spirit and fight their battles with the fruit of Your Spirit, which is love, joy, peace, patience, kindness, goodness, faithfulness, gentleness, and self-control. I thank You that they speak the truth in love and are peaceful with themselves, with You, and with others.*[28]

We love you and want to take care of you. There's money set aside for you, there are people to help guide you, and here's everything we've done to provide for that.

Our financial wealth is held in trust, with a trustee appointed to watch over that money and see that it does the most good over the longest time and fulfills its highest and best use.

It is important for you to know that a significant portion of the trust assets come from our life insurance policies. Because of this, it is our life insurance policies that are ensuring you know how much we love you. We gladly paid each and every premium and have used the cash value to start a business, invest, and cover emergencies. These policies have given us tremendous peace of mind knowing that we have done all we could to ensure you have the life we wanted to create for you if we were still with you.

You will not have all the money right away. The trustee will manage these funds entirely to ensure you have the schools, church, relationship and experiences, nutrition, and nurturing, supportive, and wholesome upbringing that we would choose for you.

It is our hope that you will see your relationship with the trustee as a symbiotic one in which you are working together to fulfill the stated vision and goals of the trust. Please maintain a good working relationship with the trustee, and it is our hope that you will come to see them as family. We were very intentional in choosing and trusting who would serve as trustee, and if you work with them and not against them, you will greatly benefit your life and that of your children.

While the money we have put in trust will be used to care for all your financial needs, and there will always be enough, always remember that God was, is, and will be your ultimate source of provision. While we value earning your own way in life, never believe that you have what you have simply because you alone deserve or earned it. And always be grateful for all that you have.

You will ultimately be held accountable for how you steward these assets. Seek counsel from wise people (see below), wisdom from God, and live honorably.

Your loving father and mother,

Lucas and Rachel Marshall

It's hard to read those words without tears welling up in my eyes. But never have we considered the worst in a way that brought the most unfathomable peace to my own heart.

Now It's Your Turn!

Use our letter as a template to share your most real thoughts and feelings with your loved ones who will inherit what you are currently building. Your recipient may be your spouse, children, or even another family member or charity.

Write down everything you'd want to communicate directly to them in the instant that you are no longer living on earth. Summarize what you already tell them in real life that you never want them to forget.

Then, evaluate how your financial assets would transfer to make possible everything you hope for them. Consider how life insurance could supplement everything else you're building to become the greatest gift of love you could possibly give.

Over the next few chapters, we'll discuss how life insurance is a key piece of our financial foundation that allows us to accomplish our goals while we're living and paints that hope across the sky for those we love after we're gone.

24

MULTIPURPOSE

Living Better, Enjoying More, and
Having a Bigger Legacy

Rather than managing complex portfolios with accounts that serve only one purpose, I want financial tools that save me time and energy by doing lots of jobs at once. If I can manage money simply, it cancels the noise and frees me up to focus on what matters most. That's why I want my money to multitask and serve many purposes like a Swiss Army knife.

The iconic red Swiss Army knife was invented to meet a specific need. In the late 1880s, a Swiss soldier needed a knife, a reamer, a screwdriver to disassemble the M1889 Swiss service rifle, and a can opener to easily access canned meals in the field. To make it easier to keep track of their tools and lighten their load, the Swiss Army purchased cross-functional pocketknives— one tool that could do all four tasks.[29]

Later, additional attachments were added to the design, and now, the Swiss Army knife comes in more than 100 different models, with as many as seventy-three features in a single knife, including tools as specialized as a fish scaler, scissors, pliers, corkscrew, tweezer, and nail file.[30] Today, over 34,000 of these multipurpose knives are shipped around the world from the Victorinox factory in Ibach, Switzerland, every day, and companies like Leatherman compete for the demand of everyone from off-grid survivalists to the average Joe who wants to open an Amazon box.

Like the multipurpose knife that does it all, I want financial tools that do the heavy lifting of multitasking. Instead of running ragged and managing lots of separate things, I want one hub where I make changes that percolate over to improve every other area of my financial life.

But hold on, we're getting ahead of ourselves. Before heaping on the capabilities in any area, I need to know my goals *first*, or I get crazy shiny-object-syndrome and pulled in a zillion directions with all the awesome things I was never looking for in the first place. Sound familiar?

Yeah, I figured! That's why it's critical to define the purpose of your money.

THE PURPOSE OF MY MONEY

If I'm on the quest for one financial tool that acts like a Swiss Army knife, the piercing question becomes, what exactly are the jobs I want my money to be able to do?

For me, I need cash I can touch and take. I don't want any emergency to make me nervous because I can't pay for it. And, let's be honest, we've all lived long enough to know that car maintenance and replacing a water heater aren't really emergencies and shouldn't catch me off guard.

But beyond that, I want to build up as much investible capital as possible, so I can continue building income with assets on my journey to creating financial independence. And while I'm storing that cash, I want it to be growing as quickly as possible without the risk of it evaporating like melted cotton candy. When I'm ready to use the money to grow my business, start a new one, buy real estate, hire another coach or assistant, or invest marketing dollars, I want the guarantee I can access my money quickly without having to qualify or prove anything to a third party. I need to preserve my capital with as little loss as possible to factors like fees and taxes. And I want an ideal way to channel my financial wealth through the aqueduct to the hands of my children and posterity so it can water the land of their lives and produce as much fruit as possible.

> WITH CASH RESERVES, NO EMERGENCY IS A FINANCIAL EMERGENCY. AND WITH INVESTIBLE CAPITAL, YOU CAN CONTINUE BUILDING INCOME WITH ASSETS TO CREATE FINANCIAL INDEPENDENCE.

How did I discover these financial essentials for me and my family? Honestly, it was through failing to recognize and meet those key needs.

Ultimately, we learned that whole life insurance isn't just an insurance product—it's a highly potent savings tool you can use to create stable, liquid reserves. That's when we realized the secret to having money so we could weather emergencies and invest in opportunities when the timing was right was saving money in a whole life insurance policy.

But, you didn't think I learned these giant lessons by having everything go picture perfectly, did you? That would be a really boring story. Instead, let me tell you the real story in all its nail-biting, plot-twisting, disappointing glory.

How I Discovered My Financial Swiss Army Knife

Lucas and I were a newly married couple fresh out of college trying to save money so we could invest. We really wanted to create financial freedom so we wouldn't have to depend on job security for our livelihood or accept an income ceiling.

We landed in the job market right as the Great Recession of 2008 was heating up. Because the financial world was so unstable, we wanted to be able to store and preserve wealth, and ultimately, we wanted to control our time.

The thing is, we were afraid of systemic financial failure during the stock market crash and housing crisis of 2008. We were almost frozen with a scarcity mentality that caused us to hunker down and hoard instead of focusing on production and creating value. That meant we couldn't take productive steps toward financial freedom, let alone control our time.

To make things worse, I felt terrible because we were saving almost half of our income in precious metals to have a long-term store of value, taking on the risk of speculation, thinking that their price would soar as the economy crumbled. But we didn't anticipate needing access to capital later, right at the time the bottom fell out for gold and silver prices.

I felt even worse about the situation because I had quit my job to be a stay-at-home mom, and right when we went from double income, no kids (DINK) to a one-income household plus extra expenses with a baby and starting a business, Lucas stopped getting paid one day per paycheck, and we ended up ringing up credit card debt just to make ends meet.

I felt defeated with the world crashing in on our hopes of financial freedom. The problem was that just when we needed capital to start our insurance business, our only reserves lost half their value at the same time! This made it hard to get the capital to build our business, and we were worse off than if we'd just buried the money in the backyard. That meant we weren't getting closer to financial freedom; we were sliding fast in the opposite direction!

See, this body slam of a lesson showed us the absolute need for *liquidity*. It didn't matter how high our net worth figure was if we couldn't get to and use our money.

The problem was that there didn't seem to be a good solution to have our money growing as fast as possible while at the same time plugging the drain so that none of the value could leak out and giving us the ability to reach in and pull out our money whenever we needed to. If bank savings were a car, the low-interest rates felt like an engine missing a few cylinders. Instead of that satisfying power lurch when you press the gas, it felt like it was shuffling along feebly. Even CDs, online savings accounts, and money markets didn't pack much punch. If we dipped over into the equities markets to get a higher growth rate, we opened ourselves up to the risk of losing money. Home equity wasn't a surefire way to grow our reserves, either, because it could lose value with a housing market correction, and we'd need to qualify to take out our own equity.

Then, as if by chance, something amazing happened. That's when I discovered a secret buried in the technical jargon of the health and life insurance producer's exam we were preparing for: a little line about the guarantees of whole life insurance cash value. It seemed so simple. I could almost have blinked and missed it. Lucas had a flashback to something else he'd heard about cash value life insurance several years earlier and started digging deeper.

WHOLE LIFE INSURANCE ISN'T JUST INSURANCE—IT'S A HIGHLY POTENT SAVINGS TOOL THAT YOU CAN USE TO CREATE STABLE, LIQUID RESERVES.

So, we read Nelson Nash's book, *Becoming Your Own Banker*,[31] and it became crystal clear to us how to get better growth on savings, keep it liquid, *and* invest in other opportunities without interrupting the growth, earning a return in two places at the same time. We learned that whole life insurance isn't just an insurance product, after all, but a powerful tool for saving and storing cash.

So, we started reading everything we could find about whole life insurance. But we didn't stop there. We sought out advisors and asked an embarrassing volume of questions over a ridiculous number of meetings. After that, we started moving money from precious metals into whole life insurance to fund our very first whole life policy.

Suddenly, we were more secure because we had our reserves in an asset that wasn't speculative and couldn't lose value. That meant we'd be storing cash we could use for anything—investments, college, business coaches—plus it had better growth than any other savings tool, and we could lean on the guarantees that our money wouldn't ever lose value. It wouldn't even shrink through taxes because if we used it right, we'd never pay tax after we put it into the policy.

Now we were talking! This was a tool that gave me everything I was searching for—an all-in-one package, just like a Swiss Army knife!

Whole Life Insurance Is a Financial Swiss Army Knife

Solving all our greatest financial needs translated to the stability and confidence that allowed us to settle down and make better decisions. And this was even *before* we had our own awakening to the value of the death benefit. For us at the time, getting a death benefit seemed like the icing on the cake, a peripheral *nice-to-have*.

STRAIGHT TALK ABOUT WHOLE LIFE INSURANCE

Your brain may be shifting down a gear to compensate for the uphill climb you've just encountered.

You may have opinions about whole life insurance already, and the emotion makes it hard to see clearly. You may never have been exposed to the infinite capacity of whole life insurance beyond its obvious ability to pay out a death benefit. Or you may have already written off your need for life insurance because you have so many other assets, investments, and net worth that it seems trite in comparison.

For a couple minutes, I invite you to set aside your prior perspective and look with fresh eyes because whole life is probably very different from what you think.

Let's shoot straight. Yes, you can buy life insurance from me. So yes, I can personally benefit when you use this strategy.

But the reason I want you to hear me is that I want you to have the most *and* best life insurance you can get, *whether* you work with my team or not. Why?

Because I want you to get the tremendous benefits that I have right now while I'm *alive*, so you can steady your own life and gain a longer-term perspective. Because I want you to feel the solid ground of having certainty and guarantees beneath your feet when the markets tumble or credit freezes. When your need for capital is overwhelming, I want you to know you have a war chest that can suffer deep draughts without flinching, and I want your head to sleep heavy on your pillow instead of whirring, worried about how you're going to make it all work out.

And because when you do, you'll give each one of your beloved family members the greatest gift with infinite and eternal returns. And because I know from that fateful day when I came a hairsbreadth away from needing my own life insurance that so much financial pain and hardship could be erased if families had life insurance *before* they needed it. And because it's the most tangible way I know how to bring your love into high definition to make everything you dreamed real for your family, whether or not you're here to experience it with them.

This book isn't long enough for me to step into teacher mode and explain to you everything about how and why it works.

For now, in this brief space, I'll introduce you to the profound capacity of this ancient strategy that it would be wrong for me not to share.

Then, the decision is yours to do what you like with the knowledge. And I won't judge you, no matter what you decide, m'kay?

One Financial Tool to Do the Work of Ten (or Twenty)!

Whole life insurance is permanent. That means it gives you a death benefit that will pay out to your loved ones whenever you pass away, even if you're 107 years old. That means its claims-paying guarantee doesn't expire as you get closer to the statistical possibility of needing it. And that means your loved ones will for sure receive the death benefit, and you can stake every other financial decision around the fact that your life insurance will transfer your legacy, and you don't have to reserve any other assets to do that work. And that means you get to spend more of your own money and enjoy your days more while you're here.

In addition, whole life builds up cash value that you can use while you're living. That means this tool isn't just for your loved ones. It's for you, too, right here and right now. That means you get a tank of cash you can use for literally anything and everything: investments, business, or a last-resort source of income.

When it's specially designed, this policy provides high early cash value you can use today without sacrificing the most long-term growth through interest and dividends. This translates into an internal rate of return inside the policy that far exceeds any other similar safe place to store cash, even if you just buy it and let it sit on the shelf.

But better than just that, you can strategically use your cash value through policy loans that are guaranteed to you as an owner benefit. That means that whenever you request a loan, the insurance company will send you a check within a few days without requiring paperwork or investigating your intentions with the money or your ability to repay. So, you have liquidity and can use your money freely for whatever you want.

And these loans—you decide how, when, and how frequently you want to repay them. That means this isn't a tyrant creditor breathing down your neck demanding you pay up. If you want to pay back monthly over two years or ten—or not at all and then all at once five years later—it's completely up to you.

This ease of getting liquid capital means that you can find opportunities to increase your cash or income and invest in those strategically with life insurance loans. And when you use your life insurance this way while you're living, it's like adding a second workhorse to the harness pulling towards time and money freedom. You're stacking, double-dipping, or getting your money to multitask. That's because you can earn a return on the same money in two places at the same time!

Infinite Banking:
"The & Asset"
(Returns in two places at the same time)

That's why we call this kind of whole life insurance the *And Asset*. While it's still growing *inside* your whole life policy, giving you an *internal* return, it's also working *outside* your policy, earning an *external* return in another investment. That means your money works harder, and you get higher returns on your investments without adding risk. And no matter how many times you use your own capital this way, your policy keeps chugging along without interruption like a trusty steam engine, gaining ground with its compounding power.

WITH THIS *AND ASSET*, YOU CONTINUE EARNING COMPOUNDING RETURNS WHILE YOU ALSO PUT THE SAME DOLLARS TO WORK SOMEWHERE ELSE, EARNING RETURNS ON THE SAME MONEY IN TWO PLACES AT THE SAME TIME.

Adding an extra measure of dependability, whenever your cash value and death benefit grow, the growth sets a new floor, and your values cannot drop below that point in the future. That means you have safety that your money won't evaporate, which means you can count on money being there, safe and sound, in the future. And that means the bedrock of your financial future is as predictable as the sunrise, showing up every morning and giving you an accurate way to measure where you'll be in the future and when.

So, this special kind of whole life insurance is not only the optimal storage tank for your savings that gives you safety, liquidity, and growth, but it also improves every other area of your financial life and makes every financial situation better.

And, on top of that, it also graces you with the finest method of transferring your legacy, tax-free, to future generations. That's because you have a death benefit that will ensure you'll have the most money to pass on to your loved one when you depart, no matter when that day arrives.

That's how this multitasking powerhouse plays a key role in your financial foundation that helps you reach your goals easier and faster.

INFINITE BANKING

In case you'd like a label, I've just described Infinite Banking, a strategy popularized by the late Nelson Nash, that banks, corporations, and the wealthy—including names you'll recognize like the Rockefellers, Walt Disney,[32] Max and Verda Foster (founders of Foster Farms),[33] Doris Christopher (founder of Pampered Chef),[34] JC Penney,[35] Leland and James Stanford (who founded Stanford University),[36] and our current President, Joe Biden—have been using for nearly two centuries to build wealth.[37]

After starting my own Infinite Banking system, I was not only able to have a war chest of cash that's growing faster than any bank account, with vault-like safety that will never drop in value that I can access any time I want, for any reason, no questions asked—I've also been able to stop watching the market with anxiety or hoping I've gambled correctly with my hard-earned money because I have confidence that every time I save money, I'm gaining ground and chiseling another step on my path to time and money freedom.

And in the end, all of this means I'm now able to relax, be productive and focused in my work, enjoy being present with my kids, and have peace right where I am, knowing that every step I take is bringing me closer to having complete control of my time.

NOW IT'S YOUR TURN!

Now the next step is up to you.

Maybe you've seen how life insurance could help you live better, enjoy more, and have a bigger legacy. You can start with the goal of using Infinite Banking to build up as much quick-access cash as your current income and savings permit and then supplement with as much term insurance as you qualify for. You'll want to talk with an advisor who understands Infinite Banking and Human Life Economic Value.

And, if you're still figuring out what you want to do with the information, you don't have to plunge in headfirst before you're ready. You can start slowly by getting as much convertible term insurance as you can buy now. When you do, you prop open the door to use this strategy in the future by locking in your current health status. Any time while your term insurance is in force, you can convert it in chunks over to whole life. And even if your health record becomes tarnished over the years, your new policy gets to reach back to the healthiest olden days when you first started your term policy and use that label, so you avoid the concerns of the added cost of insurance or even potential uninsurability.

If you want to learn more about Infinite Banking with whole life insurance, we have hundreds of podcast episodes, articles, videos, a free guide, and a course for you at The Money Advantage, so you can go as deep as you would like. We've curated our best Infinite Banking resources for you in the bonus content for this book, which you can access from the Resources page in the back.

Or if you'd like to get started with Infinite Banking personally, book a call with our team to start the conversation here: https://themoneyadvantage.com/calendar.

Now, while life insurance solves many problems, it can't guarantee a lasting legacy. That's because there's a silent burglar that has taunted families of means for millennia, causing wealth to vanish within just three short generations. But a few families have grown stronger over time, proving that long-term family wealth is possible.

So, just what was their secret? Stay with me as you dive into the next chapter.

25

THE BLESSING

How to Break the Curse of the Wealthy

The Lord bless you and keep you. Make His face shine upon you and be gracious to you. The Lord turn His face toward you and give you peace. May His favor be upon you and a thousand generations, and your family and your children, and their children, and their children.

—Kari Jobe, "The Blessing," based on Numbers 6:24–26[38]

Since we're talking about money—the fuel or volume of financial means to propel your legacy—I'd be remiss if I didn't point out the glaring problem of the curse of the wealthy, and how you can cancel the curse.

Here's the thing: most wealth doesn't last—not for *lifetimes*, and certainly not for *generations*. In fact, it almost seems impossible to create a legacy at all. No volume of wealth, investments, net worth, life insurance, or money, even the most well-planned and well-preserved, is enough to create a legacy. Instead of infusing strength into children and their children, success and achievements often come with a worrying cost to future generations. That's because great wealth can fling open the door for lavish spending and destroy the industry and stewardship of the ones it should have served.

James E. Hughes Jr. writes in *Family Wealth*,

Family wealth is not self-perpetuating. Without careful planning and stewardship, a hard-earned fortune can easily be dissipated within a generation or two. The phenomenon of the fleeting family fortune is so well-recognized that it inspired a proverb: "Shirtsleeves to shirtsleeves in three generations." Vanishing wealth is not unique to the United States, and variations of this proverb are found around the world, from Asia to Ireland. The Irish variant—"Clogs to clogs in three generations"—depicts things in the following way. The first generation starts out wearing work clogs while digging in the potato field, receives no formal education, and, through very hard work, creates a fortune while maintaining a frugal lifestyle. The second generation attends university, wears fashionable clothes, has a mansion in town and an estate in the country, and eventually enters high society. The third generation's numerous members grow up in luxury, do little or no work, spend the money, and fate the fourth generation to find itself back in the potato field, doing manual labor.[39]

So, how do you break this curse? How can you stop money from becoming a crutch that cripples your family lineage? Is it possible to hold back the tidal wave of poverty that seems to crash over and rip apart the legacies, money, and relationships of every family that breaks above the ranks and builds substantial wealth?

Could you instead maintain wealth that ripples out and expands in future generations? And more importantly, how can you live so that the blessing you enjoy continues blessing your children and their children, and their children?

To find out, let's uncover an incredible secret buried deep in the stories of three of the world's richest families, all whose names you'll probably recognize.

A Tale of Three Wealthy Families

Rothschild

In Frankfort, Germany, Mayer Amschel Rothschild was born to a Jewish family. It was the year 1744. He got his start by handling the financial affairs of the German Prince of Hesse. This prestigious position later became the launchpad of his own banking business in the 1760s.

Mayer then made a profitable move that earned him the title: *the founding father of international finance.* He strategically expanded internationally into the five main European financial centers of London, Paris, Frankfurt, Vienna, and Naples. And he did so by financing and installing each of his five sons in startup banks.[40]

Later, when Mayer died in 1812, his legacy never dimmed. In fact, the Rothschild name was just getting started. Today, the Rothschild family holds around $400 Billion in cumulative wealth and is represented across many diverse industries—financial services, real estate, energy, mining, agriculture, winemaking, and even nonprofits. And as a testament to their long-standing wealth, their palaces and estates still grace the countryside of northwestern Europe.[41, 42]

Vanderbilt

In 1794, across the ocean (from Mayer) in Staten Island, New York, Cornelius Vanderbilt was born. He quickly rocketed to riches as a transportation tycoon during the Civil War era. He amassed a fortune through transportation and shipping, first with a ferry service where he earned the nickname *The Commodore.* Then he expanded to regional steamboats, an ocean-going steamship line, and ultimately, to railroads across the northeastern part of the United States.[43]

At the time of his death in 1877, his estate was worth $105 Million. Factoring in inflation, his net worth was over $2 Billion in today's dollars, ranking him as *the world's richest man.*

But there were problems brewing. Favoring his oldest son but considering his youngest a wastrel, he left most of his money to his oldest son. By comparison, he gave his wife, younger son, and daughters next to nothing. Legal disputes contested his will and divvied up the assets further. Sadly, his wealth vanished not long afterward.

A cousin, Arthur T Vanderbilt II, had this to say in his book *Fortune's Children: The Fall of the House of Vanderbilt.*[44]

> This fabled golden era, this special world of luxury and privilege that the Vanderbilt's created, lasted but a brief moment. Within thirty years after the death of the Commodore Vanderbilt in 1877, no member of his family was among the richest people in the United States . . . . When 120 of the Commodore's descendants gathered at Vanderbilt University in 1973 for the first family reunion, there was not a millionaire among them.

ROCKEFELLER

Not far away, in upstate New York, John Davison Rockefeller Sr. was born in 1839. He settled in Cleveland, Ohio, where he began bookkeeping at the age of sixteen. Then, he formed several business partnerships in his 20s, mostly in oil refining. Eventually, he founded Standard Oil Company in 1870, completely revolutionizing the petroleum industry and controlling 90 percent of the oil industry in the U.S. at a time when the demand for kerosene and gasoline skyrocketed. As a side effect, he even gained influence over the railroad industry needed to transport oil.

But in 1911—ironically, the same year the Titanic was built—Standard Oil also looked like it was doomed to sink when the company violated antitrust laws. As a result, Standard Oil was ordered to shut down. But instead of losing market share, the business restructured into two new companies: ExxonMobil and Chevron. This move dramatically increased revenue and share price, with both companies rising quickly to become household names and maintaining a position of domination for over a hundred years.

Rockefeller Sr.'s net worth peaked at $900 Million in 1913, amounting to over $400 Billion in today's inflation-adjusted dollars before he died in 1937.[45] And what happened then?

The trend continued. Today, the Rockefeller family still owns some of the leading positions of wealth and influence in America. The family has maintained wealth over seven generations and still possesses substantial wealth today. Almost a hundred years later, in 2020, the family came in at an $8.4 Billion net worth spread over more than seventy heirs.[46]

So, why did I share these three stories?

I wanted to give you proof that it's possible to overcome the proverbial "shirtsleeves to shirtsleeves" and create wealth that outlasts you. Of these three families who all achieved the ranks of the rich and famous, the Rothschild and Rockefeller families have maintained wealth through the generations.

British author and journalist, Harry Mount, wrote this about them:

> That is what makes these two dynasties so exceptional—not just their dizzying wealth, but the fact that they have held on to it for so long: and not just the loot, but also their family companies.[47]

On the other hand, the Vanderbilt name was a flash in the pan, representing a lost opportunity for wealth preservation. The obvious question becomes, what caused this difference? What allows some families to prevail above the entropy that usually pulls apart family legacies in three generations?

THE SECRET OF LONG-TERM WEALTH

The key to multigenerational wealth is not the volume of money in your family but the *people*.

THE KEY TO
MULTIGENERATIONAL
WEALTH IS NOT THE
VOLUME OF MONEY IN
YOUR FAMILY BUT THE
PEOPLE.

Let me say that again, just in case you missed it. The people, not the money itself, are what propel and sustain your legacy. The people are the shoulders on which everything else rests—the active ingredient of long-term wealth.

That's why it's critical to build your family culture and teach your children and grand-children the principles of value creation, enterprise, success, and stewardship. When you focus on developing people, you'll build and continue growing wealth in each generation. But if you over-look the people, your financial accomplishments will barely do any good beyond boosting your ego and standard of living.

With a quick glance at the Vanderbilts, you can see that their relationships were fraught with mistrust and skepticism. But you don't have to look far to see that the Rothschilds and Rockefellers empowered family members instead. They believed so much in their people that they even sunk vast start-up capital into their family's endeavors, even before their investments had proven profitable.

One interview with Rockefeller Sr.'s grandson, David Rockefeller Jr., highlights the way this family still nurtures the bonds of relationships and invests in the people.[48] The family still gathers for family meetings twice a year, where as many as 100 people across the generations come together in one room. They discuss challenges, values, direction, projects, new members, and family news related to careers or important milestones, share family history, and maintain the strength of the family unit.

This shows that the *only way* to create a perpetual family legacy that lasts for generations is to invest in people and equip them with the tools to create wealth for themselves. And that's why the people, what they do, and the relationships between each of them matter oh so much more than the money itself.

An even older story suggests that this truth of creating legacies through people is sewn into the very fabric of our humanity.

ABRAHAM'S NEED FOR A SUCCESSOR

It was around 2066 B.C., and Abraham had lived a full life. For nearly a hundred years, he had experienced success and wealth that had filled whole valleys. The land and flocks and herds were plentiful, and he had armies at his command. But despite all that, one primary question weighed on his mind, robbing him of the thrill of experiencing it all.

Who would carry on his legacy after him? He and his wife Sarah remained childless. He knew that none of his possessions would matter if he had no successor. And more than just adding a son to the family, he longed for someone to love and give his name to. He wanted someone to share his stories and victories with, teach the wisdom he'd gained, and entrust with his wealth so that it would last.

Seeing the question weighing heavy, God tapped him on the shoulder, led him outside under the far-flung night sky, and tipped his gaze upward.

Can you count them?

No, why? Abraham shrugged and shook his head.

And there, speaking straight to Abraham's heavy question, God motioned to the stars with a sweeping arc of his arm. *Do you see all this?* He whispered. *Your children and their children will be more than these. In number, yes! But, oh, so much more than that! Your family line will last through the ages, as vast and established as the stars that stay fixed in their place.*

Abraham's gaze sunk downward. God, how? How are you going to make all of that out of nothing?

But the God of the heavens leaned his head back and laughed, an outright roar of deep-seated and outrageous joy. He'd been in the business of establishing whole worlds out of nothing. It was right within his wheelhouse to reward his friend of relentless faith with children who would carry out the monumental task of shaping history beyond the line where his own life would reach.

Abraham went on to have a son—several, in fact. Today, he is known not just as the father of many sons but of many *nations*. See, not only did Abraham gain a successor, but an entire posterity. That's because his son became a bridge to future generations.

And then, Abraham did something truly remarkable. He participated in the thread of patriarchs who transferred wealth *through* the generations.

How exactly did Abraham do this?

With a *blessing*.

ABRAHAM'S BLESSING

With a blessing, Abraham granted land, honor, possessions, an inheritance, and a prophecy of strength to Isaac.

And this blessing wasn't just platitudes and mere words. Instead, this profound blessing was the language of *investing* in his children. Abraham prepared and equipped his son to receive his wealth so that his son would, in turn, do the same for his children. In this way, he furthered the prospering of heirs that he would never meet.

Abraham's blessing made it possible for his son Isaac to bless his own son Jacob. And then Jacob blessed his twelve sons.[49] And now, this story has been passed on among countless Jews and Christians who count Abraham as a spiritual and ethnic father.

See, the blessing that cancels the curse of the wealthy is holistic and multidimensional. And rather than a one-time event, it's a way of life.

This transformational blessing includes:

1. Life-giving words that stem from a belief in your children
2. Provision and resources to get them started
3. Training and instruction that equips them to become stewards

$$\text{BLESSING} = \left\{ \text{WORDS} \right\} + \left\{ \begin{array}{c} \text{Financial} \\ \text{Resources} \end{array} \right\} + \left\{ \begin{array}{c} \text{Training \&} \\ \text{Equipping} \end{array} \right\}$$

It's this blessing that makes it possible for wealth to flow *through* each person, not just *to* them. That's because, instead of offloading your stuff on your kids when you die, blessing them intentionally empowers your posterity to receive your wealth and do the most with it.

WEALTH MUST MOVE *THROUGH* PEOPLE, NOT *TO* THEM

That's the secret: wealth that continues for generations is wealth that must get *through* people, not just *to* them. That means that people are *conduits*, not reservoirs. That means each person must become a *producer* and creator of wealth, not just a consumer. And that means the whole task of creating a legacy rests in how well you invest in *people*, equipping and freeing them to live out their purpose, do what they were designed to do, and produce, create, and contribute expansively because only people who join up in the chain of wealth creation can allow wealth to flow *through* them.

And that's exactly why breaking the curse of the wealthy requires you to bless the next generation in a way

> WEALTH THAT CONTINUES FOR GENERATIONS IS WEALTH THAT MUST GET *THROUGH* PEOPLE, NOT JUST *TO* THEM.

that the blessing can spill over and continue depositing from them into others' lives beyond them.

See, the one-step legacy forgets the value of the people and replaces it with the cheap alternative of valuing money itself. The problem is that no matter how much you make and no matter how much you pass on, it will never be enough to create the positive impact your soul craves.

People are all meant to participate in wealth creation, not just to spectate from the stands or benefit from someone else's work. Consuming the rewards of someone else's production is like empty carbs. They look delicious and tempting, but they're a mirage of fulfillment that leave you weak, lethargic, and mentally cloudy. The only way to gain the confidence and strength to enjoy wealth is to participate in the exhilaration of creating it. And until someone participates in the production, the fruit will never be as sweet.

That's why getting money *to* your kids is an end goal that will always be cloaked in regret. Instead, outwitting the curse requires you to wield the antidote of a blessing.

NOW IT'S YOUR TURN!

The endpoint of your legacy is not when it reaches the next generation. It isn't the dollar sum of your own net worth that makes it into the hands of your kids because you didn't use it up before you passed away.

Instead, the end point of your legacy is the endless ripple effect through thousands of people's lives and hundreds of years ahead that was started by your actions in the here and now.

It's like a golf swing—it isn't over at contact. If that was your finish line, you'd have poor form and way too many shots over par. Instead, your golf swing requires vision and execution all the way to the follow-through. In the same way, to truly create a legacy that lasts, you need to be looking way past that moment of transfer to the follow-through.

What will your legacy mean for your children's children, and their children, and their children? How do you become like the patriarchs of old who bestowed a blessing like that, propelling wealth *through* future generations?

In the next chapter, we'll uncover a powerful way to deliver this blessing in a way that builds people. It gives you the power to invest in your family and integrate them into the family mission and fulfill their potential. This blessing paves the way for you to create perpetual wealth that rides on the shoulders of an army of producers, thinkers, creators, and investors who all recognize their value, contribute to others, and flourish because they fully enjoy the fruit of their work.

26

FAMILY BANKING

Investing in Your Family

F inancial gifts have many limitations that can cause them to backfire, leaving many wise parents wary of leaving an inheritance at all. This is where family banking shines. That's because family banking overcomes the lack of accountability with gifts and the sterile nature of wealth transfers, by instead using the best system for investing in your family and teaching financial stewardship all along the way, preparing your posterity to receive an inheritance.

Let me share a story to demonstrate how.

Avie was six and hungry to earn money in a fun way. She recruited her friends to run a lemonade stand together during our neighborhood yard sale.

To get started, she needed supplies. So, we parents footed the bill to buy lemons, sugar, cups, pitchers, and materials for signs. They fresh-squeezed gallons of lemonade and advertised as "The Best Lemonade on Earth." Then, on that blistering Saturday, they proceeded to sell from their perfect location right at the entrance to our neighborhood as well as walk door to door to give out samples and offer cups for sale.

I think they made over $100 that day, which included some very generous tips and donations from supporters who admired their grit. Then they paid back their loan to their investors for the cost of supplies. When they split the profits, there were six very sweaty but happy girls.

It occurred to me that we had invested well. Not only had our loan provided the capital to launch her micro business, but we had also invested in teaching business and teamwork skills she will need to become a good financial steward of the money we will leave her someday.

To share the wealth you've built and leave it in the hands of the family who come after you, you may be tempted to think immediately of gifts. Gifts are good. They're part of transferring a legacy. But they have some limitations that cannot be overlooked.

THE PROBLEM WITH GIFTS

Gifts are a transfer of money to someone else, whether by investments, life insurance payout, or cash. Gifts are given by the biggest-hearted people. They are well-intentioned, and they may even deliver to your recipient well. However, gifts do a terrible job of getting wealth *through* people. That's because gifts do not develop people. Here's why:

> GIFTS DO NOT DEVELOP PEOPLE.

First, gifts can feel like charity, elevating the giver and making the receiver feel inferior.

Then, there's also the problem that as soon as the gift leaves your hands, the strings of accountability are cut, leaving the recipient to do whatever they want with the money. That may work if they're already wise stewards and managers who will invest well. But if they're ungrateful, entitled, and irresponsible prodigals who live high on the hog—or if they simply haven't learned good stewardship yet—nothing prevents them from wasting your gift.

That's because a gift is a one-way street. It may benefit the one who receives it, but it has no way to guarantee that money will do the good you intend and contribute to growing family wealth in the future.

On top of that, there's the dilemma of fairness. Do you give equally to each family member, knowing full well that some will handle it better than others? Do you give based on need, or are you obligated by your own stewardship to give more to the ones who will manage it better and risk the ensuing jealousy and contention that will haunt your family as a result?

And most perplexing of all, gifts don't provide satisfactory answers for how to instill values, character, and stewardship in the first place. So, each gift is a blind gamble with your fingers crossed.

So, just like we discussed in Chapter 17 about keeping assets in trust, gifting your inheritance outright to family members can end up depleting family wealth or even decimating it completely. That's no way to build a legacy that lasts! Rather, it's the same slippery slope that's bested most families, fating them to lose all their money in just a few short generations.

Here's a solution that helps you give the next generation an unfair advantage while teaching them stewardship at the same time. It's called *family banking*.

CREATING MULTIGENERATIONAL WEALTH

Family banking fixes the problems of financial gifts. That's because, instead of doling out presents like Santa Claus, family banking uses the banking industry's mechanism of providing and accessing capital via *loans*.

This simple shift pays huge dividends.

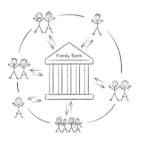

Family Banking

1. First, it makes the family money sustainable because it is continually being replenished, no matter how many times it's used.

223

2. Secondly, it is the best training wheels for developing the skillset of discerning stewardship. That's because it moves children from a position of minimal liability to increasing responsibility until they can take over as trustees and shareholders of the whole pot of family capital.

That means family banking is a financial mechanism to deliver wealth to future generations in a way that develops people. Let me show you just how this works.

In traditional banking, the bank extends the loan. Then the borrower puts capital to work, repays the loan, and replenishes the bank's stores, delivering more capital that can be loaned out again. Family banking is the same—except that it's the family who creates and holds reserves that the family members can access.

FOSTERING ACCOUNTABILITY

But rather than a free-for-all buffet, the family bank is a sealed vault. And the only key that opens the door—is *accountability*.

That means a borrower must answer to the family in advance for why they should be able to use family resources and then again afterward for how they used them. Before gaining access to family money, a family member must go through a vetting process to qualify on the gatekeeper's terms and earn the approval of the board, who presides over the fund. That means they will need a solid business plan with a compelling case to answer to the family for why they are deserving in the first place. They'll have to deliver a well-developed proposal, justify the use of capital, and prove their character and ability to repay. Then, they'll have to commit to a repayment schedule and interest.

See, here's the magic of accountability: It's the guide rails you need to protect the family bank and create the highest likelihood of learning for the borrower.

Strengthening the Family Team

With family banking, family members are no longer disconnected individuals who make decisions in isolation and live in their own respective silos. Instead, family banking brings together everyone on the same team, where they win or lose together. That's because if a borrower manages a profitable endeavor, the family bank shares in the victory. If they miss the mark and default on a loan, the whole family bears the loss together.

> FAMILY BANKING BRINGS EVERYONE TOGETHER ON THE SAME TEAM, WHERE THEY WIN OR LOSE TOGETHER.

Incentivizing Mentorship

The most important goal of family banking is to provide capital to qualified borrowers who will add back to the family's financial wealth. That means that you need good loans to approve. And because you're not searching amongst a sea of strangers to find them, but within the intimate circle of your own family, it's up to you to lead the relationships with your children that will eventually support this kind of trust.

If your children are still young, you'll want to prepare them ahead of time. That means teaching financial literacy and equipping them with the knowledge and skillset for savvy business ownership and investing. Even more importantly, you need to cultivate the integrity, character, responsibility, and discipline they'll eventually need to earn the approval of the family bank.

If your children are grown and ready to begin using the family bank, your mentorship will look different. You have the power to approve or deny a loan application. But you also gain a third option of choosing to *improve* their business plan when you recognize undeveloped potential.

Family Banking Is Investing in Family

Family banking changes everything. See, family banking solves the giant question of how to *develop people, invest* in your family, and get wealth *through* them. Children and grandchildren who want to use family money must accept the responsibility to grow family wealth and become net producers and creators.

That's why family banking is an indispensable tool of generational wealth used by the ultra-wealthy for centuries.

How to Practically Implement Family Banking

Getting started with family banking is easy. All you need are these two key components:

1. Cash reserves
2. Process for vetting, approving, providing, and repaying loans

You can use any cash storage account as the holding tank for your family bank if it provides preservation of your principle and accessibility through loans. In addition, an account with the maximum internal return will give you additional leverage over time because of the compounding growth.

Now, while any cash storage account can serve as the holding tank for your family bank, *specially designed whole life insurance* with high cash value can step in and double your efforts. So, this same tool we've already discussed can be a warehouse to store your savings—cash you can use for anything from buying a house to paying for college to funding a new business—and this same policy (or system of policies) can also multitask as your family bank. That's because, in a contest amongst all the tools for holding cash—savings account, checking account, money market, CDs, or home equity—life insurance offers the most safety, growth, and access of any other tool.

And that means that in addition to all the other personal benefits you gain from whole life insurance, you also layer on the capacity to use your wealth as a tool to equip the stewardship of your children and future generations. In this way, Infinite Banking can truly become infinite. When each policy pays out, if it is used to buy more whole life insurance for the next generation, you create infinitely growing, and dare I say, *perpetual* wealth for generations!

FAMILY BANKING IS LIKE CONCRETE

There's a striking resemblance between family banking and concrete.

Douglass Lodmell, one of our team's asset protection attorneys, once told me that concrete never stops hardening. There's an initial set time of about 24 hours before you can walk across it. Then, after about a twenty-eight-day curing period, it's considered to have reached maximum industrial strength. However, concrete continues to harden because it keeps getting denser, even 100 years after it's been poured.

Family banking using life insurance is just like that. It also continues improving with time. Here's why:

- First, after your initial capitalization phase, the cash value in your family bank will be more than you paid in and will continue to rise for the rest of your life.
- Then, when the founding generation passes away, there is a leveraged-up death benefit that's always far higher than your premiums to pour capital into the storehouse of the next generation.
- Finally, as the death benefit of one policy is used to capitalize a new policy on another family member, the second policy will be much larger than the first. When this process is repeated for generations, you'll grow monumental wealth.

That means that whole life insurance alone can single-handedly guarantee an ever-expanding family bank in the generations ahead. That's why the most profound use of life insurance is as a long-term generational wealth builder. And that's without mentioning all the other ventures you and your family will embark upon to create capital and cash flow throughout your lifetime.

When you have capital, a whole world of opportunities opens up because you have the means to buy investments when the market drops and those assets go on sale. And these external returns outside your life insurance policies contribute to growing your family's banking system over time. This goes to show that the longer you've had your family banking system, the more powerful it becomes.

PRACTICAL APPLICATION

To see this process in action, I want to show you how my business partner, Bruce Wehner, has used family banking for his whole life. When he was a young child, Bruce's parents purchased a whole life insurance policy on him. Later, when he became a young adult, they transferred ownership to him, so he could access and use his policy.

This first whole life policy has been the source of cash for starting multiple businesses, buying his first house, and investing in real estate. Then, over time, he's added several additional policies on both him and his wife. Although they have no children, they have listed their nieces and nephews as beneficiaries so that their estate will continue to benefit those after them.

Another colleague, John Moriarty, has used his family banking system over the course of the past twelve years. He's put over $1.9 Million into four policies and has borrowed over $2 Million against it for everything from business expansion to personal loans to family members.

GENERATIONAL TAX BENEFITS OF LIFE INSURANCE

In addition, family banking creates massive tax benefits. That's because the initial policy grows income tax-free with interest and dividends. And then the death benefit passes on income tax-free.

If the proceeds are then used in another investment, you'll need to pay tax on the growth of the investment purchased with the death benefit. But if you put the proceeds into premiums on another policy, they maintain their income tax-free status.

There is a possibility that if you grow your estate large enough, you will owe estate taxes (it depends on the estate tax thresholds at the time). Because you have more in death benefit than you pay in premiums, you can use the leveraged-up death benefit to pay the estate taxes. In this way, family banking can be a strategic tax planning tool to minimize the impact of estate taxes.

With this long-range view, it's almost impossible to mess it up. Even if all other trust assets get used up, the family wealth bucket will get filled back up with life insurance.

HIGH NET WORTH DOESN'T MEAN YOU'RE OVERQUALIFIED

Many people believe that when their net worth is high enough, they outgrow the need for life insurance because they can self-insure. The problem is that self-insuring is far more expensive because you need to use up assets to fund your legacy.

But properly structured life insurance will always give you an advantage over self-insuring because the death benefit is always more than what you pay in. In addition, it protects your income so that all along the way during your lifetime, if something happened to you, the money would be there to keep growing your family legacy the way you were.

Life insurance makes any financial situation better. It means you'll have the most money at the endpoint of your life, whenever you meet it. And it's the catalyst that best passes the baton of stewardship over the family wealth to the next generation.

Our Family Bank

Family banking is one of the best ways to overcome the odious proverb and let future generations stand on the shoulders of your success. And that's exactly why we've built family banking into our own legacy.

Creating a family banking system may seem lofty and complex. That's why I want to break this down into simple terms and show you exactly how we're putting this into action, so you can see how practical and tangible this wealth creation engine really is.

We're using our cash value whole life insurance as the holding tank for our family bank. We're funding as much whole life insurance as our cash flow allows and adding policies as our cash flow increases. Then, we're taking loans for profitable business opportunities and investments and repaying the loans to free up the cash value to use again.

This growing cash value is available for us and our children to borrow. That means it can be used for college tuition, business ventures, or investments. And we've asked that most loans be repaid or paid forward into a fund for their children.

When we pass away, our trust is directed to purchase as much whole life insurance as possible for our children to continue building the capital within our family banking system. Each generation benefits by having access to the cash value. They'll also gain the payout of the death benefit that will be used to re-invest and purchase more life insurance. With this process, we've set in motion a perpetual wealth system that will continue to grow as each generation follows the map that we've laid out to build their own wealth on the foundation of cash-value whole life insurance.

Here's the excerpt from our *Memorandum of Trust* outlining the financial management of trust assets with family banking:

We believe that true wealth is a meaningful and fulfilled life now. Our desire is that more than money, you would carry on the financial wisdom that we have gained through years of reading, mentors, and financial experience and business.

Our goal is that you would become wise stewards, producers, and contributors to the family wealth.

We would like to purchase as much high cash value, dividend-paying, mutual whole life insurance as possible on each of our children as age, underwriting, and insurability allow, and invest in opportunities that grow their financial capital without prohibiting the trust from having sufficient liquidity to fulfill its intent and purpose.

Once our beneficiaries reach adult age, we have outlined scenarios in which we wish that at least a portion of distributions be repaid or put into a fund or cash value life insurance for future beneficiaries. In the event our beneficiaries reach adult age and take distributions where we have directed that money be paid back or put into a fund for future beneficiaries (paying it forward) and they willfully/intentionally do not make an effort to fulfill this requirement, we direct the trustee(s) to stop future distributions until proof that beneficiaries have upheld our wishes. Again, we leave this 100 percent to the discretion of the trustee, as there could be circumstances that we cannot foresee.

While we have done our best to make our wishes known, this trust is set up such that the distribution of trust assets is 100 percent left at the sole discretion of the trustee. We have selected trustees we trust will do what is in alignment with our desire that our beneficiaries do not become dependent on this trust for life, but that this trust helps them become productive self-sufficient members of society, go farther in life then we have, and realize their full potential.

The trust will cover your living expenses up to age twenty or as long as you are in full-time college. This includes large-ticket items such as a car, home, travel to visit family, and starting a business. Higher education costs are an investment that we would want to be paid forward, as outlined below.

After age twenty, or after you have completed a degree program, we have an expectation that you would have your own source of income to provide for basic needs. At that time, you may continue to utilize the trust for large-ticket items when you have full faith and confidence that you will be able to pay at least a portion of it forward. Notable exceptions are for your wedding and a yearly vacation to get the family together, which will be funded as gifts. Here is the way we ask that you pay it forward:

Our intent is that our beneficiaries have skin in the game and are willing to pay it forward, and to that end, we leave it to the trustee to decide if full repayment or only partial repayment is required.

Before making financial decisions to spend and invest above basic needs, please seek the counsel of the trustee, Bruce Wehner, or Ryley Smith. We ask that you listen to *The Money Advantage* podcast, read the articles, watch the videos, and study the materials, resources, courses, and books we have provided to clients.

Our philosophy:

- Always pay yourself first (10–30 percent+ goes directly to an emergency/opportunity fund).
- Outside of basic living expenses, hold cash, maintain at least six to twelve months (or more) in emergency reserves; stay liquid.
- Purchase investments you know and can control only after careful consideration.

We have created a family bank utilizing our life insurance cash value as the capital and a board to oversee the distribution of the capital and set the repayment terms to the family bank. We are the current board members, but as you age, it is our intent to add you to our board. The purpose would be to aid the family in making investments and starting businesses, to benefit both the individual and the family, over time, creating a bigger bank to fund future generations' endeavors.

It would be our intent that you would use life insurance as the foundation of your family's wealth and continue the family banking concept we have started for ourselves and our family. Life insurance cash value should serve as your emergency and opportunity fund and ultimately ensure our and your legacy passes on.

We're using this practical tool of Infinite Banking with whole life insurance as the method to carry out family banking. It allows us to strategically invest family capital in the next generation and provides a tactical way for us to teach freedom with responsibility that's at the core of our family DNA. In addition, it paves the way for perpetual wealth that increases with each generation.

See, instead of just setting up our whole life insurance policies for ourselves and leaving them on the shelf to accumulate cash value, we're *using* our cash value. We're personally leveraging our cash value to invest in profitable ventures, and we're building the capital reserves that our children can also borrow from to fund their opportunities.

We've set up the guidelines for the wealth we're creating today and left instructions for how to steward and manage the wealth we leave behind. With these simple actions that anyone can put in place today, we're investing in the future of our family and turning the tide of poverty by creating life-giving perpetual wealth. Instead of just creating means, we're ensuring those means are used to stoke the fire of a multigenerational legacy of more than money.

NOW IT'S YOUR TURN!

Like those who planted a copper beech tree that wouldn't fully mature for at least thirty years, starting a family banking system is a small action that will continue investing in your family's future for generations to come. You're planting a seed that will become a mighty forest in the lifetime of children and grandchildren after you, and those future generations will reap the greatest benefit of your actions.

As you're creating the most you're capable of, ask good questions. Where are there holes in your strategy? What is your end goal? Do you want to have the means to travel? To not be a burden to your children in your later years?

If you're only looking at what you can get *out of* your financial wealth, your vision isn't big enough. That's because you're part of an eternal story, writing the script that will live past you. So, how will you make sure your work has the greatest impact? Do you have a successor to continue your work after you? How are you investing in them so they can stand on your shoulders?

You can turn your success and achievements into a catalyst that creates a blessing that overflows to the rest of your family as well. What are your plans to overcome the problems of losing wealth and falling into obscurity? As you grow your financial wealth, how will you ensure your efforts and accomplishments benefit and bless seven generations in the future? How will you maximize your efforts to develop the stewardship and capabilities of your successors? What seeds are you planting in the lives of others that will increase their knowledge, skills, and relationships and eventually grow to full maturity, increasing the value that *they* can provide?

Those after you, whether they be children, other family members, students, mentees, a business successor, an organization, or a charity, are craving your practical love and support so they can thrive and reach their full potential. Decide today how you will invest in those relationships and foster their ability to create, grow, and enjoy wealth. Today, you can start using the capital building and lending system of family banking to overcome the entropy of eroding wealth and become the inflection point to set in motion perpetual wealth that lasts for generations. The honor will rest on you as the benefactor, the fountainhead, and the bestower of an endless river of blessings.

YOUR FAMILY LEGACY

Now that you've come so far, let's zoom out to gain perspective and celebrate your progress.

You picked up this book because the idea of creating a legacy for generations to come has drawn you to be ultra-intentional about how you live, the activities you choose, the lessons you teach, and the priorities you invest time in. Before you began, you loved your children with a relentless love and wanted the most for them, and you wanted to make the biggest difference with your life.

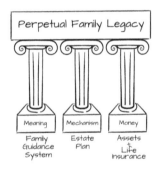

Now, you've seen how to build Pillar 1, where you articulate your WHY as a family. By spelling out your *ideals* that counter gravity, the *values* that point you to your true north in everyday life, the *mission* that's your family's job today, and the *vision* that's your long-term life aim, you craft a guidance system that will lead your family today and for centuries to come. Like designing the plans for your aircraft, this step reveals what exactly your family legacy means.

Then, we've discussed building Pillar 2, where you determine HOW you will legally transfer your legacy from your hands to the next generation. This is where you create the mechanism of the formal legal documents you need as the bones of your *estate plan*, draft the *Memorandum of Trust* that will be the spirit and power of your gift, and lean in and open up to the Gorilla Glue *relationships* you'll need to keep your legacy intact. Like building, staffing, and scheduling your airplane, this step transfers your assets in a way that accomplishes your goals.

And finally, you've gained the insight to build Pillar 3, where you've discovered how to put the fuel in your airplane so that it can fly the furthest by guaranteeing the most money possible at the end of your life. You've seen the value of specially designed life insurance in guaranteeing a death benefit while benefiting your family along the way and providing a way to teach stewardship and welcome each member of the family into the ranks of wealth creators.

With these three pillars, you create the foundation for a family legacy that lasts. Not just a memory. Not just money. But a lever that begins today to hoist the capability and possibility for every single person who follows in your wake.

If you want to implement the Seven Generations Wealth and Legacy Formula easier and faster, so you can gain all of this ground in your family, hop on our calendar here:

https://sevengenerationslegacy.com/strategycall

I imagine a world lit up with the light of families doing this brave work. Like pinpricks of cell phone flashlights in a dark stadium, this light will pierce the darkness. These lights will join together with other families who also are wrapping their giant love for their children into a practical and tactical plan that keeps pumping that love, like an infinite supply, through the people in your family long after you're gone.

By now, you know that Olivia and I both lived. But, in the last two chapters, let me tell you how it happened because it was one of the greatest lessons I needed to receive as I lived through this experience.

KEY CHAPTER TAKEAWAYS

- Life insurance guarantees that when you pass away, your estate will be the greatest possible. It is a gift of love that ensures that what you want to make possible for your children will happen, whether you're there or not.

- The best way to communicate to your children/heirs why you purchased life insurance is to write a love letter to be delivered along with the check at your passing. Here, you can memorialize everything you believe about them and want them to know forever, and tell them exactly why you are giving them this money.

- Whole life insurance isn't just an insurance product with a death benefit. It's also a highly potent savings tool with maximum safety, liquidity, and growth that allows you to create stable reserves to access for emergencies and opportunities. In addition, it provides guarantees, tax advantages to you and your heirs, increased returns because it is an "And Asset" that allows you to continue earning inside the policy while also deploying capital to work in another investment at the same time, and is the ideal estate transfer tool.

- The curse of the wealthy is that most wealth is lost by the third generation. However, families who have maintained wealth for many generations value the people, so they invest in developing people and strengthening family bonds. The secret that allows you to create multigenerational wealth is blessing your children with life-giving words that stem from a belief in them, the provision and resources to get them started, and the training that equips them to become stewards. This allows wealth to move *through* people, not just *to* them.

- Financial gifts can backfire because they lack accountability, and they are a one-way street that depletes resources.

Instead, family banking replenishes family money, making it sustainable for generations, and it's the best training wheels for developing stewardship, allowing you to invest in people.

CONCLUSION

Putting Your Perpetual Legacy in Motion

Perpetual Family Legacy

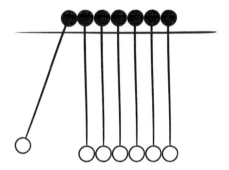

Family wealth and flourishing
that grows with each successive
generation

27

MIRACLE IN ROOM 3404

Mercies During the Worst Week of Our Lives

Over the next two days, I learned two lessons that make legacy creation possible. The first was to look for the beauty in the midst of the greatest difficulties, because everything works out for your good. The second is that you cannot do anything great alone. These are the same two lessons you need to learn as you build your seven generation legacy.

Let me tell you now about the first lesson.

I spent the rest of the day in ICU, quietly and steadily gaining strength. The lactation consultant helped me pump nutrient-dense colostrum to send upstairs for my baby for the rest of the day. The ICU nurses, Linda and Samantha, celebrated the fact that they could start emptying my catheter. And as I overheard the staff talking with hushed amazement about my case, I clung to every word, trying to remember the details.

They said something about neurological recovery. I asked if that meant my brain was working right, and the nurse said, "Yes, wonderfully! You're joking and have a sense of humor!" It struck me then that there had been a chance I would have lost my mental capacity.

My pastor, Grant, found out about our situation through the grapevine and came to pray with me.

Later that afternoon, Lucas left to pick up Avie so she could meet her baby sister. After soaking up the snuggles and treasuring "the one and only baby cuteness," she'd been thanking Jesus for over the last nine months, Avie came to see me in ICU. Lucas had sheltered her from knowing the full details, but he told her I was very sad and sick. Her eyes were saucers as she stared at me lying in the hospital bed with all the medical lines and tubes. I knew she was scared for me, but I squeezed her tight to reassure her that everything would be okay.

Hospital policy prevented additional children from staying overnight at the hospital, so we'd planned for Lucas to be home with Avie during the nights, and I'd be with Olivia. But now, I was more patient than a caregiver, stranded across the hospital from Olivia. That meant Lucas would care for Olivia in the mother-baby recovery room, and Avie would need to spend the second night with Jackie, the lead teacher at her school. It was far less than ideal to have all of us separated when we longed to be together. But we were doing the best we could under the circumstances and leaning hard and heavy on friends who stepped in and became like family to us in those delicate hours.

I rebounded dramatically. By that night, the ICU nurse removed the last of the lines and announced that I was ready to return upstairs. I watched the yellow hospital socks move for the first time that day as the nurses lowered my feet to the floor to transfer me to a wheelchair. On the way out of the glass doors, I finally could see the nurses' station which was the hub of the ICU, and several familiar faces that had surrounded me that morning. They were all smiles now, telling me how much better I looked!

The wheelchair took me up the elevator and down the labor and delivery hall to Room 3404. On the other side of that door, there was a dark and quiet reunion. I was frail from labor and the day's events, sapped from being severely anemic, and drained from having nothing to eat since the peanut butter I'd snuck during early labor. But I was reunited with my Love and my dewy and swaddled newborn, and everything was right with the world.

During almost exactly twenty-four hours since Olivia's birth, I had bungee jumped into a head-first free fall, stopped just short of certain death, and sprung back as the gears of my biology had engaged and unbelievably spun back to life.

Later, I confessed to Lucas how heartbreaking it was to have missed the first day of her life. Ever my anchor, he reassured me, "It's what's given you the ability to get the rest of your lives together."

I saw how exhausted and drained Lucas was from being up all Monday night, fearful for me, and being both dad and mom to a newborn on her first day. I knew I had nurse Kaylen to help me remember how to use my legs, steady me to walk to the restroom, and lift Olivia in and out of the crib. So, I sent Lucas home to get some real sleep.

He barely kept his eyes open during the twenty-minute drive and once home, fell headlong into the bed without undressing. A few short hours later, his phone dragged him from the deepest sleep. It was Jackie texting to tell him that Avie was sick with vomiting and diarrhea.

He groaned, mustering every ounce of energy to push back the overwhelm and choose rational thoughts to solve yet another monstrous problem. Hopefully, it's just something she ate, or homesickness from the stress, or a twenty-four-hour bug. He buckled his seatbelt behind the wheel again, judgment impaired by worry and sleep deprivation. He called me, and together we tried to juggle another impossible situation. He couldn't leave her, bring her to the hospital, or be with Olivia and me. He had his hands full and had to trust that barely 24 hours after he'd kissed my face with relief, he was powerless to help me, and I would be okay on my own.

The next day, my pastor's wife Brittany visited like a ray of sunshine to welcome baby Olivia and let me know I was not alone. Anna, the bubbly nurse with the warm smile, lingered a few extra minutes as we connected about podcasting and her deep concern for women's health.

By Wednesday morning, I was strong enough to move about unassisted, and Olivia was getting the hang of nursing. However,

I had a gnawing concern about the wisdom and safety of bringing a newborn home to a sick family, especially in my compromised state. When my friend Joanna visited with the car seat she'd gifted us, she invited me to stay with her until Avie recovered.

By Thursday, what we thought was a twenty-four-hour bug had no sign of letting up. Avie was too sick to leave the house, both uncontrollably and violently ill and completely lethargic. Thursday night, Lucas took her to urgent care and then to the emergency room to rehydrate with IV fluids. They said she had Rotavirus.

My friend Rose came to comfort me and give me someone to talk to and process my swimming thoughts as I dealt with so many unknowns and impossibilities. She, too, had delivered a baby during household sickness and helped me bear the mental guesswork.

That night, I was healthy and strong enough to be discharged from the hospital. In less than 72 hours after the crisis of a lifetime, my body had healed and stabilized, to the utter astonishment of the medical staff.

Olivia, however, had yet to pass a ninety-minute car seat test to ensure her tiny body would maintain sufficient oxygen while strapped in. She had already been tested twice on Thursday and had failed both tests within the last few minutes, both times because she was holding her breath to poop. I was informed of the new plan to take her to the children's hospital via ambulance for a car bed test before discharging her, and if she failed that, she'd be in for another five-day hospitalization.

Along with my discharge, I would not be receiving more meals. While Olivia was still a patient, now I was just a guest. I'd need to fill my own water and order my own meals. To do so, I would have to leave Olivia in the nursery.

I filled pages with notes, checklists, and details as I frantically administrated birth records, ordered a Social Security Number, scheduled and rescheduled the pediatrician visit required for release three times, and tracked feedings and diaper changes, all the while, coordinating around the ninety-minute tests in the nursery. I barely had time or energy to squeeze in my own showers, pack up my bags, and remember to take my iron supplements. When the hospital photographer stopped in, I had no more bandwidth to think about scheduling newborn photography.

I wasn't cleared to drive. So, while Lucas was caring for Avie's desperate condition and couldn't do anything for me, I was frantically coordinating my transportation either for discharge or to the children's hospital, not knowing which we'd need. I'd texted several friends, but the problem was that I didn't know when I'd be released or where we would be going, so it was impossible to plan.

On top of that, my supply of protein-packed snacks I'd brought to the hospital—almond butter, sweet potatoes, broccoli, chicken, cheese, hard-boiled eggs, hummus, and organic blue corn chips—had just run out, and the hospital room refrigerator was empty. I didn't know where my next meal was coming from. That was terrifying because the massive breastfeeding hunger gnawed at me and left me shaky.

I was tormented by the knowledge that Lucas and Avie had been stuck in a never-ending nightmare of sickness all night. Then Olivia screamed for three hours through the night and wouldn't nurse. At the same time, my milk came in with excruciating pain and fever. I tried to pump off the excess milk but instead blistered and bruised my breast in the process. I was shaky with lack of sleep and still dangerously anemic, in great pain from the engorgement, worried about the car seat test, afraid of being unable to nurse, scared of getting mastitis and not being strong enough to care for Olivia, frightened of not having a satisfying meal in the morning, anxious about Avie's health and feeling so frustrated that I couldn't be there for her, concerned for Lucas being able to withstand the trial of watching his girls suffer, and feeling completely alone, helpless, and terrified. Everything was outside my control.

I didn't share these details with Lucas at the time, knowing he had enough stress of his own. Instead, I attempted humor to reassure him that Olivia was now more capable of passing her car seat test. If she had initially failed for lack of lung capacity, she'd just developed it in the last three hours of screaming. And if her failure was because of discomfort, she'd just passed the last of the meconium, so her stomach would be more settled.

The last sermon I heard was about overcoming through worship. I didn't know what to do, so I sang aloud through sobs to a God who carried me. I knew that somehow God's presence and goodness would make a way, that He would meet me at the end of myself. Right where my human strength and wisdom failed, His would be sufficient, and that His grace would be more than enough. Then, I finally succumbed to sleep at 2 a.m.

Despite the difficulty, one prayer was being answered in a very tangible way. Because of the trauma my body had endured, there had been a concern that my milk supply would be delayed or may not come in at all. In addition, Olivia might not latch because she'd spent most of her first 24 hours on a bottle. But not only did my milk come in, it was earlier than expected, and she took to nursing wonderfully.

At 4 a.m., after just two hours of sleep, Lauren, the nurse, came in to do yet another test. There were so many blood tests for me, bilirubin checks for Olivia, medication for my uterus to clamp, and so on throughout the days and nights that I'm not sure which was which. I asked for help, and before I knew it, I was sobbing in front of her. I had reached the point of more than I could bear.

"Oh, honey! Let me help you!" she exclaimed and stepped into the role of a lactation consultant to help me survive the night. She brought me life-preserving supplies: ice packs, salve, and the most blessed invention of a nipple shield. She coached me through nursing, then brought me apple juice and apple sauce that took the edge off my electrolyte-depleted hunger. I could only conclude she was an angel.

In the morning, there were new mercies at every turn. I received breakfast. Dr. Greely, the neonatal specialist from the children's hospital, arrived and decided to do the car seat test one more time. He injected a measure of confidence that Olivia would pass the test this time. My friend Kara offered to drive me wherever I needed to go, including a side trip to the drugstore to pick up a probiotic that would prevent thrush. Joanna was ready for me to stay at her house. She let me know she'd already laid out baby sleeping gowns and would have dinner waiting. Viola, the hospital's dining attendant, made sure I was served lunch. Olivia passed the car seat test! Each person was a gift, each provision was manna from heaven, and each time, I wept aloud with gratitude.

In case you needed a reminder—you can trust that God is for you, things are working out beneath the surface, people are good, and we are designed to serve and support each other. As you turn to the last chapter, you'll see exactly how important this mindset is as you embark on your journey to build a multigenerational legacy.

28

FENNEL AND FRIENDS

Why Wealth Is a Team Sport and How to Assemble Your Team

The bigger your vision for your legacy, the more you need others to help you accomplish it. That's because a healthy mindset about the world and others accepts your own limitations and recognizes that humility gives you the greatest strength.

I know, because I lived it.

Olivia was discharged about 12:30 p.m. on Friday afternoon.

Kara grabbed my bags and snapped photos of Olivia and me that we'd completely missed in our chaos. While she drove my car from the hospital to Joanna's house, she asked, "Rachel, does your family know how bad it was?" She had just lost her sister earlier that year to post-delivery heart failure.

With all our extended family out of state, Lucas and I had sent just a few texts at critical moments, but the fortress-like walls had blocked most of our cell signal, making communication difficult. Every spare minute and ounce of energy had been conserved to navigate the immense administrative challenge. I realized that beyond a few general details sprinkled through group texts, my own family didn't know the severity of my condition. It seemed so overwhelming just to survive those dark days that communicating the details had seemed beyond my capabilities.

For the next few days, I recovered in Joanna's home with her and her three beautiful children. They witnessed my raw frailty as I moved gingerly, reclining all day holding or nursing the most delicate-looking newborn I've ever seen outside the NICU, her tiny five-pound body swimming in the newborn clothes I'd packed. Rose stopped by with a basket of preemie clothes that Olivia would wear for the next six weeks.

I felt like I was staying in a bed and breakfast. Joanna set out fresh flowers in my room, cooked lovely meals, forbade me to help with dishes or clean up, and made the space for me to relax and heal while I created some of the first memories with Olivia.

One day, the house was empty and quiet. Joanna had taken her kids to baseball practice, and Olivia was napping, so I had the house to myself. I pulled the leftover Southern chicken out of the fridge and heated myself a plate in the microwave. As I sat down at her square table in the dining room, the distinctive flavor and aroma of fennel, carrots, onions, apples, celery, and thyme wrapped and held me in the most tangible comfort. I was safe, alive, present, and loved. There, with my bare feet on the hardwood, gulping down the most satisfying food, I heaved huge sobs of gratitude—for the grace that had carried me, sustained me, and delivered everything I needed through the hands of beautiful people who lavished me with the generosity of friendship during the darkest days of my life.

I still wasn't strong enough to drive, and Avie was still sick. I postponed Olivia's pediatrician visit again and surrendered to a few more days of waiting. It was during those healing days of safe, retreat-like calm while Olivia slept on her topponcino on the olive-green patio chair next to me that I called my sister Twyla. For several hours over the next three days, she listened, breathless, as I relayed the details of my delicate story. It was there that my emotions were wide open and unreserved, and the tears flowed freely. I asked her to share with the rest of the family until I was able to reach them all, one by one.

"Treasure your truths," midwife Blaine had said in that dim hospital room somewhere in the foggy days during recovery. "You'll hear stories of maternal mortality, and you'll relate to it all, but your ending was different. And the emotion will come out of nowhere. Don't let anything rewrite your truth."

I didn't have my computer with me, and typing out the details of the story on my iPhone notes app with my thumbs was tedious and slow. I requested a notepad and began to write down every detail, pressing it firmly into my memory.

And when I was tempted to wonder if everything that I'd experienced had just been a dream, every time I showered, I found more bruises and sticky residue across my hands, arms, shoulders, and chest left over from the sensors and medical tape and blood draws and IVs that had been my lifeline, reminding me of the trauma I'd endured. The marks on my body faded, but the scars were forever seared across my soul.

I finally gathered the strength for a walk down the street a few days later. Gradually, Avie recovered.

As we waited forty-eight hours post-symptoms to plan my homecoming, Lucas got sick. I nearly suffocated with anxiety that he would get sick and wouldn't be able to care for Avie while going through sickness as aggressive as she'd had. Graciously, his only symptom was a low-grade fever for 24 hours, but it set back our timeframe for returning home yet again, giving us unknowns and snatching the control out of our hands. I sent Melissa, another dear friend who had taken our glowing maternity photos just a week earlier, to bring him supplies.

REUNITED AT LAST!

Finally, the sickness dissipated from our house on Sunday morning. We waited for another 48 hours.

Lucas sanitized everything. Joanna loaded my hospital suitcase, diaper bag, coolers, the bag of hospital supplies, and the car seat with my tiny precious Olivia. I'd never been so thankful in all my life that I'd overpacked because those supplies had lasted me over a week! And then I tucked myself into the driver's seat that felt so foreign. I drove home in what felt like a marathon to my weak and wobbly body, stopping at the pediatrician's office for Olivia's newborn visit *en route*.

It was Tuesday, eight days after Olivia's birth, and a full seven days since we'd all seen each other. Avie and Lucas had missed Olivia's first week, and we'd all carried unbearable mountains of worry about each other. I'd been listening to "We Raise a Hallelujah" all morning, and it came on the radio as I rounded the corner into my neighborhood. My eyes flooded with tears that poured in rivers off my chin as I wept aloud at the extravagant mercy, blanketed grace, and profound goodness of God. It was an emotional reunion! I nearly crumpled in Lucas's arms, winded, weary, and relieved.

On the night we returned home, Lucas had a recurrence of some of the symptoms of Rotavirus, and the monster of fear raised its ugly head again. I was terrified of Olivia getting sick, which could be deadly to a newborn, or of my health failing and not being able to care for her. The happy reunion turned tense. Lucas slept on the couch and was afraid to touch Olivia or me. I was scared to move about the house freely and re-sanitized everything in my path. However, I felt the Lord reminding me to trust, and at every turn, the fear slowly subsided.

On her due date, a full ten days after Olivia was born, I finally finished writing out the story to announce her birth to friends and family who still had no idea we'd delivered our baby.

> Beginning this week on Wednesday morning, we slowly, tenuously, cautiously became a family again, able to snuggle and kiss and hug and hold and share our affection.

> Through the physical and emotional toll of the hardest week of our lives, we have been sustained, held, and surrounded by the close, tangible presence of Jesus, an enveloping peace and overwhelming gratitude for life itself, angels in human form who ministered to us, the goodness and provision of God at every turn, the supernatural strength and healing, and the beauty of friendship when we needed help and God taught me about

valuing my life the way He does and receiving the kindness and care and love from literally at least a hundred people. It's just so overwhelming!

We have so much to be grateful for. The gift of each breath and heartbeat, these four lives that have been united into a family, the opportunity to see each sunrise and sunset, the love spilling over and erasing the limits and boundaries of our hearts, and the great Author of Life who holds us together.

Our lives have been transformed by the addition of this beautiful life. God's plans are astoundingly great for this wee little one.

YOU AREN'T MEANT TO DO THIS ALONE

There is one simple meal that means more to me than Christmas dinner. It's the fennel chicken recipe that I ate alone in Joanna's dining room. I make it at least once a year, every summer, around Olivia's birthday. And every time, my heart catches with a cascade of emotion. The smell of roasted fennel is almost sacred to me, a concrete reminder of how the gift of friendship ministered to me so deeply during the most fragile week of my life.

It was the people whom I'd broken bread with, with whom we'd shared life, meals, joys, struggles, comfort, and encouragement that gave me a safety net of human connection that caught me during that crisis.

Look, we aren't meant to do hard things alone. We aren't meant to survive trauma, make giant life decisions, or create a legacy by ourselves. We need others to lift our arms when we are weak, who do with us what we can't do alone, who see our blind spots, and whose strengths complement ours to multiply our efforts.

This, like so many other life truths, seems exactly the opposite of everything we've ever been told. Grind, force it, muscle your own way, depend on yourself—it's the popular line, but it doesn't work. To do superhuman things, you need to stop trying so hard and let go.

Wealth, like life, is a team sport. Building a legacy that fulfills your potential to create the most financial means and human flourishing in your lifetime and for generations afterward is a task that requires the strategic coordination of every area of your financial life.

There are so many components that you need to work together to make an efficiently running financial system. There's maximizing profitability, achieving your cash flow goals with your investments, getting the most income throughout your entire lifetime, tax strategy to reduce taxes for your whole life, getting the best insurance at the lowest cost, saving for your kids' education, choosing the right mortgage and business financing strategy, and saving in the best bank that gives you the most growth, access to your money, safety, and options. Then, there's building an estate plan and business legal structure to protect your assets against creditors and lawsuits.

Why You Can't DIY Your Own Comprehensive Financial Strategy

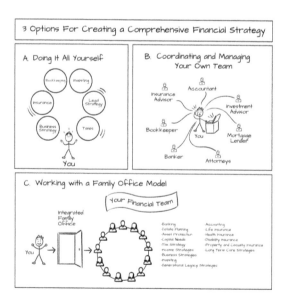

Look, you can try to do everything by yourself, but you'll exhaust yourself in the process.

There are two ways people DIY their wealth creation.

TRYING TO DO ALL THE WORK THEMSELVES

One way is that they guess their way by doing all the work themselves. These people usually do their own bookkeeping, file their own taxes, and pride themselves on the money they saved by not hiring a professional.

Doing It All Yourself

Bookkeeping · Investing · Insurance · Legal Strategy · Business Strategy · Taxes

You

But the journey is tedious and lonely because you're heaping the back-breaking burden of becoming the expert in every area on your shoulders and struggling under the weight. If you get into a bind, you can waste a lot of time trying to untangle everything. And with so much guesswork, you can end up with a lot of false starts and failures.

VOLUNTEERING TO COORDINATE YOUR OWN FINANCIAL TEAM

The second way well-intentioned good people struggle and fall short of their financial potential is that they recognize the need for professional support, so they hire help but pencil themselves in as the quarterback. They hire the banker, the accountant, the investment advisor, the insurance agent, and the attorney.

Coordinating and Managing Your Own Team

Insurance Advisor · Accountant · Investment Advisor · Bookkeeper · You · Mortgage Lender · Banker · Attorneys

The problem is that *your* job description requires coordinating dozens of individual strategies and relationships that are all separate, distinct, and invisible to each other. You wind up the hub holding everything together, educating one, explaining what the other told you, making sure each does their job well, and in the end, you're the one holding the responsibility to make sure you communicated everything that needed to be said to stitch together your entire financial system.

And that can create a hodgepodge of disjointed financial strategies and products that work against each other—often in direct opposition, conflict, or competition with each other. Not to mention you get a migraine from the mind-numbing minutia of being the liaison between professionals who don't communicate with each other.

A COORDINATED FINANCIAL TEAM

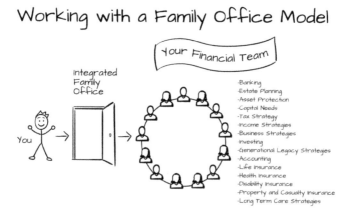

Working with a Family Office Model

To write out your plan, design the legal structure, and fund the plan, you'll need help. That's because maximizing your wealth creation requires strategies in every area of your financial life that are synchronized, working together in one efficient system. Like the inside of a motor, you want everything to coordinate smoothly, not clunking, sputtering, or flying apart. That way, there isn't one strategy counteracting another and canceling out its benefits.

At the bare minimum, to create a multigenerational legacy of more than money, you need an estate planning attorney and a financial advisor who integrates life insurance to help you. But rather than operating in their own silos, you need them to work closely together, aware of your goals and what you want to accomplish, so their efforts complement and strengthen each other, not cause the other parts to break down.

This is only possible when you recognize that your wealth is a team sport. Your investments need to maximize your tax strategy. Your tax strategy needs to support your business objectives. Your estate plan needs to lean on life insurance. Your financial freedom strategy needs investments that support your income needs. And you need capital you can rely on to support your investing and stabilize your financial foundations to give you confidence today and tomorrow.

No one advisor can do all of that well. If they say they can, I promise you they aren't good at everything. You can't rely on just one advisor dabbling in everything with a surface knowledge of a lot but lacking the expertise and skill to serve your needs well.

That's why we provide a family office model. We bring the family office, usually accessible only to the ultra-wealthy, to those who are building wealth so that you can get the same advantages. That means you get a network of financial specialists who understand your goals and needs, who have developed a depth of knowledge, and who work together, on the same team, towards the same goals. And with our unique ability teamwork approach, each person does what they do best. We always have at least two people sitting together at each meeting so that there's a built-in contingency system. That means rather than having a one-man band who knows you and what you want, there's always another team member who can step in and take over right where they left off. And instead of you quarterbacking this team, we do that for you. That means you aren't communicating the same thing to several people to bring them up to speed. And you aren't wearing yourself out being the middleman.

To do your most important life work, you need to work with a team that helps you optimize every area of your financial life. That's why it's critical to build the relationships now that work together to support your long-term goals.

To do that, you need to recognize and value your own unique ability and protect your ability to stay in your own lane, so you can do your best work. To find excellent people to journey with, you must let go of your ego and realize there are so many things you don't know. Rather than the admission being your kryptonite, it will become your superpower that launches you way past yourself.

WHERE TO GO FROM HERE

Now that I've shared my story of crisis, recovery, and building a legacy, you have a choice. You can keep going as you have been without an adequate plan, or you can start taking action, one step at a time, to change your future and your children's future. I hope you feel the same tension I felt when I realized I was called to do everything in my power to carve out this legacy that would love and hold my children and grandchildren for as long as eternity.

And more than just nice ideas, I hope that I've given you enough of the feet-on-the-ground, practical tools to wrestle through your own family guidance system, estate planning, and financial planning to set your legacy in motion.

But I can only share so much in a book. If you would like additional help and guidance to implement these strategies, you can take the first step to working with your own coordinated wealth team today by booking an introductory conversation here:

https://sevengenerationslegacy.com/strategycall

There's just one more thing you need to know. It's that you can't wait. Your life is far too precious to leave this work until later.

None of us have a single guarantee of another minute. Instead of that scaring us, it should compel us to live up to our best every moment.

Even if you aren't exactly sure what to do, take action. Even imperfect action is a thousand times better than doing nothing. You'll gain momentum and clarity while you're in motion.

Before I say farewell, I want to say thank you so much for joining me here on these intimate pages. You have no idea how much it means to me that you've found value in my story and the power it has to transform your own life and legacy.

This process of creating our three-pillared legacy was a beautiful thing for me and gave me so much peace and confidence. I'm excited to walk this out over the days, years, and decades to come and to watch the impact of these decisions continue to unfold.

In writing this book, I realized for the first time that it truly was possible that my hellish week, hanging in the liminal space between life and death, was meant not only for my good but for yours too.

I would love nothing more than to know how you are walking this out beside me, choosing to be the inflection point of your own multigenerational legacy of more than money. Would you please take one minute to tell me what this book has meant for you by leaving me a review wherever you purchased your copy?

I'm so glad you've joined the legacy creator's tribe! Your story is just getting to the good stuff.

My team and I are here to help you should you choose to contact us.

RESOURCES

Access the following book bonuses you received along with the purchase of this book here:

Get the *Seven Generations* book bonus content

QUICK GUIDE: How to Get Started with Your Family Guidance System—Start brainstorming your Family Guidance System with some starter questions to consider your family values, mission, and vision.

QUICK GUIDE: How to Get Started with Your Estate Planning—Jumpstart your estate planning with a few clarifying questions to make sense of what matters to you as you protect your family and pass on assets.

Four Secrets to Building Resilient Relationships—Use these four keys to build "Gorilla Glue Relationships" that you can depend on to carry your legacy beyond you.

Infinite Banking Secrets Guide and Mini-Training—How to earn a return on the same money in two places at the same time, so you can boost investment returns without taking on more risk.

ACKNOWLEDGEMENTS

Thank you to the enterprising families that I am lucky to know and who will always inspire me: The Eide family, who built a family business, brought family members into the business, and cherished family dearly. The Zetterberg family, who's multigenerational legacy I saw up close and personal and was invited to their welcoming table, where they served and ministered to all kinds of people. The Dizons, who have taken the best from their parents and started their own remarkable family culture. The Stocketts, whose extended family I was included in as they got together with aunts, grandparents, and cousins for holidays and annual Easter egg hunts. The Hammond family, who keeps growing and celebrating each other. The Hunt family, who invested a love of music in their children and performed together as a family, and taught me the best way to parent well is to live your passion in front of your kids and have an amazing marriage.

Thank you for the amazing care of the Labor and Delivery team, ICU staff, and friends who loved me well during the hardest week of our family's life, including: Adrea, L., S., Ericka, L., H., T. K., K., L., R., V., T., Claudia, Kelly, Joanna, Kara, Twyla, Rose, Debbie, Melissa, Lindsay, Kara, Kodie, Aaron and Adrienne, Brooke, Bob and Holly, Laura, Carly, Cyndi, Nnene, Cy and Cindy, Bill and Jody, Tom and Terri, Maureen, Grandma Sally Montagne, Jared and Petra, and Lucas's work team.

To the family who have gone before us and made our life possible. We are just beginning to uncover your legacy.

To my co-author, co-business owner, co-family leader, and husband, Lucas Marshall, who's thought leadership, insight, and wisdom has made this book everything it is.

To my beta reader team, whose attention to detail and unique perspective have polished this book to make it all that it is: Twyla Franz, Cece Corujo, Stephen Haynes, Gina Dizon, and Kelly Storrs.

To the friends, professionals, coaches, and authors who shaped my perspective, or helped me become who I am: Brad Montagne, Teri Alen, Kenneth Marshall, Ruth Marshall, Brian Hopper, Marshall Rosenberg, Brett and Molly Hildebrandt, John Lenhart, Mike Michalowicz, Robert Kiyosaki, Rabbi Daniel Lapin, Russell Brunson, Cheri Dunnigan, Rick Randall, Michaela Nicolaison, Steve Lentz, Andrew Weinhaus, Andrew Howell, Stephen Haynes, Keith Whitaker, Jeremy and April Pryor, Jefferson and Alyssa Bethke, Craig Ballantyne, Rich Litvin, Nelson Nash, Dr. Robert P. Murphy, Bruce Wehner, John Moriarty and the team at e3 Wealth, Sally Hogshead, Dan Sullivan, James E. Hughes Jr., Susan E. Massenzio, Dennis Jaffee, Tom Michler, Mitzi Perdue, Garrett Gunderson, Napoleon Hill, Wallace Wattles, Jackie Hill, Jeff and Laura Sandefer, Connor Boyack, Dustin Griffiths, Aaron Fletcher, Jim Edwards, Joe Yazbeck, Peyton Roberts, John Assaraf, John C. Maxwell, Marie Forleo, Brendan Burchard, Simon Sinek, Patrick Donohoe, Don Blanton, Mark Bertrang, Bob Burg, John David Mann, Bryan S. Bloom, Tom Love, James Neathery, Ryan Griggs, Bob Wheeler, Steve Sims, Scott McCright, Dave Zook, Dr. Wade Phau, Todd Langford, and Chris Voss.

Thank you to those who believed in me and this project and offered encouragement, criticism, and feedback that helped shape this book: Lucas Marshall, Bruce Wehner, Ryley Smith, Stephanie Smith, Helen Abernathy, Jonathan Dison, Lee Matthis, Randy Singer, Nnene Mbonu, Gary Boomershine, Julia Jordan, Tina

Lovejoy, Joanna Ragon, Wendy Carter Custer, Douglass Lodmell, Mark Podolsky, Mike Kitko, Cesar Quintero, Michael K. Cobb, Dave Chase, Mikkel Thorup, Jon and Missy Butcher, Barb Stackhouse, Keith Whitaker, Ross Stryker, Eileen Wilder, Craig Ballantyne, Anna Kelley, Jack Gibson, Richard Wilson, Rodney Mogen, Jeff Ganthner, Brian Dixon, Moses Seuram, Ron Phillips, Kevin Clayson, Amber Zetterberg, Paul Moore, Martha Krejci, Joe Evangelisti, Jason Rink, Terry Cook, Blake Brewer, Sabrina Starling, Dylan Ewing, Brittany Schanck, Chase Hunter, Trevin Jacobson, and the Peaceful Profits team, including Suzanne Burns and Meredith Trunkett.

Special thank you to Richard Wilson for writing the foreword to this book and being a part of this message.

Thank you to my illustrators: Andres Arturo Chavez Montoya, Mikey Marchan, Mikael Kevin Marchan, Ronald Cruz, Ma. Jenica Alexis Llanes, Louie Gio Ocsena, and Evan Joshua Tiu Ng with DesignPickle, and Zahra Tariq.

Cover design: Debbie O'Byrne

Thank you to the whole team at Author Academy Elite for direction and guidance on my proposal, manuscript, editing, marketing, and the entire process of authorship: Kary Oberbrunner, Daphne V. Smith, Erin Casey, Abigail Young, Brad, Tony Colson, Michel Longpre, and Jill Ellis.

ENDNOTES

Find endnotes online at https://sevengenerationslegacy.com/endnotes.

1   Baumann, S., Neidhardt, T. & Klingauf, U. "Evaluation of the aircraft fuel economy using advanced statistics and machine learning." *Springer*. 19 June 2021.

2   "How Much Fuel Does a Jumbo Jet (Boeing 747-400) Burn?" *Flight Deck Friend*. https://www.flightdeckfriend.com/ask-a-pilot/how-much-fuel-does-a-jumbo-jet-burn/. (accessed 24 February 2022).

3   "How Much Fuel Does an International Plane Use for a Trip?" *How Stuff Works*. (19 May 2021) https://science.howstuffworks.com/transport/flight/modern/question192.htm

4   Hughes, James E., Keith Whitaker, and Susan E. Massenzio. *Complete Family Wealth*. Hoboken, NJ: John Wiley & Sons, Incorporated, 2018.

5   Prov. 13:22 (NASB)

6   Spector, Nicole. "100-Year-Old Companies Still in Business Today." *Yahoo*. https://www.yahoo.com/video/100-old-companies-still-business-170025835.html. 6 March 2021.

7   Hughes, James E., Keith Whitaker, and Susan E. Massenzio. *Complete Family Wealth*. Hoboken, NJ: John Wiley & Sons, Incorporated, 2018.

8   Hughes, James E. *Family: The Compact among Generations*. New York, NY: Bloomberg Press, 2007.

9   Hughes, James E., Keith Whitaker, and Susan E. Massenzio. *Complete Family Wealth*. Hoboken, NJ: John Wiley & Sons, Incorporated, 2018.

10 Hoyt, Richard. "The Growth of the Beech Tree." *HomeGuides.* https://homeguides.sfgate.com/growth-beech-tree-67489.html. (accessed 24 February 2022).

11 "European Beech." *Arbor Day.* https://www.arborday.org/trees/treeguide/treedetail.cfm?itemID=790. (accessed 24 February 2022).

12 The Constitution of the United States. *National Archives.* https://www.archives.gov/founding-docs/constitution-transcript. 17 September 1987.

13 Strong's G703. *Blue Letter Bible.* https://www.blueletterbible.org/lexicon/g703/kjv/tr/0-1/. (accessed 24 February 2022).

14 Arête. *Britannica.* https://www.britannica.com/science/arete-glacial-landform. (accessed 24 February 2022).

15 Prov. 22:6 (NASB)

16 Gal. 5:22-23 (NASB)

17 Butcher, Jon and Missy. *The Money Advantage podcast.* https://themoneyadvantage.com/building-family-wealth-jon-and-missy-butcher/. 21 September 2020.

18 Bartsch, Christine. "How Long Does Probate Take? These 5 Factors Can Make All the Difference." *HomeLight.* https://www.homelight.com/blog/how-long-does-probate-take/. 28 June 2019.

19 Probasco, Jim. "Estate Tax Exemption, 2022." *Investopedia.* https://www.investopedia.com/estate-tax-exemption-2021-definition-5114715. 23 February 2022.

20 "Instructions for Form 706." *IRS.* https://www.irs.gov/instructions/i706#idm139646239255744. September 2021.

21 "Federal Estate and Gift Tax Rates, Exemptions, and Exclusions, 1916-2014." *Tax Foundation.* https://taxfoundation.org/federal-estate-and-gift-tax-rates-exemptions-and-exclusions-1916-2014/. 4 February 2014.

22 Weinhaus, Andy. *The Money Advantage podcast.* https://themoneyadvantage.com/estate-planning-for-everyone-with-andre-weinhaus/. 28 September 2020.

23 US Debt Clock. https://www.usdebtclock.org. (accessed 24 February 2022).

24 Strong's H5397. *Blue Letter Bible.* https://www.blueletterbible.org/lexicon/h5397/kjv/wlc/0-1/. (accessed 24 February 2022).

25 Genesis 2:7. Bible Hub. https://biblehub.com/commentaries/genesis/2-7.htm. (accessed 24 February 2022).

26 York, David R., and Andrew L. Howell. *Entrusted: Building a Legacy That Lasts*. Salt Lake City, UT: YH Publishing, 2015.

27 Whitaker, Keith. *The Money Advantage podcast*. https://themoneyadvantage.com/complete-family-wealth-keith-whitaker/. 7 September 2020.

28 Inspired by the following verses: Eph. 6:10-18, Gal. 5:22–23, Phil. 4:8, Josh. 1:9, Matt. 21:21, 2 Cor. 10:5, Col. 3:2, Rom. 8:38–39, Eph. 4:15, and Phil. 4:7 (NASB).

29 "Swiss Army Knife History and Facts." *Alpenwild*. https://www.alpenwild.com/staticpage/swiss-army-knife-history-and-facts. (accessed 24 February 2022).

30 "Swiss Army Knives." *Victorinox Swiss Army*. https://www.swissarmy.com/us/en/Products/Swiss-Army-Knives/c/SAK?ScrollPosition=176&maxResults=60. (accessed 24 February 2022).

31 Nash, R. Nelson. *Becoming Your Own Banker: The Infinite Banking Concept*. Birmingham, AL: Infinite Banking Concepts, 2008.

32 Koenig, David. *Mouse Tales: A Behind-the-Ears Look at Disneyland*. Irvine, CA: Bonaventure Press, 2006.

33 Our Story. *Foster Farms*. https://www.fosterfarms.com/all-about-us/our-story/. (accessed 24 February 2022).

34 Dyke, Barry James. *The Pirates of Manhattan: Systematically Plundering the American Consumer & How to Protect Against It*. Hampton, NH: 555 Publishing, 2008.

35 Curry, Mary E. *Creating an American Institution: The Merchandising Genius of J.C. Penney*. New York, NY: Garland, 1993.

36 The Spectator, a Weekly Review of Insurance. New York and Chicago, Thursday, February 14, 1918

37 Joseph Biden Executive Branch Personnel Public Financial Disclosure Report (OGE Form 278e). *White House*. https://www.whitehouse.gov/wp-content/uploads/2021/05/Biden-Joseph-R.-2021-Annual-278.pdf. July 2020.

38 "The Blessing," "The Blessing," sung by Kari Jobe with Cody Carnes, Written by Chris Brown, Carnes, Steven Furtick, and Jobe, Produced by Austin Davis, Cody Carnes, Henry Seeley, released October 23, 2020, via Sparrow Records

39 Hughes, James E. *Family Wealth: Keeping It in the Family.* Bloomington, IL: Indiana University Press, 2004.

40 Cook, Jennifer. "A History of the Rothschild Family." *Investopedia.* https://www.investopedia.com/updates/history-rothschild-family/. 11 June 2021.

41 "Rothschild Family Net Worth." *Celebrity Net Worth.* https://www.celebritynetworth.com/richest-businessmen/rothschild-family-net-worth/. (accessed 24 February 2022).

42 Morton, Frederic. *The Rothschilds: A Family Portrait.* New York, NY: Diversion Books, 2014.

43 "Commodore Vanderbilt's Life." (PDF). *The New York Times.* https://timesmachine.nytimes.com/timesmachine/1877/01/05/80358542.pdf. 5 January 1877. Retrieved 11 March 2022.

44 Vanderbilt, Arthur T. *Fortune's Children: The Fall of the House of Vanderbilt.* New York, NY: William Morrow, an imprint of HarperCollins Publishers, 2013.

45 Sumner, Scott. *Money Illusion: Market Monetarism, the Great Recession, and the Future of Monetary Policy.* Chicago, IL: University of Chicago Press, 2021.

46 #43 Rockefeller family. *Forbes.* https://www.forbes.com/profile/rockefeller/?list=families&sh=19385a75430e. 16 December 2020.

47 Mount, Harry. "Rothschild and Rockefeller: their family fortunes." *The Daily Telegraph* (London). https://www.telegraph.co.uk/finance/9300205/Rothschild-and-Rockefeller-their-family-fortunes.html. 30 May 2012.

48 Frank, Robert. "4 Secrets to Raising Wealthy Kids, According to the Billionaire Rockefeller Family." CNBC. https://www.cnbc.com/2018/03/26/david-rockefeller-jr-shares-4-secrets-to-wealth-and-family.html. 26 March 2018.

49 Genesis 13:2, 24:35, 15:1-5, 12:2-3, 26:12-13, 25:5, 27:28-29, 30:43, 49:1-28 (NASB)

ABOUT THE AUTHORS

Lucas and Rachel Marshall help enterprising families recognize, codify, and live into the contribution they are meant for so that the money they leave behind will keep on giving, empowering future generations.

When Rachel's near-death experience shook their family to the core, they found their calling to build a flourishing family team that lasts for generations.

Now, they are spearheading the Seven Generations Legacy movement with a mission to help a million families create a multigenerational legacy of more than money.

For the past ten years, Lucas and Rachel have been entrepreneurs in the wealth industry. Frustrated with status quo financial rhetoric that robs people of financial control, they charted a new course to build time and money freedom by creating cash flow from assets, maximizing tax advantages, and planning generationally.

Lucas and Rachel Marshall are authors, speakers, coaches, and Co-Founders of The Money Advantage, a team of financial architects for wealth creators. They serve clients across the United States with a family office model, coordinating strategies for cash flow, business, investing, insurance, Infinite Banking, permanent tax reduction, estate planning, asset protection, and more. Their podcasts, articles, videos, resources, guides, and courses have been widely praised for their disclosure and simplicity, helping independent thinkers gain clarity so they can make decisions.

Learn more about the Seven Generations books, courses, programs, resources, consulting, and coaching at www.Seven GenerationsLegacy.com and www.TheMoneyAdvantage.com.

BOOK YOUR LEGACY WEALTH STRATEGY CALL

Let's Map Out Your 90-Day Legacy Wealth Plan

In just 30 minutes, we will work together to help you map out a crystal clear strategy to help you remove the fear of money ruining your kids, without stress, overwhelm, or having to give everything away, and find out if and how I can help you exceed your generational wealth and legacy goals . . .

Schedule My Legacy Wealth Breakthough Session

BLOCKCHAIN
VERIFIED IP™

Powered by Easy IP™

Milton Keynes UK
Ingram Content Group UK Ltd.
UKHW020943011223
433598UK00014B/140/J

9 798885 832267